Becom

For Paul,

With gratitude for the understanding
I've gained from your book,
but also for the satisfaction of
your understanding of mine.

Dec. 2014

Continuum Studies in Ancient Philosophy
Series Editor: James Fieser, University of Tennessee at Martin, USA

Continuum Studies in Ancient Philosophy is a major monograph series from Continuum. The series features first-class scholarly research monographs across the field of Ancient Philosophy. Each work makes a major contribution to the field of philosophical research.

Aristotle and Rational Discovery, Russell Winslow
Aristotle's Ethics, Hope May
Aristotle's Metaphysics, Jeremy Kirby
Aristotle's Theory of Knowledge, Thomas Kiefer
The Enduring Significance of Parmenides, Raymond Tallis
Happiness and Greek Ethical Thought, M. Andrew Holowchak
The Ideas of Socrates, Matthew S Linck
Parmenides and To Eon, Lisa Atwood Wilkinson
Plato, Metaphysics and the Forms, Francis A. Grabowski III
Plato's Stepping Stones, Michael Cormack
Pleasure in Aristotle's Ethics, Michael Weinman
Pythagoras and the Doctrine of Transmigration, James Luchte
The Socratic Method, Rebecca Bensen Cain
Stoic Ethics, William O. Stephens
Stoic Virtues, Christoph Jedan

Becoming God

Pure Reason in Early Greek Philosophy

Patrick Lee Miller

continuum

Continuum International Publishing Group

The Tower Building
11 York Road
London SE1 7NX

80 Maiden Lane
Suite 704
New York NY 10038

www.continuumbooks.com

First published 2011
Paperback edition first published 2012

British Library Cataloguing-in-Publication Data
A catalogue record for this book is available from the British Library.

ISBN: HB: 978-1-8470-6164-5
     PB: 978-1-4411-5270-1

Library of Congress Cataloging-in-Publication Data
Miller, Patrick L. (Patrick Lee), 1970-
Becoming God : pure reason in early
Greek philosophy/Patrick Lee Miller.
   p. cm.
ISBN: 978-1-84706-164-5
1. Philosophy, Ancient. 2. Reason. I. Title.
B505.M64 2010
180–dc22   2010011586

Typeset by Newgen Imaging Systems Pvt Ltd, Chennai, India
Printed and bound in Great Britain

To

Jack & Jean, Mother & Father

CHIASMUS

No
twice
stepping into
the same river,
this specious now, this
very one, now gone, alas,
not even once, if truth be told,
nor can it be, truly, for knowing grasps
a thing, no thing, each thing is nothing in itself but
a waxing palimpsest, this selfsame text, myself no less,
waning at best before your very eyes, each blink
effacing, the drying ink tracing these echoes,
these dying refrains of infant palindromes,
returning again imperfectly somewhere
new, sometime over or under,
whenever yields never the
same word twice, unless,
maybe, now, this
once:
Yes.

Contents

Acknowledgments

This volume matured over several years and took some surprising turns along the way. Looking back over them all, I see how each depended on the influence of other people—sometimes colleagues, occasionally students, often friends—and recognize how different the final product would have been without their help. In that spirit, and because this is my first book, I want to begin by acknowledging five teachers who read none of it but nevertheless imprinted it with their indelible instruction: Charles Taylor, Alasdair MacIntyre, Kenneth Reckford, Jerzy Linderski, and Paul Brinich.

The first version was a short paper written for a conference hosted by Randall Styers, and I would like to thank him formally for that invitation. The proceedings of that conference are being published by Vandenhoeck & Ruprecht (*Light against Darkness: Dualism in Ancient Mediterranean Religion and the Contemporary World*), which has permitted my contribution to appear here as well, divided into parts of the third and fourth chapters. Once I had a fuller manuscript, which I sent to Continuum thanks to the recommendation of Jim Fieser, my editors there (Sarah Campbell, Tom Crick, and David Avital) remained remarkably patient with me as I changed it severely. I am likewise grateful to my readers from the University of North Carolina for their wisdom as well as their patience. Among the many, I must mention William Race, William Lycan, Ram Neta, Thomas Holden, and Graham Pardun.

After leaving Chapel Hill, my research and writing was done with the support of two institutions. The Harvard Center for Hellenic Studies, under the direction of Gregory Nagy, invited me to spend a year as a Junior Fellow, and I am deeply indebted to the many people who made my time there so rewarding. Of them all, I must name Pascale Brillet-Dubois for the sharp comments she made on my drafts, as well as the warm companionship she brought with her family. Thanks are also due to Duquesne University for granting me that year's leave, but more importantly for sustaining the kind of philosophical community that has enlivened my work since I arrived there. Of its many fine members, three stand behind this particular book.

The devotion to philosophical conversation of both Robert Guerin and Louis Butler helped bring to light some of its ideas (not to mention its bibliography and index), while the tireless efforts of James Swindal have made such conversations a daily feature of our department. His trust has emboldened me to take intellectual risks, first in my teaching, and then eventually in my writing.

Without similar encouragement from Jonathan VanAntwerpen, who shepherded my initial thoughts about Heraclitus onto *The Immanent Frame,* the superb academic blog he founded, the second chapter of this book would not have been written. William Connolly read these thoughts there, and it was his seasoned interest that convinced me to expand them and bring them into the same story with Parmenides and his rival tradition. Marina Hall introduced me to Anna Lea and the Society for the Preservation of the Greek Heritage, whose invitation to speak helped me to crystallize this volume's conclusion. Along the way to that conclusion, when it was still obscure, Melissa Goldthwaite wisely reminded me that poetic diversion from scholarly work can help us reveal what otherwise remains concealed. Similarly, Rachel Singpurwalla, Rebekah Smith, and Lauren Freeman nudged me with kind words.

Finally, there are three people whose influence I see on nearly every page. James Lesher agreed to read my first writing on the Presocratics, saving me often from embarrassing errors. Since then he has helped me on many occasions, and not just by reviewing my manuscript. This is not to say that he agrees with the final result, but only that this volume would have been much worse—and its author far less secure—had he not been its selfless guide. David Reeve has for a decade been my most careful reader, at times my sternest critic, and in the end my most important teacher. For his generosity, prudence, and friendship, my words of gratitude are not enough. My deepest thanks go to my wife, Sarah Alison Miller. With a final reading she purged of its excessive humors a book that owes to her more than any other its monstrous birth.

Chapter 1

Introduction

No longer doomed to die, nor even to pass through a succession of mortal bodies, Empedocles claimed to have escaped the wheel of reincarnation and become divine: "I go about you an immortal god."[1] Such a declaration, were it made nowadays, would elicit all sorts of emotion, but never our belief. Fifth-century Greeks, still infused with the stories and values of Homer, would have been equally incredulous. "Gods may appear at times in human form, men may share at times in the divine attribute of power," wrote E. R. Dodds, "but in Homer there is nevertheless no real blurring of the sharp line which separates humanity from deity."[2] Yet in the philosophy of this period—indeed, throughout the history of Greek philosophy—the ambition to become god, or at least godlike, was common. Empedocles was in many ways a Pythagorean, and one of Aristotle's students wrote an account of this influential school that reported, "every distinction they lay down as to what should be done or not done aims at communion with the divine."[3]

Plato adopted some of the Pythagorean distinctions—between soul and body, limit and unlimited, a good cosmic principle and something that resists this good—and also preserved their divine ambition.[4] "A man should make all haste to escape from earth to heaven," he wrote in *Theaetetus*, "and escape means becoming as like god as possible."[5] The escape route, he adds, is to become "just and pure, with understanding." Justice receives a thorough explanation in *Republic*, where Plato also addresses purity and understanding, not to mention divinity and the route to it. To become godlike, according to this dialogue, we must become philosophers. Philosophy is a special technique, dialectic, that develops and defends accounts of justice, the pure soul, and rational understanding, among other things. But more importantly, as these very accounts reveal, philosophy sits at the summit of justice, the purest activity of the soul, divine understanding itself. This is a persistent theme of Plato's dialogues. "No one may join the company of the gods," according to *Phaedo*, "who has not practiced philosophy and is not completely pure when he departs from life."[6] *Republic* elaborates this purifying and divinizing vocation: "the philosopher, by consorting with what is orderly and divine, becomes as divine and orderly as a human being can."[7]

Striving to be as rational as possible, the philosopher learns that he is the divine activity of pure reason itself. Socrates teaches this lesson in the first dialogue of the ancient Platonist curriculum, *Alcibiades.* "To know itself," he begins, the soul must look at another soul, "and especially at that region in which what makes a soul good, wisdom, occurs."[8] Comparing self-inquiry to examining oneself in a mirror, Socrates argues for the importance of dialectic by suggesting that another's reason reflects our own. After all, we see ourselves as an image in the part of another's body which sees, its best part, namely the pupil of his eye.[9] Correlatively, we know ourselves by contemplating the part of another's soul which knows, its best part, namely his divine reason. "Can we say that there is anything about the soul which is more divine," asks Socrates, "than that where knowing and understanding take place?"[10] To know ourselves, we must contemplate divine reason. "Someone who looked at that and grasped everything divine," he concludes, "would have the perfect grasp of himself as well."[11] Contemplating divine reason, then, we know ourselves. Self-knowledge is theology; theology, self-knowledge.

But what is this pure reason, whether in god or ourselves? This volume will present the diverse answers to this question provided by the early Greek philosophers. Before turning to these answers, we should emphasize their historical importance by noting that later Greek philosophers would adopt them, sometimes adapting them, but nearly always maintaining them as roads to divinity. Indeed, in a scholarly era when philosophers justified their thinking by appeal to its ancient heritage, Platonists went so far as to tamper with the dialogues in order to make this summons more explicit. Into *Alcibiades*, for example, they inserted passages such as the following: "the way that we can best see and know ourselves is to use the finest mirror available and look at God."[12] But in late antiquity the equation of god, self, and reason did not require forgery; it had contemporaneous authority too. Seven centuries after Empedocles, Plotinus advanced a variety of Platonism—refined by his encounters with Aristotle and the Stoics—that promised divinity with a rival confidence. "Our concern is not to be sinless," he wrote, "but to be god."[13] Faithful to Plato, Plotinus argued that our escape from earth to heaven must follow the road of pure reason and self-inquiry.[14]

Similarly faithful to Plato's program of divinization and purification, despite some departures from his teacher, Aristotle celebrated the philosophical and contemplative life at the summit of this program. "Such a life would be superior to a merely human life," he wrote, "for someone will live it not as a human, but as having something divine within."[15] This is pure reason (*nous*). "If pure reason is something divine in comparison with the merely human," he adds, "the life of pure reason is divine in comparison with a merely human life."[16] Thus epitomizing his theology, psychology, and ethics in one of the only passionate injunctions of his extant corpus, he urges us "not to follow the proverbs and think human things because we are human, nor mortal things because we are mortal, but rather to become immortal and divine insofar as this is possible and do everything for the life of the supreme within."[17] Aristotle did not advertise this fidelity to Plato's Pythagorean program, the way Plotinus later would, but he nonetheless helped carry into late antiquity the philosophical revolt against Homeric religion that began in the period we shall examine here.

Disguising their revolution, Greek philosophers of all periods interpreted the traditional myths to agree with their novel ambitions. Aristotle thought that the story-tellers preserved the most ancient truth about the divine by embellishing it with myth aimed at popular persuasion.[18] Approaching Homer in the same spirit, Plotinus interpreted the myth of the two Heracles as a poet's version of his own abstract doctrine of the divided soul.[19] After the hero's immolation, one ancient story put him in Hades, whereas another had him join the gods on Olympus. Homer synthesized them, dividing Heracles' mortal shade from his immortal self.[20] According to Plotinus's interpretation of this synthesis, the descending Heracles represents our lower soul, which must tarry in a mortal body until it dies, whereas the ascending one represents our higher soul, pure reason, which remains divine. Had he been a philosopher, apparently, Heracles' ascent would have left nothing behind. "Because he was an active and not a contemplative person," however, "there is also still a part of him below."[21] This distinction matched the sophisticated psychology Plotinus himself synthesized from Plato and Aristotle, but the philosophical attention he paid to Heracles stemmed from the most ancient Pythagoreans.[22]

Aiming at communion with the divine, they naturally revered Heracles. Myths told not only of his travels through their region, southern Italy, but also of his travels to Hades, where he received a warm welcome from Persephone, who permitted him to retrieve dead souls.[23] Through Heracles' intervention, as they understood this story, one could escape death. Escaping death, however, was normally the privilege of the immortal gods. Writing a victory ode to a Sicilian tyrant, Pindar integrated both Heracles and Persephone into a myth of reincarnation which promised the truthful "company with the honored gods."[24] Reaching Olympus, they would be imitating Heracles himself, if not his precise labors, for these labors earned him that summit. There he served, writes Walter Burkert, as "a model for the common man who may hope that after a life of drudgery, and through that very life, he too may enter into the company of the gods."[25] Empedocles not only claimed to realize this hope while alive, but also pretended to accomplish deeds that recapitulated Heraclean labors.[26] The Pythagorean revolution was trying, in short, to don the mantle of popular piety.

But it never really fit. Pindar described a myth of reincarnation suited to Pythagoreanism, but he also wrote the following proviso: "Do not, my soul, strive for the life of the immortals."[27] For those who would nevertheless try, he told cautionary tales from traditional mythology. "We all alike die," yet "if a man peers at distant things, he is too little to reach the gods' bronze paved dwelling."[28] Not even atop a magical horse can he hope to reach it, Pindar added, for "winged Pegasus threw his master, when Bellerophon desired to enter the habitations of heaven and the company of Zeus."[29] Next to Heracles' rare success in reaching Olympus, this tale of disastrous failure made clear the risks of trying to join the divine company. Could the risks be avoided and success ensured by those who would place their divine hopes not in mythic flights or labors but in reason alone? This seems to have been the promise of the new philosophical spirit. Challenging the unique dignity of the gods, the hero most appropriate to Greek philosophy was not Heracles, in the end, but Oedipus.[30]

Devouring the young men of Thebes, the Sphinx would not stop until someone solved her riddle: what walks on four feet in the morning, two in the afternoon, and three in the evening? No priest could help, not even wise Teiresias. "Then ignorant Oedipus came and put a stop to her," he himself boasts, "winning by thought without understanding divine signs."[31] Other mythic heroes used violence to defeat monsters. Bellerophon stabbed Chimaera with a lance; Perseus decapitated Medusa with a dagger; Jason emerged from the belly of the Dragon he sliced from within. To slay his monster, by contrast, Oedipus needed only a thought: Man. He thus appears as a new kind of hero, one of words rather than deeds, relying on human wit rather than divine aid.[32] Jean-Joseph Goux summarizes the tragedy in this terse formula: "Oedipus, an autodidact who has become an autocrat through an autoreferential response, pursues an investigation that will become more and more autobiographical." To consummate his independence, moreover, "he himself will discover that he is the guilty party, after which he will inflict punishment on himself."[33] Oedipus could be Empedocles, or Anaxagoras, or Socrates; by the power of drama, he is all three. Sophocles fashioned a character who condenses the philosophical bravado of a whole century.

As his tragedy opens, for example, Oedipus receives a representative of the grieving Thebans he now rules. Plague is decimating their city, so with the same confidence that saved his people from the Sphinx, Oedipus begins a rational investigation. He quickly reveals how contemptuous he is of irrational priestcraft, but his apparently rational procedure soon reveals that he himself is the unholy cause of divine displeasure. When this tragedy was performed, in 427, the Athenians had just suffered a grievous plague of their own.[34] Pericles had enjoined them a few years earlier to risk war with Sparta. Staying within their long walls, surrendering their farms to the continuous depradations of the stronger Spartan army, they relied on their superior navy, just as their clever leader had instructed. But Pericles' rational plan could not encompass the irrational: ships likely brought illness from Egypt and it spread like wildfire among a trapped populace.[35] Similar to Oedipus, whose investigation precipitates his own destruction, Pericles himself perished from the plague for which his rationality was partly to blame.

Anaxagoras had been his teacher, the first philosopher to give *nous* a cosmic role.[36] For this innovation, Aristotle later called him a sensible man among babblers.[37] But Anaxagoras was also the first philosopher the Athenians accused and convicted of impiety—contempt of the gods for considering the divine sun but a fiery stone—so that he was banished, likely around the time of the plague.[38] The next philosopher to be so treated by the Athenians was Socrates, who also bears remarkable similarities to Oedipus. Each receives an oracle from Delphi, for instance, which provokes a quest for self-knowledge that is ambiguously tragic.[39] Told that Apollo had called him the wisest of the Greeks, Socrates interrogated his fellow Athenians, hoping to discover from their answers what the god could have meant about him, and so about human wisdom. This quest ended with his willing administration of hemlock to himself. Self-inquiry thus precipitated his death. Was this a tragedy, as it seemed to most of his disciples? Or was it instead the divine comedy of purification and divinization he reportedly envisioned?

To become pure and divine, according to Plato, the philosopher must defeat monsters with words rather than deeds, just as Oedipus did. But the monsters slain by these words are within the embodied soul: the hydra of its appetite, the lion of its ambition.[40] Purified of them, purified of the body and its affects, reason alone joins the company of the gods. As a tale of his bodily fate, then, Socrates' death is a tragedy. It becomes comic in Plato's hands—a tale of rational ascent to the divine. Self-knowledge, as we shall see in the fourth chapter, is supposed to be the end of this ascent; self-inquiry, its means. Therein, however, lies a paradox. The uncompromising pursuit of self-knowledge will render its achievement impossible; relentless consistency will ensure contradiction. In his own dramaturgical way, Sophocles has already prophesied this paradox. At the end of *Oedipus Tyrannus*, the sort of investigation he has been prosecuting all his life has finally revealed him to be the murderer of his father and the husband of his mother. The rationality he formerly considered the means of purification has been exposed as a cause of impurity. Was it not his self-inquiry that brought him into the path of his father at the crossroads? Was it not his wit that made him brother to his own children? Blinding himself, he begs for a pitiable exile. *Exeunt omnes.*

But this is not the end of Oedipus's story. He returns in Sophocles' last play, *Oedipus Coloneus*, where he hobbles onto stage with the help of his daughter. No longer striding confidently down palace steps, contemptuous of priests and oracles, expecting to solve every problem rationally, the old hero now enters a grove and begins by enquiring about the local divinities: "Are we near a shrine? Is this holy land?"[41] Resting his weary body at last, he offers it as an apotropaic for the people of Colonus.[42] Nowhere evident is his former pretense to be an uncompromising investigator of truth.[43] His ambition to do everything by himself has been slain not by his intellect but by his suffering.[44] No longer relying on reason alone, he eventually receives a divine summons: "Oedipus, Oedipus, it has been too long, now is our time."[45] Kneeling down and kissing the ground, he vanishes: "something else, not human, came down from above and led him up high into heaven."[46] Oedipus thus ascends to the divine neither by pure reason nor the pursuit of self-knowledge, both of which nearly destroyed him.

From the vantage of his own old age, surveying the intellectual ferment that characterized his lifetime, Sophocles seems to warn of pure reason's dangers.[47] Most Greek philosophers ignored this warning and made the rational life their goal. Aristotle not only called this life divine in comparison with a merely human life, he also made its demands quite explicit. "The same attribute," he wrote, "cannot at the same time belong and not belong to the same subject in the same respect."[48] The world tolerates no contradiction; neither should pure reason. Deeming non-contradiction "the firmest principle of all things,"[49] Aristotle argued that failure to heed it destroys reasoning and discourse, making its transgressor "like a plant."[50] But this imperative to think consistently was not unique to Aristotle. A version of the same principle can be found in Plato, alongside the promise that reason thus purified is divine. "It is clear that the same thing cannot do or undergo opposites," goes his earlier version; "not, at any rate, in the same respect, in relation to the same thing, at the same time."[51] Only his Forms will meet this strict criterion, so that anyone who adopts it must think only of them.[52] This is the goal of Platonic philosophy. Purified of all contradiction, immortal reason contemplates the eternal divine.

Before both Plato and Aristotle, however, Parmenides articulated the first version of the principle of non-contradiction: "that (it) is, and that it is not possible for (it) not to be."[53] More austerely devoted to the consequences of this principle than were any of his successors, Parmenides was also the first to recognize that it precluded time. "Nor was it ever nor will it be," he wrote, "since it is now."[54] For if it is not (now), it cannot be; after all, it is not possible for (it) not to be. Saved by pure reason from the contradictory illusion of time's passage, Parmenides called those still deceived by it "equally deaf and blind, amazed, hordes without judgment, for whom both to be and not to be are judged the same and not the same, and the path of all is backward turning (*palintropos*)."[55] The target of this reproach seems to have been Heraclitus, whose style of thinking flirts with contradiction. "They do not comprehend how a thing agrees at variance with itself," he wrote; "it is a backward-turning (*palintropos*) attunement, like that of the bow and the lyre."[56]

This backward-turning style of thinking is chiastic. Named after the Greek letter *Chi* because of its criss-cross shape (χ), chiasmus is a literary figure where a pattern is repeated but in reverse order ($A : B :: B : A$). The pattern can be semantic, as in the following example from Shakespeare: "Who dotes, yet doubts, suspects, yet strongly loves!"[57] Here, a reversal of synonyms has been adorned with an artful change of consonants. The pattern reversed can also be syntactic, as in this example from Milton: "Love without end, and without measure Grace."[58] Here, a noun and prepositional phrase trade order. Again, a substitution of words introduces some pleasant variety, yet it also adds layers of concealed meaning. *Chi* became a symbol of Christ in antiquity: it was the first letter of his name, and its shape resembled his cross. By substituting "Grace" for "Love," and thereby assimilating them, Milton points to the crucifixion as sign of divine love freely given. In short, Milton communicates a Christology—a logos, or account, of his God—with the figure of chiasmus. Form matches content.

A Heraclitean aphorism provides us with an excellent example of the same technique, exploiting both semantic and syntactic chiasmus: "All things are a requital for fire, and fire for all things, as goods for gold and gold for goods."[59] In this faithful English translation the complex chiasmus of meanings shines through: $A : B :: B : A ::: C : D :: D : C$. Below this semantic pattern, additionally, is a dazzling arrangement of nouns whose syntax cannot be rendered into English. Their cases (*N*ominative and *G*enitive) and their numbers (*S*ingular and *P*lural) make the following pattern: *GS* : *NP* :: *NS* : *GP* ::: *GS* : *NP* : *GP* :: *NS*.[60] In the first half of the sentence is thus a chiasmus according to case: *G* : *N* :: *N* : *G*. In the second half, one according to number: *S* : *P* :: *P* : *S*. This is a fugue in Greek, weaving linguistic opposition into a complex unity, but what is its philosophical significance?

Chiasmus threatens to violate the principle of non-contradiction whenever its components are conjoined and opposed, whether as contraries or contradictories. This happens often in the Heraclitean aphorisms, but nowhere more flagrantly than in the following, which we shall eventually call the principle of chiasmus: "wholes and not wholes, convergent divergent, consonant dissonant, from all things one and from one all things."[61] Whatever this principle describes, contradiction is evidently involved. We shall argue in the second chapter that this is time, which is contradictory at each of its moments. Tolerant of such contradiction, without forcing us to become like a plant, Heraclitus teaches us how to think time properly, how to think about it without judging it illusory. The principle of chiasmus comes closer than any of his other aphorisms to describing time's peculiar structure, but it makes little sense on its own. Rather than standing alone as the firmest principle of all, indubitable, the necessary condition of reasonable thought and meaningful discourse, it stands at the summit of a reflection that must begin with earthier aphorisms about rivers and lyres and fires. Beginning there, accordingly, we shall aim to reach this summit by steps. Our goal will be to adopt this style of thinking—chiasmus—which affirms time by sharing its very structure. In this way, and only thus, can Heraclitus communicate his becoming god.

Visitors reportedly found him warming himself by his hearth. They hesitated to enter, but he summoned them: "Come in, and don't worry; for there are gods here also."[62] The story comes to us from Aristotle, who wrote nearly two centuries after Heraclitus, but whether it really happened or not, it nonetheless captures a truth about the theology of this enigmatic thinker.[63] He thought divinity everywhere—in a kitchen fire as much as an altar fire—because the whole cosmos is god. He defined it in the oddest way. "The god: day night, winter summer, war peace, satiety hunger. It alters, as when mingled with perfumes it gets named according to the pleasure of each one."[64] To make sense of this strange theology, we must begin by appreciating the fundamental challenges Heraclitus poses to our prejudices about language, thought, and world.

Among the deepest of these prejudices—certainly since Parmenides, Plato, and Aristotle entrenched it—is the view that thought and language should be purified of contradiction because the only intelligible and expressible world is thus pure. Writing before these philosophers, Heraclitus does not aim his aphorisms at them, but he does challenge a perennial temptation that their philosophies would later indulge: to deny time, especially the death it exacts from us all. No tradition has indulged this temptation more exquisitely than Greek philosophy. But not Heraclitus. As inscrutable as his definition of god may be to us now, its temporality is already obvious: he lists two seasons of the year, two phases of the diurnal cycle, then four stages in the changing lives of individuals and nations. Were the list of the first sentence not temporal enough, the second sentence of this definition says explicitly that god alters.

Divine change was hardly unusual for archaic Greece, whose gods changed constantly and capriciously in the drama of the epics. One change that neither Homer nor Hesiod would permit the gods to suffer, however, was death. In their traditional religion, the gods were immortal and humans mortal, without any mixture between these two pure opposites.[65] Heracles was the exception that proved this rule. Breaking the rule more boldly than any other Greek, Heraclitus immerses divinity so thoroughly in time that he mixes it impurely with our humanity: "Immortals mortals, mortals immortals, living the others' death, dead in the others' life."[66] This bewildering aphorism not only immerses immortal divinity in time, it also promises divine life to mortal humans.

"Becoming god" thus acquires two distinct but related senses in Heraclitus: first of all, his god is becoming, a god in time; secondly, he allows us to participate in its life by becoming god ourselves. The method by which we do so is self-inquiry. Heraclitean philosophers who seek self-knowledge soundly will find god, therefore, while Heraclitean theologians who seek divine knowledge soundly will find themselves. Sound thought and speech must testify to the nature of the world, even exemplify it, and the Heraclitean world is but one divine conflict. By affirming the temporality of all three— thought, language, and world—this style of thinking reveals itself as their shared structure: chiasmus. Rejecting chiasmus as contradictory, Parmenides and those who adopted his principle turned their thought instead to eternity. "Becoming god," for them would have only one sense: our striving to think divinely, purely, without contradiction, and thereby recognize time as an illusion. Following the tradition of pure reason, we discover that we are neither our bodies nor our affective souls; we are neither souls that perceive nor souls that believe; indeed, we are not even souls that reason from one proposition to another. All such motions require contradictory time. Instead we discover that we are eternal reason, contemplating all there really is, namely our divine self. We are, in Aristotle's immortal words, "thinking thinking of thinking."[67]

But how can we *discover* that we are eternal? How can we *strive* to recognize that we never change? How can we *become* who we are? From the beginning of this tradition, a chasm opens between the eternal end of self-knowledge it celebrates and the temporal process of self-inquiry it travels to this end. This is a chasm which Heraclitus and his few successors never needed to cross. In antiquity these were Stoics such as Marcus Aurelius.[68] Honoring Heraclitus as a sage, he quoted him from memory, twice alluding to the Heraclitean river. "Existence is like a river in perpetual flow,"[69] he wrote in one passage, elaborating the same metaphor in another: "Time is a river of things that become, with a strong current. No sooner is a thing seen than it has been swept away."[70] Far from dismissing the river of time as an illusion, in the manner of Parmenides or Plato, Marcus sought to comprehend it: "Let the whole of time and the whole of substance be continuously present to your mind."[71] Whereas Plato had separated reason and eternal Form from sensation's moving image of eternity, Marcus assimilated everything into one.[72] "The universe embraces all things and is one," he wrote, "and the god who pervades all things is one."[73] Like other Stoics, he eschewed eternity when invoking this one divine whole, calling it seminal *logos*, emphasizing at once both its creativity and his own allegiance to Heraclitus.[74]

Such allegiance proved rare through medieval and early modern philosophy, when Parmenides' devotion to pure reason—thanks especially to Plato's fusion of it with the Pythagorean program of purification and divinization—influenced many more philosophers. Kant, for instance, believed that "the ground of obligation must not be sought in the nature of man or in the circumstances in which he is placed but a priori solely in the concepts of pure reason."[75] He makes the practical demand of reason explicit, forbidding actions whenever they "are of such a nature that their maxim cannot even be *thought* as a universal law without contradiction."[76] Absent from this twilight devotion to consistency, however, is its original promise of divinity. Missing is any consolation at all for the immense sacrifices this devotion must involve. Kant called sexual desire "nothing more than appetite," adding that "there lies in this inclination a degradation of man."[77] Consequently, he wrote, "all strict moralists, and those who wish to be taken for saints, have sought to repress and dispense with it."[78] But sexual desire was not alone the target of Kant's contempt. If action is to be moral, all appetites and passions must be disregarded, if not dispensed with, as merely human nature. To what end?

"For me, the highest thing would be to gaze at life without desire."[79] Thus Nietzsche ventriloquizes the modern contemplative, the latter-day saint of pure reason. "To be happy in gazing, with benumbed will, without the grasping and greed of egotism," he adds, "cold and ashen in body but with

intoxicated moon-eyes!" The moon sends our world only cold and lifeless
light, whereas the sun heats it with its illumination, making life possible.
Nietzsche is ridiculing a contemplation that is pure of body and passion, an
"immaculate perception" that looks on the world without heat and life.
It has only one desire: to mirror the world. Behind the abnegation of this
mirthless ideal, Nietzsche sees a necessarily frustrated desire: the desire to
forego desire. At the historical origin of this ascetic ideal he sees many
figures, especially philosophers, but none older and more single-minded
than Parmenides. "All the manifold colorful world known to experience,"
he begins his critique of him, "are cast aside mercilessly as mere semblance
and illusion."[80] Pure reason administers this purgation, so that "truth shall
live only in the palest, most abstracted generalities, in the empty husks of
the most indefinite terms, as though in a house of cobwebs."[81] But only
pure reason survives this purgation, so that "beside such truth now sits our
philosopher, likewise as bloodless as his abstractions, in the spun out fabric
of his formulas."[82]

Aristotle's firmest formula of all, the only formula that exists for
Parmenides, is the principle of non-contradiction, which we shall eventually call simply the principle of consistency. As we shall see in the third
chapter, only the activity of this principle survives the purgation that it itself
administers. In other words, pure reason alone meets the criteria of pure
reason. "A spider at least wants blood from its victims," Nietzsche concludes,
but "the Parmenidean philosopher hates most of all the blood of his victims, the blood of the empirical reality which was shed and sacrificed by
him."[83] The Parmenidean philosopher just is the pure activity of consistency—empty of any content in the beginning, in the end contradicting even
itself. "Let us be wary of the tentacles of such contradictory concepts as
'pure reason,'" Nietzsche later wrote; "let us be more wary of the dangerous
old conceptual fairy-tale which has set up a 'pure, will-less, painless,
timeless, subject of knowledge.'"[84]

With equal vim, his Zarathustra scolds the modern believers of this
fairy-tale. "You of 'pure knowledge,'" you who find Parmenidean logic too
austere but have nonetheless been seduced by the richer version of Plato,
"you have put on the mask of a god."[85] Whatever appeal this masquerade
had in antiquity—sacrificing empirical reality, striving for eternity—has
vanished along with the god it celebrates. The devotees of pure reason now
wear the death mask of a departed god. In the same book which skewered
Parmenides, Nietzsche sought to revive a philosophy that would return us
to time and its becoming god. "The world forever needs the truth," he wrote
there, "hence the world forever needs Heraclitus."[86]

Chapter 2

Heraclitus

Socrates was said to have praised Heraclitus's book, adding nonetheless that "it needs a Delian diver to get to the bottom of it."[1] The story is likely an invention, but it gives a sense of the interpretive difficulty that the work presented to those who possessed a complete text. Because we have only fragments of it, our difficulties are that much worse. We do not know how to order these fragments, except for one. This is the book's opening passage, which begins by invoking something called *logos*: "Although this logos holds forever, men ever fail to comprehend, both before hearing it and once they have heard."[2] Already a paradox arises: if this logos is something to be heard, it would seem to be something spoken; but since it is something we do not comprehend before hearing it, although apparently we should, it would seem to be something prior to speech, something in the world.[3]

Before we dive into this paradox, we should reach for a lexicon. *Logos* is ambiguous. It derives from *legein*, to speak, and so its most basic meaning is "something spoken," thus "word," "statement," "speech," "report," or "language." By extension, it can mean "account," "explanation," "definition," "proportion," "structure," and "reason."[4] Deliberately exploiting such ambiguities whenever he invokes the logos, Heraclitus is able to mean both his own speech and the structure of the world—its reason—which this speech conveys. Consistent with this complex meaning, the best Heraclitean aphorisms exhibit the very structure they ascribe to the world. This is more than literary finesse; it is the essence of his approach, without which his philosophy degenerates quickly into dogmatism and cliché. With this unity of form and content, he can demonstrate an identity between our logos and that of the world.

2.1 Fluent Logos

The most famous of the Heraclitean aphorisms, the so-called river fragment, is a perfect example of this unity of form and content: "As they step into the same rivers, other and still other waters flow upon them."[5] The Greek is artful in several significant ways: *Potamoisi toisin autoisin embain-ousin, hetera kai hetera hudata epirrei.* First of all, before the comma the repeated sigmas of its datives sound together like the sibilant babbling of an interrupted stream, whereas afterwards its aspirated vowels—finished by an aspirated *rho*—sound like the rush of waters returning to their customary flow. Secondly, the Greek words for "the same" (*toisin autoisin*) could be associated with either "rivers" or "they" or both.[6] In this particular English translation, these words are associated with "rivers," so that although their waters are perpetually different, these rivers are nonetheless the same. In an alternate translation, "the same" is associated with those who are stepping into rivers: "On the same (people) going into rivers, other and other waters flow."[7] According to this version, the steppers are assumed to be stable things, but the rivers' waters flow so quickly that they pass by the moment the steppers go into them.

When there is ambiguity in a Heraclitean aphorism, whether it is a matter of individual words or their relationships with one another, the multiple meanings seem deliberately balanced.[8] In the case of the river fragment, then, we should probably see stability in both subject and object—steppers and the rivers into which they step—despite the instability of the flowing waters that surround the one and compose the other. Indeed, we should not miss similar stability in the very aphorism that exhibits a parallel insta-bility of meaning.[9] Despite the syntactic ambiguity of "the same," the river fragment hints at the one stable lesson that stepping selves and the rivers into which they step are what they are—in a word, the same—only by some kind of flowing, some kind of perpetual change or otherness.

Another Heraclitean aphorism on rivers helps us to elaborate this contra-dictory lesson: "Into the same rivers we step and do not step, we are and we are not."[10] In the next section, we shall try to understand what Heraclitus is doing generally with such contradictory aphorisms; in the section after that, using our understanding of Heraclitean contradiction, we shall return to this specific one, investigating Heraclitus's ephemeral self.

2.2 Illogical Logos

Another way of revealing Heraclitus's logos is to examine his aphorisms on fire, which he assigns the same cosmic role as the logos itself. "The ordering [*kosmos*], the same for all, no god nor man has made," he wrote, "but it ever was and is and will be: fire everliving, kindled in measures and in measures quenched."[11] The Stoics and many Heracliteans since them have taken this doctrine for a physics, believing that fire was for Heraclitus the prime substance of the cosmos, just as water and air were proposed by his immediate predecessors, Thales and Anaximenes.[12] But whether or not Heraclitus had a physics, he is certainly using fire as a prime example, a paradigm of the paradoxical pattern he sees everywhere. Fire is "need and satiety," according to one report of his thought, and such paradoxes have given him a reputation for flouting the hallowed principle of non-contradiction.[13]

"The same attribute," writes Aristotle, "cannot at the same time belong and not belong to the same subject in the same respect."[14] He goes so far as to call this "the firmest principle of all things," claiming that if one fails to heed it—as many in antiquity thought Heraclitus failed to do—then one cannot have any knowledge at all.[15] Ignoring for now the genealogy of this principle, let us consider instead whether Heraclitus heeded Aristotle's formulation of it.[16] Initially it appears that he did not. Here are three representative examples: (i) "The way up and the way down are the same"; (ii) "The sea is purest and foulest water: for fish drinkable and life-sustaining; for men undrinkable and deadly"; (iii) "Cold things grow hot, a hot thing cold, a moist thing withers, a parched thing is wetted."[17] Despite initial appearances, however, each of these aphorisms heeds Aristotle's formulation of the principle of non-contradiction by appealing to one of its three qualifications.

The first aphorism appears contradictory because it says the same attribute (e.g., up) at the same time belongs and does not belong to the same subject (e.g., a mountain road): the way up and the way down the mountain are the same. But in fact the attribute "up" belongs with respect to one direction (from the bottom to the top), whereas it does not belong with respect to the other direction (from the top to the bottom). Aristotle is careful to qualify his principle, allowing that the same attribute can belong and not belong to the same subject *in different respects*. Similarly, it allows for contradictory attribution *to different subjects*, and this qualification accommodates the second Heraclitean aphorism above: sea water is drinkable to fish but undrinkable to humans. Finally, Aristotle's formulation allows for contradictory attribution *at different times*: something may be cold at one moment but not-cold at another. By appealing to one or more of these qualifications, in this manner, commentators have resolved the apparent contradictions of many aphorisms, exonerating him from the charge of obscurity that has stuck to him since antiquity.[18]

But there are a few aphorisms that cannot be resolved so easily, beginning with the one that calls fire need and satiety. For if fire were needy and satisfied at the same time (now), with respect to the same thing (its fuel), the attribute of satisfaction would both belong and not belong to the same thing, as would neediness; it would therefore violate the principle of non-contradiction. The Stoics saved Heraclitus from this contradiction by making his fire—which became their prime substance, and thereby their whole cosmos itself—oscillate between conflagration and extinction.[19] At one time, according to them, the cosmic fire is satisfied with a holocaust; at another time, it becomes needy and is extinguished. Imagining a perpetual cosmic cycle between these extreme stages, the Stoics anticipated the doctrine of the Eternal Recurrence some readers find in the writings of another Heraclitean, Nietzsche.[20] But no such elaborate cosmology is necessary to save Heraclitus from irrationality; in fact, as with Nietzsche, cosmologies generally distract attention from the deep lessons available upon careful contemplation of something more common.[21] "Heraclitus's aim is not to improve the Milesian cosmology," writes Kahn, but "by meditating on the fire one who knows how to read oracular signs can perceive the hidden harmony that unifies opposing principles not only within the cosmic order but also in the destiny of the human psyche."[22]

In this spirit, let us consider the humble candle flame: it is need and satiety, at the same time (now), and with respect to the same thing (its fuel). After all, for any given moment, if it were not satisfied by its fuel at that moment—having insufficient fuel to continue burning—it would be extinguished; and yet, if it were not also needing that same fuel at the same time—not consuming the requisite fuel to continue burning—it would likewise be extinguished right then. The candle flame's burning thus requires it to be needy and satisfied with respect to the same thing, a contradiction, at each moment. Unlike the other aphorisms we have examined, this one about fire cannot be resolved by appeal to Aristotle's qualifications upon the principle of non-contradiction. The same attribute—whether satisfaction or need, it does not matter which—at the same time belongs and does not belong to the same subject (the candle flame), in the same respect (towards its fuel). The point is difficult to grasp, but only because it demands that we do something impossible: freeze the flame in a moment. Fire cannot be frozen in a moment because it is, above all, a process. For fire, in other words, there is no now.

More than anything else, except perhaps a river, fire draws our attention to the fact that time is not composed of frozen moments, of "nows." Aristotle himself would later provide an argument to this effect in his *Physics.*[23] Roughly, he observed that if time were a succession of moments, each moment would have to perish, for only so could these moments yield to one another and produce the flow of time. But when could a particular moment perish? In which moment could it do so? Not in itself, for then it would both exist and not exist; nor could it perish in any other moment, for then it would be simultaneous with a different moment.[24] Both options, in short, would violate the principle of non-contradiction. Indeed, the contradictory options available to anyone who freezes time in this way resemble nothing so much as the dilemmas produced by the paradoxes of motion Aristotle considers elsewhere in his *Physics*, which were crafted by a follower of Parmenides, Zeno of Elea.[25]

Of Zeno's four paradoxes of motion, or change, the most relevant for our purposes is the so-called Flying Arrow.[26] As we tried a moment ago to freeze the Heraclitean fire, this paradox similarly invites us to freeze the flight of an arrow. If time is composed of moments, what happens to a flying arrow frozen in each of them? Aristotle agrees with Zeno that it must be at rest: "If everything when it occupies an equal space is at rest, and if that which is in locomotion is always in a now, the flying arrow is therefore motionless."[27] So compactly stated, this paradox requires some explanation. Were we to freeze a flying arrow in a "now"—catching it on film with a high-speed camera, for example—it would occupy a space equal to itself. For if it should occupy a space longer than itself, so to speak, it would be moving, not frozen. In our photographic analogy, it would be as if our shutter speed were too slow: rather than catching the flying arrow at a moment, we caught it over several moments, creating a blur. Catching it in a "now," we would find it occupying a space equal to itself, which is to say motionless. In every "now," at every moment, it must be motionless. Yet at each moment it must also be moving. After all, it is a *flying* arrow: if it never moves, it cannot fly. In sum, then, at every moment it must be both moving and still.

Like a burning fire, the flying arrow would seem to violate the principle of non-contradiction. But according to Aristotle, such an absurd "result follows from the assumption that time is composed of moments: if this assumption is not granted, the conclusion will not follow."[28] In other words, if "time is not composed of indivisible nows,"[29] but is instead infinitely divisible, there is no freezing the flying arrow in a moment. Without freezing it in a moment, however, there is no way to generate the contradiction of simultaneous stasis and motion. Cameras tempt us to think that there are moments, real "nows," and that fast-shuttered cameras catch them on highly sensitive film. But if time and motion are in fact continua, as Aristotle believes,[30] then even the fastest-shuttered camera using the most sensitive film will only diminish the blur, perhaps to the point of indiscernibility—either by us, the camera, or both. For, if a motion happens over time that is infinitely divisible, every division of its duration should reveal it to be moving. While moving, it must always occupy a space longer than itself, only less so with each finer division. With no final division, there is no moment at which the arrow turns out to be still. One solution to this paradox, therefore, is to claim that time is not composed of "nows"; instead, it is infinitely divisible.

Is the same Aristotelian solution available to the paradox of fire? Yes, but with profound philosophical consequences that will preoccupy us in one way or another for the rest of this volume. Fire, as a process, is ever-changing, a sort of motion. Dividing the duration of its burning—where this burning is parallel to the arrow's moving—we shall never reach a moment when it ceases to burn, anymore than we shall reach a moment when the arrow is still. The parallel is important to keep in mind, since the same photographic temptations arise for fire that arose for the flying arrow. We imagine capturing a fire on film; with the image of such a fire before our minds, we are tempted to think that we have frozen it in exclusive satisfaction, the way we were tempted by Zeno to think of the arrow as perfectly still in a "now." But if time is infinitely divisible, however finely we divide the duration of the fire's burning, it is no more exclusively satisfied in this division of its duration than was the arrow perfectly still in its own. In every division, no matter how fine, the flying arrow is moving. Correlatively, in every division, no matter how fine, the fire is burning.

This burning is a satisfaction with fuel, lest it be extinguished, but it is also a need for fuel, lest it be static. Fire cannot burn in a moment, anymore than an arrow can fly in a moment, and so it should come as no surprise that the effort to imagine it doing so creates a contradiction. In order to stay aflame in a moment, fire would have to be both need and satiety with respect to the same bit of fuel, violating the principle of non-contradiction. But thanks to the analyses of Aristotle and Zeno, we can say more precisely that the logical offense occurs only when we conceive of time as divisible into "nows." Immersed in the flow of time, surrounded by changes, motions, and processes, we have learned from Heraclitus that these processes appear contradictory only when we conceive them as happening by distinct moments. Indeed, as Aristotle argues, time itself appears contradictory when we conceive it this way.

Yet there is a deep irony here that Aristotle himself does not seem to recognize: the principle of non-contradiction itself encourages us to conceive time and change this way. It demands that we freeze time in a moment in order to examine whether the attributes of anything analyzed are consistent with one another. If this principle really is a necessary condition of knowledge, knowing any object must require freezing it. But if knowing demands that we freeze the object of knowledge, then processes, changes, and motions must be unknowable as such. They cannot ever meet knowing's necessary condition: the principle of non-contradiction. Recognizing this entailment, we should not be surprised to find philosophers who make the principle of non-contradiction a necessary condition of knowledge—namely, Parmenides, Plato, and Aristotle—also making the proper objects of knowledge unchanging, timeless, eternal. Once the proper objects of knowledge have been placed outside of time, the subject who knows them must take up residence in eternity as well, for only in that way can the knowing subject grasp the known object. This is an argument we shall explore in subsequent chapters.

Long before we come to these philosophers, though, we must understand the rival principle that their tradition began by rejecting. In the following section, accordingly, we begin our ascent to the ultimate principle of Heraclitus, his immanent god.

2.3 Divine Conflict

The logos may not freeze time in contradictory moments, but it nonetheless affirms as one a world that appears full of contradictions. "It is wise, listening not to me but to the logos," writes Heraclitus, "to agree that all things are one."[31] How can we affirm as one both life and death, war and peace, hunger and satiety, along with all the other opposites of this world? What sort of logos affirms unity in the midst of so much difference? Is such a logos logically possible? That will depend on our logic. The principle of non-contradiction precludes it, to be sure, but perhaps such a logos becomes possible according to another logic, where the principle of non-contradiction plays an important role, but is not the firmest principle of all. The Heraclitean aphorisms speak not only of the oppositions in the world, but also of their situation in the river of time. Properly understood, according to this logos of time, the contradictions of this multifarious world become one.

Heraclitus notoriously revels in such contradictions, going so far as to exalt conflict and divinize war: "War is father of all."[32] This was a Homeric epithet of Zeus;[33] by appropriating it for war, Heraclitus transfigures war into a god. This is easily misunderstood as bellicose, as a perverse celebration of violence, but instead of worshipping a malicious god he recognizes an indifferent cosmic principle. "One must realize that war is shared," he writes, "and conflict is justice, and that all things come to pass in accordance with conflict."[34] Although this aphorism also evokes the bloody war and greedy conflict denounced by his epic rivals, Hesiod as well as Homer, Heraclitus is highlighting a principle according to which every unity is a tension of warring opposites, while every battle of opposites hides a deeper unity.[35] His simplest examples are bow and lyre: each must strain in opposite directions just to be the unity it is. Contemplating both, he thinks, we see "how a thing agrees at variance with itself; it is a *harmoniē* turning back on itself."[36]

Before joining him in this contemplation, we should become aware of the polysemy of this Greek word. Once we have done so, as we did earlier with logos, we can adopt an Anglicized equivalent: harmonia. In the end, we shall discover, they are but two different ways of speaking of the same structure, whether found in language, thought, or world. In the meantime, though, we should note how *harmoniē* can mean at least three things: a physical arrangement of parts, a musical harmony, or a reconciliation between opponents.[37] For simplicity's sake, let us call these the physical, musical, and political meanings. Not surprisingly, when this word appears in the Heraclitean aphorisms, it reverberates with all three, showing how diverse meanings can agree at variance with themselves when they are strung artfully.[38]

This is nowhere more evident than in an aphorism whose translation obscures its artistry. *Harmoniē aphanēs phanerēs kreittōn:* "Harmony concealed rather than revealed is greater."[39] We can begin to appreciate this artistry by considering the three meanings suggested by the polysemy of *harmoniē* alone. In political arrangements, the unwritten constitution of habit is stronger than many written laws; in musical arrangements, the ratio of tones is more fundamental than the many manifest chords; but of all arrangements, according to Heraclitus, the best is that of the physical world—the cosmos—and its many apparently chaotic events.[40] Beneath its appearances of randomness, according to another aphorism, lies order: "The fairest order [*kosmos*] in the world is a heap of random sweepings."[41] Of the three resonances of *harmoniē* audible in this aphorism, then, Kahn highlights the third, writing of "the divine unity that structures the world."[42] Insofar as this unity is concealed beneath the world's contradictory appearances, he adds, *harmoniē aphanēs* might be taken "as a general title for Heraclitus's philosophical thought."[43]

We have yet to understand the nature of this divine unity, this logos of the whole cosmos, but we have just begun to see how this very aphorism— itself a logos too—conceals a marvelous arrangement. Three features make it an instance of the very harmonia it describes. Besides the polysemy of

harmoniē, there is also the ambiguity of *kreittōn*—like "greater," it can mean
better or stronger. The second sense, writes Kahn, "brings with it the deeper
interpretation" because it resonates with other aphorisms about the hidden
strength of the divine one.[44] This resonance establishes another link
between the concealed harmonia and the divine logos. Counting simply
the multiple meanings of its two most ambiguous words, moreover, we have
already six literal English translations of this sentence. But the aphorism is
more than a skein of intertwined meanings. Unifying this semantic plurality
of parts is their syntactic arrangement. The antonyms *aphanēs* and *phanerēs*—
"unseen" and "seen," most literally—oppose each other across the middle
of this perfectly balanced sentence, while *harmoniē* and *kreittōn* surround
them, so that the unity of arrangement for this sentence, the harmonia of
this logos, is symbolically greater than the opposition it contains.

    This logos therefore agrees at variance with itself. Once we have revealed the
artistry of its arrangement, in fact, this agreement seems hardly to have been
concealed at all: four simple words, straightforward syntax, all together
forming one harmonious logos. Such a hardly concealed but nonetheless
deep harmonia agrees with the logos with which Heraclitus opens his book,
which warns how "men ever fail to comprehend, both before hearing it and
once they have heard."[45] Warned further that the unseen harmonia is greater
than the seen, we should turn back to its two initial signs—bow and lyre—
which conceal deeper unity in difference than first appeared, as does the
aphorism that links them. For in its full version it signals another parallel
between harmonia and logos, beginning with words that turn back to the opening aphorism: "They do not comprehend how a thing agrees at variance with
itself; it is a harmonia turning back on itself, like that of a bow and lyre"[46]

    To be what it is, for instance, the lyre needs the initial opposition of its
frame and strings, the particular arrangement of its diverse parts. But furthermore, this arrangement can produce not just single notes but also the
simultaneous opposition of many. This musical harmony, in turn, may
oppose the voice of a singer to achieve a richer unity, which is further
enriched when he opposes his voice to that of a chorus. Singing together,
they may accompany a feast, celebrating the reconciliation of opponents.[47]
And so on, just as with the bow, which is both like and unlike the lyre. For,
to be what it is, the bow also needs the opposition of its frame and strings.
Like the lyre, which must be plucked to produce its notes, the bow can
shoot an arrow only when it is drawn in opposite directions by the archer.[48]
If he uses it in a hunt, it participates in the harmonious conflict of organic
life; if he uses it in war, it thwarts the reconciliation of opponents. In both
cases, it kills. Compounding this integral unity of opposites, *bios* is Greek
both for life and for bow.[49] Exploiting another opportunity to show the

logos at work in language as well as the world, Heraclitus observes that "the name of the bow is life; its work is death."[50]

Carrying the bow as a weapon of war and the lyre as an adornment of peace, Apollo embodies this harmonious logos.[51] "The lyre and the curved bow shall ever be dear to me," he says the moment he is born, adding, "I will declare to men the unfailing will of Zeus."[52] His declarations of Zeus's will and his paradoxical prophecies exemplify the logos as much as do his contradictory accoutrements. "The lord whose oracle is in Delphi," writes Heraclitus, "neither declares nor conceals but gives a sign."[53] More oracular than the Delphic god, he has likewise given us paradoxical signs. Whereas Apollo's utterances were obscure prophecies whose meaning would nonetheless become clear in time, Heraclitean ambiguity goes deeper. His logos must remain forever ambiguous in order to report faithfully the logos of a world whose own ambiguity never ends.[54] His harmonious logos is greater when concealed, if only because the "nature" it aims to exemplify as well as convey "loves to hide."[55] We may wish Heraclitus had eliminated its ambiguities and then demonstrated its universal claims from universal premises, but instead he has given us only these concrete and paradoxical aphorisms. By the end of this chapter we shall understand better why he has chosen this frustrating route, but for now we must register his evocation of Apollo: both speak the divine logos of Zeus.

Our interpretive task is nonetheless to reveal this concealed logos, for it is far from obvious that the pattern now evident in bow and lyre—the pattern of unity in opposition—is a universal feature of the cosmos, rather than something to be found only in a few concrete examples. To show that it is such a feature, even if Heraclitus is never so explicit, we must highlight something that permeates the world, something that would by its universal presence make everything in it, indeed the world itself, a unity in opposition. The following section argues that this feature is time. As we have seen, when a temporal unity such as fire is frozen in a moment, it will oppose itself. But as long as fire remains immersed in the flow of time, whose perpetual difference makes it the same, it remains unified. The most fundamental unity is the world itself; it too flows in time. This one world, unified by time's reconciliation of its opposites, is Heraclitus's god.

2.4 Divine Unity

Heraclitus is careful to use appropriate names when speaking of the divine, as were other Greeks who trembled before gods both vain and fickle:[56] "the wise is one alone, unwilling and willing to be spoken of by the name of Zeus."[57] This contradictory aphorism, like the god it invokes, stands at the intersection of several lines of Heraclitean thought. One such line connects the aphorisms on wisdom, one of which begins with the same three words: "The wise is one, knowing the plan by which it steers all things through all."[58] Repetition of these neuter and abstract words (*hen to sophon*) encourages us to combine the two aphorisms, turning back from the one to the other as we have already done with earlier reverberations. God, we find, is neither vain nor fickle. He is not one among many others like him. He—or better, it—is something impersonal that knows and executes a rational plan, a *gnōmē*, an insight.[59]

This rational plan and insight correspond to the logos, which is not only a report of the world's reason, but is that very reason itself. This correspondence warrants the following substitution of terms: the wise is one, knowing the logos by which it steers all things through all. "It is wise, listening not to me but to the logos, to agree [*homo-logein*] that all things are one."[60] It is wise, then, to agree with the logos—that is, to say (*legein*) the same (*homo*) as the speech that all things are one, but also to think the same as the thought that all things are one, and ultimately to become as unified as the world in which all things are one. In other words, Heraclitus is encouraging his listeners to bring themselves into agreement with the logos of the wise one, of god. Agreeing with our earlier argument, this logos is also a harmonia, a unity of opposites, a justice in conflict, so that now harmonia is also revealed as the divine plan.

Bringing all these names together, we can more easily see how they invoke in different ways the wise one alone (*mounon*), who is thus understandably unwilling as well as willing to be spoken of by the name of Zeus. This aphorism about naming god, which appears so contradictory on its surface, conceals a deeper consistency by unifying opposing syntactic roles for *mounon* ("alone" or "only"). The Greek word floats more freely through the original aphorism than does any of its equivalents through an English rendering. We have already witnessed Heraclitean words playing an ambiguous syntactic role in the river fragment; Graham shows how this technique recurs in several other aphorisms.[61] As for *mounon*, we should recognize that it can be taken with what precedes or what follows it.

Taken with what precedes, "the wise one," it produces the translation quoted earlier—"the wise is one alone, unwilling and willing to be spoken of by the name of Zeus"—indicating that there is only one such being. On this surface reading, god may be willing to be spoken of by the name of Zeus, insofar as that name signals the highest honor in Greek theology, but is unwilling to be identified with him because of the anthropomorphism of the epic poets. Such thinking would put Heraclitus in agreement with Xenophanes, who not only criticized anthropomorphic theology,[62] but also wrote of "one god" (*heis theos*) who was "greatest among gods and men."[63] Heraclitus criticizes Xenophanes almost as harshly as he does Pythagoras,[64] so it might surprise us to find him adopting both of their doctrines. But whether he exploits the harmonies of the one or the henotheism of the other—not to mention the cosmologies of the Milesians—he enriches every doctrine he adopts from his predecessors according to his own logos.[65]

Beneath the surface reading of the aphorism on the naming of god, accordingly, his logos suggests a deeper translation. For when *mounon* is taken with what follows, it can modify either the infinitive ("to be spoken of") or the noun ("the name"). Taking it with both, we derive this composite English paraphrase: the wise is one, willing alone to be spoken of by the name of Zeus, but unwilling to be spoken of by the name of Zeus alone.[66] In other words, none other than this god should be known by the name of Zeus, since none other is worthy of such high esteem. But also, because even this name is inadequate for such an impersonal and indifferent deity, this god should also be known by other names.

We introduced Heraclitus's theology under the name of war, the divine conflict that is justice.[67] This conflict is harmonia, unity in opposition, the logos. As a result, god not only knows the logos by which it steers all things through all; god is this logos. It is therefore wise to recognize that all things are one, declares this logos, which is itself the unity of all things in their harmonious opposition, in the conflict that is justice, in the "cosmos" that "ever was and is and will be: fire everliving, kindled in measures and in measures quenched."[68] On the growing list of divine names, then, we find Fire, War, Conflict, Justice, Harmonia, Logos, and Zeus. Anyone who is wise, Heraclitus thinks, will recognize them all as both adequate and inadequate names for the wise One.

2.5 Becoming God

This One, as we have seen, "steers all things through all,"[69] but it does so not as a god transcending what it governs; rather, it is immanent—the world itself as deity. "This is monism with a vengeance," writes Kahn.[70] We shall eventually complicate this description, after we have noticed that the Heraclitean aphorism which appears most explicitly monistic conceals a contrapuntal pluralism, holding both monism and pluralism in a harmonia that is paradoxically both one and many. Before we come to this supreme paradox of Heraclitean philosophy, though, we can see that its monism is far from the static one of pure being, which we shall find Parmenides developing in the next chapter.[71] If Heraclitus is a monist, his One is dynamic: one world perpetually becoming according to a divine order.

The name "fire" suits this order as well as any other, especially when he emphasizes its judicial role. "Thunderbolt pilots all things,"[72] Heraclitus writes, invoking at once the purest fire of the heavens and the traditional accoutrement of Zeus, arbiter of justice.[73] Were the judicial role of pure fire not clear enough from this aphorism alone, Heraclitus also writes that "fire coming on will discern and catch up with all things."[74] Such a fire discerns not simply malfeasants, but seizes everything. With so indiscriminate an indictment, however, what sort of judgment does it render, what sort of sentence does it deliver, and how can it do so justly? The justice of cosmic fire, as we shall now argue, is what it suffers and itself exemplifies: time.

We first approached Heraclitus's illogical logos through an analysis of fire, producing the contradiction of "need and satiety" when we froze it in a moment. Contradiction and conflict is similarly the fate of everything temporal at every moment in this *kosmos* of time. The world is one and ever-living, but it is nonetheless a cauldron of many things, all becoming and perishing. Some of these things are becoming while others are perishing, to be sure; more importantly, though, each of them is becoming and perishing at once. At every moment of its burning, fire perishes from its own satisfaction yet becomes thanks to its need: kindled in measures and in measures quenched. Moreover, when we articulated Heraclitus's illogical logos of time with the help of later philosophers, we found Zeno's flying arrow at every moment to be both moving and still, while Aristotle's "now" proved to be both present and absent.

As time passes, generally speaking, everything it encompasses must age; as everything ages, as it moves through time, it must suffer contradiction at every moment. This is true of a river, but also of a mountain range, and even of "the god [*theos*]: day night, winter summer, war peace, satiety hunger. It alters, as when mingled with perfumes it gets named according to the pleasure of each one."[75] This is the only extant aphorism in which Heraclitus defines his deity, but now that we have surveyed the other divine names we can see how his definition draws upon them. Indeed, by comparing his god directly to an altar fire which provokes different names according to the different pleasures or scents of the different perfumes mixed with it, Heraclitus has woven into the definition itself an explanation for the assignment of many different names to the one god.[76] According to this aphorism, these many names are not those we have examined so far, such as "fire" or "harmonia," each revealing in its own way the concealed divine nature—but rather the names common in Greek religion, which he roundly criticizes.[77]

War and peace, for instance, were popularly considered separate and opposing gods,[78] but Heraclitus unites them under the rule of one god: "War is father of all and king of all."[79] Although he appears to be contradicting himself by privileging one opposing god over the other, in truth he unites these two popular conceptions of deity in one hidden god who is neither war nor peace, at least as commonly conceived, but rather both in harmonia— not unlike the bow, the lyre, and the god who makes them both his signs, Apollo. The same critique of popular piety is more explicit in his definition's conflation of "day night." After all, both were divinized by Hesiod, whom Heraclitus rebukes for dividing and thus misunderstanding the one god.[80] "The teacher of most is Hesiod," he writes with scorn; "It is him they know as knowing most, who did not recognize day and night: they are one."[81] They are so unified in the Hercalitean definition of god, in fact, that their names stand next to one another in blunt asyndeton, without a conjunction, as though in apposition rather than opposition. Popular piety, by contrast, opposes Day and Night, and thus overlooks the divine unity in their opposition.

Approaching the fire of the divine altar, analogously, thoughtless worshippers name it "myrrh" or "cyprus," or "rose," according to the scents of the perfumes mixed with it.[82] They thus overlook its concealed nature, its unity of opposing need and satiety, its harmonia. "Most men do not think things in the way they encounter them," Heraclitus protests, for most are like these thoughtless worshippers who fail to "recognize what they experience, but believe their own opinions."[83] These opinions are the perfumes they mix with the divine, concealing its logos according to the pleasure of each. Exploiting these opinions and pleasures, the Heraclitean logos of god, his definition, is thus a list of things carefully arranged—a harmonia— according to their positive or negative value from the human perspective (or at least that of sixth-century Greeks and their religion).[84]

Daylight stands for life (positive), nighttime for death (negative); winter is the stormy season (negative), summer the season of growth (positive). Switching from these two prominent cosmic cycles, Heraclitus next lists two dramatic human cycles. War destroys (negative), whereas peace preserves (positive); satiety is what we work to achieve (positive), while hunger is what we struggle to avoid (negative). Taken together, then, the values of these oppositions form the following complex pattern: $+ - - + \mid - + + -$. Within the cosmic cycles, first, there is a chiasmus $(+ - - +)$; within the human cycles, next, the order of values is reversed (– + + –). Ultimately, then, the definition unifies an opposition between cosmic and human. Chiastic unity, we shall see, is Heraclitus's god. We should not be surprised to find the divine concealed beneath such a complex pattern of human valuations, for "although the logos is shared, most men live as though their thinking were a private possession."[85] In the midst of these private possessions, god is the harmonia that unifies their oppositions.

If this harmonia were to be one thing, it would be time. Time unifies day and night, winter and summer; time is an ordering, kindled in measures and in measures quenched; time, it therefore seems, is Heraclitus's god. For only by perpetually becoming, in time, can this god encompass the simultaneity of need and satiety, the absence and presence of every moment, as well as the simultaneous birth and death of every thing. That said, definitively naming this god—whether by "time" or any other single noun—would be a mistake. "Grammar," Nietzsche writes, "is the metaphysics of the people."[86] We the people are tempted by its distinction between noun and predicate, for example, to assume a real distinction between lightning and its flash when we hear that "Lightning flashes."[87] In the reality described by this simple sentence there is not the lightning, on one hand, and its flash, on the other. The lightning just is the flash: "there is no 'being' behind the doing, effecting, becoming."[88] With grammar as our metaphysics, however, we are tempted by nouns into thinking of the things they designate as static. "Fire" and other nouns seem to refer to something stable—a nugget, so to speak—although we have seen how they misrepresent their referents by doing so. Apparently recognizing this temptation, Heraclitus eschews a simple definition of god and instead provides a logos that lists nouns in polar opposition.

Such a definition suggests that god is not one static thing to which these nouns refer, but rather the temporal process of opposition between them all. To dispel further the illusion of stasis fostered by nouns, Heraclitus switches in the second sentence of his definition to verbs, which in Greek may stand alone without any explicit subject: "[It] alters, as when mingled with perfumes [it] gets named according to the pleasure of each one."[89] Had Heraclitus been less artful, and more inclined to neologism, he might have anticipated Heidegger and written not of god but of "godding," or something to that effect.[90] Besides its awkwardness, such a ruse stumbles on the fact that verbs (not to mention participles, which are verbal nouns) may also trick us into ossifying the world, into thinking processes themselves as stable. When we think of flowing or burning, for example, how often do we think of them as processes or things that could exist in a moment without contradiction? Without practicing Heraclitean meditation—reminding ourselves perpetually of the passage of time, and of the absurdity produced by trying to thwart its greed—the candid answer must be: nearly always.

To disrupt such thinking, Heraclitus juxtaposes his definition's two sentences in a unity of perfect syntactical opposition. "The first consists of nine nouns in the nominative, with no syntax, simply a list of names," as Kahn observes, whereas "the second sentence is all syntax, with three finite verb clauses but no subject noun."[91] In sum, Heraclitus uses grammar itself to dispel the illusions of grammar. Defining god not by one sentence or the other, but rather in the harmonia between the two, he reports a logos that exhibits what it conveys. His becoming god is the unity of all these opposites, a god that "rests by changing,"[92] a god that is the unity of this opposition as it processes through thought, language, and world.

2.6 Becoming Oneself

To find ourselves in the becoming god, we must first search for our selves. Doing so, we follow in the footsteps of Heraclitus himself: "I went in search of myself."[93] Yet contradiction arises the moment such a search begins. If Heraclitus is searching for himself at a moment, he must both be himself and not be himself, for he is both the searcher and the sought. As searcher, he must be present to himself; as sought, he must be absent. "This is as straightforward a paradox as any in Heraclitus," writes Kahn, who summarizes it with a simple question: "How can I be the object of my own search?"[94] This simple question will be elaborated throughout the ancient philosophical tradition, first by Plato, then by Aristotle, culminating in the version of the Skeptic Sextus Empiricus.[95] We get a sufficient sense of it for the purpose of interpreting Heraclitus once we recognize how a moment of self-inquiry requires the searcher to be "absent while present."[96]

Described in these terms, Heraclitus's paradox of self-inquiry resembles his contradictory description of fire as need and satiety. Accordingly, we should not be surprised to learn that this contradiction too can be avoided by refusing to freeze self-inquiry in a moment, by understanding it as a temporal process. As much as this process resembles fire, though, it differs inasmuch as it is self-reflexive. Fire burns fuel, something other than itself; self-inquiry inquires into itself. When it does so, however, it must find itself to be this very activity of self-inquiry. Otherwise there would arise a distinction between this activity and its object, so that the activity would not be a self-inquiry, properly speaking, but instead an inquiry into a distinct object. As with the flash of lightning, we should not be fooled by grammar into performing two inquiries, one into the self and another into its characteristic activity, self-inquiry. Our investigation of this activity is tantamount to an inquiry into self because the self is nothing other than this activity: its thinking about itself must be a thinking of its own thinking, a thinking of its own thinking of its own thinking, and so on *ad infinitum*.[97]

The next section will attempt to grasp this infinite regress, ultimately arguing that it is not nearly so narcissistic as it first appears because it involves a contemplation of the whole cosmos. Before grasping this elusive conclusion, though, we can already see how a self that is identical to self-inquiry would increase itself, and do so infinitely: it inquires into itself, then inquires into itself inquiring, thence into itself inquiring into itself inquiring, and so on, infinitely elevating the height of its self-reflection. This vertiginous result matches two of the few extant Heraclitean aphorisms about the self. First: "To the self belongs a logos that increases itself." And second: "You will not find out the limits of the self by going, even if you travel over every way, so deep is its logos."[98] It is the activity of self-inquiry that travels over every way, as we shall see, but we have already argued that this activity is the self itself. The logos of the self is thus without limit because its activity is equally so. To understand the nature of this infinite self, in sum, we must grasp the nature of this infinite activity.

This is a difficult activity to grasp, and not only because of its infinity, for grasping it—like grasping fire—seems to demand that we freeze it in a moment. But this would generate the contradiction introduced above: because the self (as subject of the inquiry) investigates the self (as object of the inquiry), these two selves must be different for there to be a genuine *inquiry*, but in the same moment they must also be identical for the self truly to inquire into *itself*. Perhaps this contradiction will disappear, as did the similar contradiction of frozen fire, once we introduce the flow of time. Fire is nothing more than the immanent logos of its burning, the simultaneous unity of its opposing need and satiety, the paradoxical harmonia of its being kindled in measures and in measures quenched. Fire, in short, is a temporal process. Frozen in a moment—like a fire, a flying arrow, or time itself— you too must be simultaneously becoming and perishing, moving and still, present and absent. Although this, your complex harmonia, may be concealed from yourself, Heraclitus seems to think you reveal its hidden strength whenever you go in search of yourself.

Searching for yourself, you move through time, just as you do while reading this sentence: moving from the self that thinks through the thoughts at its beginning to the self that thinks through those at its end, not to mention the self that now thinks about itself thinking, then thinks about itself thinking about itself thinking . . . When you move through any sentence—but most obviously when it is as complex and self-reflexive as the previous one—you have stepped into a river of thinking, so to speak. Whereas the waters of a literal river flow around you, however, the thinking of a sentence flows through you, just as your thinking flows through it. There is a confluence of logos and logos, quite literally, so that when you understand its thinking, when the confluence is complete, the subject and object of your thinking become one. Such confluence is most obviously perfect when the object of your thinking is the self-thinking that is your very self. When the object of someone's inquiry must be the very subject that is his self-inquiry, as we have seen in Heraclitus's search for himself, or the search of any self for itself, the logos of one must be indistinguishable from the logos of the other.

In the activity of self-inquiry, then, as in the burning of fire, the contradictions of any frozen moment become a harmonia, a unity in opposition, through the passage of time. By self-inquiry, in short, one becomes one self.

2.7 Grasping Oneself

The unity of thinking's subject and object is nowhere more prominent in the Heraclitean aphorisms than in the one that resembles the logos of god: "Graspings [*syllapsies*]: wholes and not wholes, convergent divergent, consonant dissonant, from all things one and from one thing all."[99] The logos of god begins likewise with a noun and then defines it by a list of oppositions: "the god [*theos*]: day night, winter summer, war peace, satiety hunger."[100] In Kahn's view, "both in form and content these two fragments serve as complements to one another, providing a kind of summary of Heraclitus's thought."[101] Linked by their common form, in fact, they invite a comparison of their parallel elements. What is the relationship, for instance, between *theos* and *syllapsies*, god and graspings? Recognizing this particular relationship—this identification, we shall argue—turns out to be the highest activity of Heraclitean philosophy, and it is tantamount to recognizing oneself. To promote this recognition and identification, we should begin by examining the other parallels between these aphorisms.

Most importantly, this new logos replaces the concrete and manifest oppositions of the logos of god—day night, and the others—with concealed and abstract oppositions.[102] The former are not exhaustive, after all, but merely examples; to their list, other aphorisms add disease and health, weariness and rest, living and dead, waking and sleeping, young and old.[103]

Rather than providing examples, then, the abstract oppositions describe the concealed structure of their unity in opposition, the ubiquitous harmonia of our temporal cosmos. By both expressing and exemplifying this harmonia, this abstract logos poses the most direct challenge to the exalted status of the principle of non-contradiction. To be precise, it does not threaten its value for sound thinking; instead, it dethrones it as the supreme arbiter of rational thinking, the purest activity of reason itself, the firmest principle of all. For, according to this logos, when we understand "day night" not just as a manifest opposition but as a concealed unity, what we grasp is both whole and not-whole: "day-night" is a whole unifying the not-whole of "day versus night." The object of our understanding is thus neither the one nor the other—neither the unity nor the opposition, neither the whole nor the not-whole—but both at once.

Correlatively, when we understand fire not just as a revealed unity but as a concealed opposition, we perform the same combined activity, grasping the whole that is need-satiety as well as the not-whole of need versus satiety. Whether we seek to understand fire or river or anything else in this temporal cosmos, therefore, we must not only analyze it into distinct moments—where it is contradictory, not-whole, divergent, and dissonant—but also synthesize these moments into a temporal continuity—where it is consistent, whole, convergent, and consonant. Neither by analysis alone nor by synthesis alone do we understand, Heraclitus is thus saying, but only by both together, a combined activity he calls *syllapsies*.[104] The logos that defines this combined activity does not exclude the principle of non-contradiction because it does not exclude analysis, which is this principle in activity. Instead, it reveals analysis as merely one of the opposites unified by understanding. To understand, according to Heraclitus, we must synthesize as well as analyze—not just alternately, but simultaneously—with one complex activity he calls *nous*.[105]

Lest this activity seem too complex, perhaps impossible, Graham compares it to looking at the duck-rabbit drawing popularized in philosophy by Ludwig Wittgenstein.[106] Looked at in one way, the drawing appears to be of a duck; looked at in another, though, it appears as a rabbit. The drawing remains unchanged, yet we alternate between seeing it one way and then another, back and forth, often quickly, and sometimes involuntarily. When we willfully contemplate not just the drawing but also these very alternations, though, we can rise to a higher level of reflection, coming to see the drawing as duck-rabbit, a unity in opposition. Similar epiphanies occur when we study contrapuntal music. Listening to a Bach fugue, for example, we can with disciplined effort discern not only one theme or its counter-point, nor only both in alternation, but both at once. Beyond this difficult accomplishment, the highest understanding discerns ultimately the concealed harmonia of their conflict. To fully appreciate the fugue, in other words, we must hear the unity in opposition that is Bach's composition. Studying Heraclitean aphorisms with as much discipline as a musicologist studies fugues, we learn likewise to see their concealed harmonia, complex composition, and unity in opposition.

This is the logos they exhibit, but it is also the logos of the world they describe. Heraclitean aphorisms share the logos of the world; their goal is to help us share it as well. To the extent that our thinking is already a temporal process, like everything else in the world, it already does. *Syllapsies* is accordingly ambiguous between two English meanings: on one hand, the "comprehensions" germane to thinking's subject; on the other, the "collections" in the world that are thinking's object. "*Syllapsies*," Kahn writes, "will denote the pairwise structuring of reality and also the act of intelligence by which this structure is gathered together."[107] His commendable effort to carry this ambiguity into English is "graspings," which he believes can signify objective collections of things in the world as well as subjective comprehensions of it. Close as this translation may come to preserving this delicate ambiguity, though, it tips the balance toward the subjective side. To restore that balance to equilibrium, let us introduce another neologism. After "logos" and "harmonia," then, we shall adapt a final term directly from Heraclitus's Greek: "syllapsis."[108]

Whichever term one prefers to denote this complex activity, one must preserve this crucial ambiguity. For when understanding is achieved, according to Heraclitus, the thinking subject exhibits the very same activity as the object understood, the activity we now call syllapsis. Insofar as it is a temporal process, as we mentioned above, our thinking is always participating in this activity, just as a fire must do to burn. Yet some fires grow weak either by excess or deficiency, by need or satiety, whereas other fires burn brighter thanks to their more perfect unity in this characteristic opposition. A much later Heraclitean makes this analogy himself, twice comparing the virtuous self to "a bright fire that appropriates whatever you throw into it and from it produces flame and light."[109] We might elaborate his analogy a little, adding that virtuously thinking selves exhibit a perfect unity in the midst of their characteristic opposition—analysis versus synthesis—and this unity is *nous*, which likewise grows stronger with every appropriation.

Guiding our thinking exclusively by the principle of non-contradiction, we arrest whatever we contemplate in a moment and generate contradictions. Contemplating fire, for instance, we see only opposition, divergence, and dissonance, thereby misunderstanding fire's full nature. Were we to abdicate analysis, however, we might see unity, convergence, and consonance—the way we see a fire when we use it to cook, for example, without considering it as a complex process—but we would also misunderstand fire's full nature. Thinking only synthetically about it, we could not know what opposition, divergence, and dissonance it unified, reconciled, and harmonized. To think at once of its unity and its opposition, indeed of its unity in opposition, the self must think both synthetically and analytically, which is to say syllaptically.

This requirement of understanding becomes crucial when the self tries to understand itself. For, as we saw in the previous section of this chapter, self-understanding requires that thinking's subject be the same as its object. Were such a subject to think only analytically, on one hand, contradiction and fragmentation would afflict it as well as its object, just as we found when we analyzed the apparently banal but truly paradoxical aphorism: "I went in search of myself."[110] On the other hand, anyone who searches for himself without the help of analysis will assume he is a unity, as we humans usually do before we have been awoken from our self-neglect, either by the paradoxes of self-inquiry or, as is more often the case, the frustration of inner conflict.[111] To consider oneself a unity in this way, without also seeing oneself as opposed to oneself, is to misunderstand what kind of unity one is: the only kind there is, according to Heraclitus, a unity in opposition.

If a thinking subject is to understand itself—indeed, if it is to become one self—it must exercise both analysis and synthesis. In other words, it must think according to a more comprehensive principle than the principle of non-contradiction. For the moment we shall call this the principle of syllapsis: "wholes and not wholes, convergent divergent, consonant dissonant, from all things one and from one thing all."[112]

To think according to this principle is the ultimate goal of Heraclitean philosophy; this is its version of reason. To anyone who holds the principle of non-contradiction to be the firmest principle of all, needless to say, this version of reason will appear impure. It is contradictory, after all, for the same subject to think both analytically and synthetically at the same moment about the same object, just as it is contradictory for the same object to be both whole and not-whole, not to mention all the other opposites named in the more comprehensive principle. Yet purely analytic thinking, according to the principle of non-contradiction, has also revealed itself as contradictory, ironically, whenever it turns to anything temporal, but most of all when it turns upon itself. Self-thinking according to the principle of syllapsis, by contrast, surpasses its contradictions, because its fragmentation, divergence, and dissonance are together only one component of this complex activity. The other component simultaneously achieves reconciliation, convergence, and consonance. If this synthesis be considered impossible—as it must be by anyone who exalts the principle of non-contradiction above its secondary status—then so too, remember, must be the burning of fire.

Searching for oneself is not impossible, of course, because self-thinking, like the burning of fire, is in time. Accordingly, we may reconstruct the following movement in the self-thinking of syllapsis. Thinking of itself by first exercising analysis upon its simultaneous unity of synthesis and analysis will indeed elicit a contradiction. Analysis fragments the self into the divergent activities of analysis and synthesis. But since this self-thinking is truly syllaptic, such fragmentation serves only to summon a reconciliation. From this additional unity of analysis with synthesis, however, a subsequent analysis elicits still another contradiction by breaking this unity into parts that will summon still another synthesis. And so on. In this perpetual motion of self-reflection, the self will achieve thinking of thinking, not to mention thinking of thinking of thinking . . . In the midst of this vertiginous self-inquiry, moreover, the self recognizes itself. For at every milestone along this infinite way, the subject and object of thinking is but the same syllapsis. In self-inquiry, in short, the self recognizes itself as this divine activity, the very activity of the whole temporal cosmos, becoming god.

2.8 Immortals Mortals

Whenever we arrest this becoming god in a moment, mixing its divine fire with our longing for stability, we give it inappropriately static names: day or night, winter or summer, satiety or hunger, war or peace. Whenever we think the temporal world, including our selves, according to the principle of non-contradiction, absurdities arise. Why do we do either? Parmenides and his philosophical heirs cannot be to blame. He may have been the first to propose this principle, as Chapter 3 will argue, but he seems to have written after Heraclitus.[113] The target of the Heraclitean aphorisms cannot therefore have been Parmenides, his principle, or the successors who honed it, but must instead have been something more fundamental in habitual ways of thinking. This target seems to have been the denial of time which the principle of non-contradiction appears to justify. Yet which pleasure (*hēdonē*) do we indulge when we deny time? None of the extant aphorisms names it directly, although from them we must expect it to be hostile to the becoming god. Naming it more explicitly than did Heraclitus himself, his philosophical heirs have since called it nostalgia.

"That it cannot break time and time's greed," writes Nietzsche, arguably the most faithful of these heirs, "that is the will's loneliest misery."[114] And why is this? Why is the will miserable before inexorable time? Every new

moment brings the death of an old one; time's greed thus consumes
moments and whatever in them we have cherished. Whenever we deny
time, then, the pleasure we indulge is the fantasy of a deathless "now," an
eternal present, an immortal moment in which nothing good is lost. With
its idea of a timeless heaven, where everything good survives, and only what
is good survives, Christianity presented Nietzsche with the purest form of
this fantasy. Diagnosing the redemption it promises as "the spirit of revenge"
against time, a resentful denial of its inexorable greed, his Zarathustra
preaches an alternate redemption, a "reconciliation with time."[115] This is
the often misunderstood doctrine of the Eternal Recurrence. Although this
book is not the place to interpret it,[116] we should nonetheless notice how
another Heraclitean anticipated both it and the diagnosis that prompted
Nietzsche to propose it.

Marcus Aurelius meditates on the passage of greedy time, not to escape it,
but to accept it. "Observe every object," he writes, "and realize that it is
already being dissolved and in process of change, and, as it were, coming to
be from decay and dispersion."[117] Preoccupied with death, not least his own,
Marcus writes with a melancholy that Nietzsche's joyful science seeks to
overcome.[118] However disparate their moods, though, both are after the
same Heraclitean goal: a reconciliation with time, a recognition that life is at
every moment intertwined with death, an acceptance of such conflict as just
and ultimately divine. Returning our attention to his aphorisms, none of
them promotes this reconciliation more directly than the one Kahn considers "in point of form Heraclitus's masterpiece, the most perfectly symmetri-
cal of all the fragments."[119] Indeed, this aphorism exhibits a complex chiasmus
similar to the one we found in the logos of god, forging a formal link with
that aphorism which its content also corroborates: "Immortals mortals, mortals immortals, living the others' death, dead in the others' life."[120]

Before discussing the content of this aphorism, let us analyze its chiastic
form, first recalling the structure of the logos it resembles. Using signs for
the positive or negative values of the terms by which god was there defined,
we discerned the following complex pattern in the first half of that apho-
rism: + − − + | − + + −. Within the cosmic cycles denoted by its first set of
nouns, there was one chiasmus (+ − − +); within the human cycles of its
second set, there was another, but the order of values was reversed (− + + −).
Thus, the first half of that logos unified a chiastic opposition between
cosmic and human, immortal and mortal. Its second half moved from
nouns to verbs, unifying syntactic as well as semantic opposites, all the while
frustrating our desire to ossify divinity.

A remarkably similar pattern emerges when we analyze this logos of life
and death. If we use "+" to stand for life, "−" for death, we get the following

pattern in its first half: "Immortals (+) mortals (–), mortals (–) immortals (+)." Its second half reverses the chiastic pattern by switching from nouns to verbs, or at least verbal adjectives, namely participles. Assigning a second set of values based on form rather than content, then, letting "–" stand for participles, "+" for nouns, we get the following chiasmus from a translation that hews closest to the Greek: "living (–) the others' death (+), in the others' life (+) having died (–)." This reversal elicits an identical pattern from these two logoi: + – – + | – + + –.[121] Each exhibits a chiasmus of chiasmus, a super-chiasmus. No matter how complex its chiastic structure, no matter how close its formal resemblances to the logos of god, this logos on life and death speaks louder with the content of its words.

Immortality was the hallmark of divinity in Greek religion: gods live forever, humans must die.[122] Thus, by intertwining life and death, living and dying, mortality and immortality—just as earlier aphorisms intertwined becoming and perishing—this aphorism implicitly conflates divinity and humanity. The conflation is so thorough, in fact, that the arrangement of the aphorism's first half makes the subjects of the participles in its second half ambiguous. Do immortals live the death of mortals, while mortals are dead in immortals' lives? Or, instead, do mortals live the death of immortals, so that immortals are dead in mortals' lives?[123] Stumbling upon ambiguity now, as so often before in Heraclitus, we need not choose one interpretation to the exclusion of the other; instead, we should see a unity in this opposition, a harmonia that is the deeper significance of its logos. As it turns out, this deeper significance is a lesson we have already learned but cannot fully digest until we have accepted its application to our selves.

Arrested in a moment, we too are both whole and not-whole, absent and present, dying and being born. Every moment of our lives is thus entwined with fragmentation, absence, and death; correlatively, every moment of our death should also be entwined with wholeness, presence, and life. "Perhaps the greatest surprise that awaits us at our death," writes Kahn, "is that things will not be very different, since we are and always have been familiar with the experience of continually dying and continually being reborn."[124] We reconcile with time, accordingly, when we accept that time is no more greedy than generous: it is each in equal measures. Such an acceptance should be doleful and buoyant in equal measures, but neither Marcus nor Nietzsche was able to maintain this difficult balance. Marcus tips it toward melancholy, with his emphasis on destructive death; with his emphasis on creative life, Nietzsche inclines toward joy.[125] Despite their different emphases, though, both are faithful to the Heraclitean logos: affirming the whole world, acknowledging the god in which we too are becoming, and grasping its conflicts whenever our thinking arrests it in a moment.

Marcus advises in one passage: "Let the whole of time and the whole of substance be continuously present to your mind."[126] To this ambitious intellectual discipline, he soon adds the following affective exercise: "the universe loves to create what is to happen . . . therefore I say to the universe: 'I join in your love.' "[127] Against the temptation to arrest time in a moment, in other words, Marcus recommends contemplating time's passage and loving its perpetual activity of creation. Combining his own meditation on time with a still more rhapsodic embrace of everything it encompasses, Nietzsche later asks, "Have you ever said Yes to one joy?" If so, he adds, "then you also said Yes to *all* pain. All things are enchained, entwined, enamored."[128] Along with his parallel meditation on the whole of time, then, Nietzsche also evokes the Stoic doctrine that all events are necessarily connected. To his own intellectual discipline, finally, he adds the following affective condition: "If you ever wanted one time two times, if you ever said 'I like you, happiness! Whoosh! Moment!' then you wanted *everything* back."[129] Sharing Marcus's enthusiasm for all things in time, then, Nietzsche likewise flirts with an eternal recurrence of all times.[130]

But whether they believe in this doctrine as a matter of cosmology, or merely propose it as a spiritual exercise—enjoining us to love time's perpetual creation so ardently as to wish paradoxically for its repetition— both philosophers are trying to elaborate the Heraclitean logos. Speaking of this logos, and quoting Heraclitus, Marcus writes that "men are at odds with that with which they are in most contact."[131] All the Stoics owe a deep debt to Heraclitus, but Marcus pays him special homage.[132] Besides quoting this and other aphorisms from memory, he twice alludes to the Heraclitean river. "Existence is like a river in perpetual flow,"[133] he writes in one passage, elaborating the same metaphor in another: "Time is a river of things that become, with a strong current. No sooner is a thing seen than it has been swept away."[134] For his part, Nietzsche alludes to the river and agrees with Heraclitus that "everything is in flux."[135] Although this doctrine has been frozen through the "hard winter" of subsequent philosophy, he writes, at long last "the thaw wind is blowing!"[136] Nietzsche fashioned himself this thaw wind, this champion of Heraclitus, for as we saw at the end of our introductory chapter he eulogized him thus: "The world forever needs the truth, hence the world forever needs Heraclitus."[137]

In this section we have turned to Marcus and Nietzsche—two Heracliteans who supplement the intellectual austerity of the extant aphorisms with emotional diagnoses—in order to understand why humans so stubbornly distort the logos, conceal its harmonia, and arrest its becoming god. The answer shared by both is that our impotence before time, and especially our death, makes us inveterately nostalgic. While Heraclitus does not promise us power over time, he nonetheless reconciles us to it by conflating life and death, mortality and immortality, humanity and divinity. We cannot freeze time, but by thinking syllaptically and thus meditating on the unity in these and other oppositions, the harmonia of their conflict, and the logos of their ever-living fire, we take consolation by grasping ourselves becoming god.

2.9 One and Many

Syllapsis is the divine dialectic of analysis and synthesis. As analysis, it brings all things out of one; as synthesis, it brings one thing out of all. The terms of this distinction are as applicable to god as they are to self, but they appear more suited to cognition than to the cosmos. Reverting to the more cosmic terms canvassed earlier, then, we recall that the first component of this divine activity is also called conflict; the second, justice. Whichever set of terms they feature, though, the Heraclitean aphorisms are usually either one of two types: some speak of contradiction, conflict, and opposition, while others testify to reconciliation, justice, and unity.[138] These two types of aphorism represent two divergent and dissonant trends in Heraclitean philosophy, but they appear no less convergent and consonant when properly arranged by a correct interpretation. To achieve this arrangement and interpretation, as we have seen, several aphorisms offer the key.[139] None does so more perfectly than the principle of syllapsis.

This one logos reports the unifying structure of all the aphorisms when they are collected and comprehended together, and this structure is chiasmus: opposition in unity, unity in opposition. Recognizing this pattern, and doing our best to avoid neologism, we may at last translate *syllapsies* by a word that is accepted English, even if it too began as Greek. Equally at home naming thought and world, it tips the balance neither toward the subject nor the object of thinking. "Chiasmus," in short, is no closer to "comprehension" than it is to "collection." Most significantly, it reveals the structure of both, the concealed harmonia of the logos itself. Accordingly, the principle of syllapsis could just as well be called the principle of chiasmus, which we called it in our introductory chapter, translating it as follows. "Chiasmus: wholes and not wholes, convergent divergent, consonant dissonant, from all things one and from one thing all."[140]

True to form, this aphorism exemplifies the structure it describes. Of its four pairs of opposites, the first and the last are joined internally by a conjunction, while the two in the middle lack one. A first chiasmus is

therefore: syndeton, asyndeton; asyndeton, syndeton. Secondly, with each
opposite in the middle expressed by one word, while many words express
most of the oppositions around them, the aphorism exhibits the chiastic
movement it reports, going from many to one before returning to many
from one. *Nous*, or understanding, is just this dialectical movement between
synthesis and analysis. As such, it must also be the movement exhibited
by any understanding of this very chiastic principle.

Whenever it is understood, it must be thinking's subject as well as its
object, exactly as we concluded earlier.[141] Indeed, as we also concluded
there, the self is but the perpetual exercise of this understanding, which is
an understanding of understanding (and so on without end). The principle
of chiasmus thus reveals itself as the logos not only of understanding, but
ultimately of divine self-knowledge.

As subject of the understanding of this principle, you must move between
parts and whole, analyzing and synthesizing, as you would in the case of any
other logos. While understanding this logos in particular, though, your
thinking must move not only between parts and whole, but also between this
whole and itself as part of a still greater whole: your self. After all, you are the
subject of understanding that is identical to its object, the principle of chiasmus; as your understanding becomes an understanding of understanding,
then, so too does the logos with which you are identical: wholes and not-
wholes both, in a perpetual dialectic between unity and plurality, moving to
ever higher levels of understanding. Once prompted—whether by the logos
of Heraclitean aphorisms, the harmonia in the world these aphorisms
report, or the syllapsis of the thinking self they enjoin us to recognize—we
identify more fully with all three. Like the fire that burns brighter by its
perfect chiasmus of need and satiety, when we consciously unify our own
opposition of analysis and synthesis, through the dialectical movement of
time, we burn brightest of all. We grasp, finally, our own divine chiasmus.

Earlier we introduced the divine as both conflict and unity: conflict and
contradiction in a moment, unity and reconciliation in the flow of time.
Now that we understand Heraclitus's god more thoroughly as the divine
chiasmus of unity and plurality, we may analyze the simultaneous contradiction as many and one, whereas the temporal reconciliation is one alone. Yet
this god is both contradiction and reconciliation, and thus more paradoxical than a simple chiasmus of unity and plurality. At this elevated stage of
analysis, in other words, this god must be many and one . . . as well as one.
The paradoxical chiasmus of many-one (or one-many) makes Heraclitean
theology difficult enough; the addition of this final one makes it seem
altogether mystical. But we have been prepared to understand precisely this

paradox by our earlier discussion of self-thinking. For at this level of divine contemplation there is indeed an additional contradiction, but higher order conflict summons a further reconciliation, provoking another conflict, generating a still greater unity, and so on.[142]

Ascent past the first level is a struggle, to say the least. While remaining here below, though, we can nonetheless see how this divine activity shares the dialectical movement of self-thinking. Divine activity exhibits the logos of self-knowledge, in fact, just as self-knowledge revealed the logos of the divine. Although this common logos is a temporal dialectic of many stages—an opposition of many unified by one, then a contradiction of one-many reconciled by a more comprehensive unity, and so on—it is tempting to see it ultimately as a unity. Thus, despite its delicate balance between conflict and justice, opposition and unity, pluralism and monism, Edward Hussey discerns in the Heraclitean logos a supreme monism. "Unity-in-opposites is a unified conception that overcomes the apparently unbridgeable oppositions of monism and pluralism," he observes, adding that "it is therefore an example of itself."[143] By now we should expect Heraclitean conceptions to be instances of themselves, but we cannot accept any formulation of the Heraclitean logos as final.

A moment's analysis reveals this one—unity-in-opposites—to be a contradiction, thereby summoning a future synthesis, which a subsequent analysis reveals as contradictory, provoking a consequent synthesis . . . If this is one logos, one activity, a perfect unity, we must nevertheless refract this one into many whenever we think or speak it.[144] Heraclitus accordingly refracts the divine one into many names, as we discussed earlier, although he is careful to add that it is unwilling as well as willing to be known by the most exalted of them.[145] Pulled farther toward the monism that is but one pole of his chiasmus, commentators have found testimony to the Heraclitean One in the aphorism that we have already scrutinized: "It is wise, listening not to me but to the logos, to agree that all things are one [*hen panta einai*]."[146] This typical translation does make the thought appear monistic, but only so long as we overlook the irony of Heraclitus inviting us to listen not to him, but to something else.[147] If this is the canonical aphorism of Heraclitean monism, it remarkably begins by distinguishing between Heraclitus and the logos, even if, in the end, it collapses all such distinctions.[148]

This particular irony recalls the first sentence of Heraclitus's book—"Although this logos holds forever, men ever fail to comprehend, both before hearing it and once they have heard"—which refers ambiguously either to an eternal logos of the world, or the account of it in words, or, as we argued earlier, both at once.[149] The same lesson can be found in the syntactic ambiguity concealed by the typical translation of Heraclitus's putatively canonical aphorism on monism. The grammar of Greek's indirect statement—where the verb is infinitive, while subject and predicate are both accusatives—does not determine whether *panta* (all things) or *hen* (one) is its subject. The most obvious meaning, thanks to the customary word-order, is that all things are one; but a concealed meaning, sustainable with this word-order, is that one is all things. Recalling first how the principle of chiasmus held both one and all in perfect balance, then remembering how the concealed *harmonia* is better than the revealed one, we cannot neglect this second meaning.[150] The price of such neglect can be very high in Greek literature, at least when the meaning is concealed beneath the deceptively obvious deliverance of an oracle.

Herodotus, for example, tells how the king of Lydia, Croesus, considered making war on the Persians, but first sent legates to consult the Delphic oracle of Apollo in order to see whether it would be wise.[151] Accustomed to ambiguous responses, as Heraclitus himself observes,[152] Apollo used the grammar of an indirect statement—at least in Herodotus's account—to conceal the meaning Croesus feared beneath the revealed meaning his hopes sought. In a common translation that follows the revealed meaning, the oracle says that "if he made war on the Persians, he would destroy a great empire [*megalēn archēn min katalusein*]."[153] This translation takes "he" (*min*) as the subject of the indirect statement, and "great empire" (*megalēn archēn*) as its object.[154] But the reverse is equally sustainable: "a great empire would destroy him." This is the concealed meaning that turned out to be true. When we neglect the concealed meaning of a Heraclitean aphorism which shares the same grammatical ambiguity that seduced Croesus, we risk offending the same god, for it was upon Apollo that Heraclitus modeled his own oracular style, going still further than the oracle by testifying ambiguously to an ambiguous world.

We should aim to "recognize what is wise, set apart from all," some unity transcending all multiplicity, but we must also grasp that whenever we try to do so our thought and speech enter necessarily into a chiastic and dialectical movement between one and many.[155] Thus, even if we acknowledge that "the wise is one," we must also understand that it cannot be the object of any final or definitive thought and speech.[156] To the many divine names introduced by Heraclitus, we have reluctantly added "Time," "Syllapsis," and "Chiasmus," aware that they each become as paradoxical as any of the others whenever we focus our thinking upon them. Perhaps this supreme divinity can be confessed—if at all—only apophatically, by signaling the presence of its absence.

2.10 Chiastic Self

Heraclitus speaks in the enigmatic style of Apollo's oracle, but the comparison between mortal philosopher and immortal god does not end with style. Above the temple walls at Delphi were several gnomic inscriptions. The two most famous were *gnōthi sauton* (know thyself) and *mēden agan* (nothing in excess). "Both maxims might reasonably be paraphrased as *sōphronei*," writes Kahn, who translates this polysemous Greek term as the command to "be of sound mind."[157] Heraclitus connected self-knowledge and sound thinking, too, when he insisted that "it belongs to all men to know themselves and think well [*sōphronein*, keep their thinking sound]."[158] The philosopher thus speaks the same logos as the god, giving the same counsel, neither declaring nor withholding it but giving a paradoxical sign.[159] How, after all, can sound thinking and self-knowledge properly belong to all men, when Heraclitus supposes both to be difficult achievements that elude the many whom he scorns as "absent while present"?[160]

This contradiction resembles the one implicit in the opening of his book. There, as we saw, Heraclitus speaks of the logos that "men ever fail to comprehend," even though "the logos is shared."[161] Noticing the similarity between these two contradictions—searching for an absent while present self, searching for an absent while present logos of the world—Kahn concludes that "self-knowledge and world-knowledge will in the end converge in this comprehension of the common *logos*."[162] After our own investigations of the Heraclitean world and self have brought us to the same conclusion, we find ourselves here at the end of this chapter back at the point of its beginning: the common (*xunos*) logos. Taking some satisfaction in the aphorism that "the beginning and end are shared [*xunon*] in the circumference of a circle,"[163] we should not overlook the contradiction of such a point, whether in the motion round a circle or in the progress of our inquiry. But neither should we forget that such points appear contradictory only when the movements that course through them, and the time that is their shared medium, have been denied.

Our beginning is self-neglect; our end, self-knowledge. We all begin living as though our thinking were a private possession; the best of us aim to grasp the shared logos. The contradictory point each of us inhabits now, in this single moment, is the ethical tension between who we are and who we could be. Heraclitus dramatizes this tension in several vivid aphorisms: "a man is found foolish by a god, as a child by a man"; or, "human nature holds onto no set purpose, but the divine has."[164] Read in isolation, these aphorisms might appear as proof-texts against the thesis of this chapter, the thesis that according to Heraclitus we are becoming god. But we have also witnessed him balancing mortals and immortals in perfect chiasmus. "War is father of all and king of all," moreover, "and some he has shown as gods, others men."[165] Reading all four of these aphorisms together, we acknowledge their tension, but refuse to judge Heraclitean ethics incoherent as a result. For this is exactly the sort of tension, the sort of chiasmus, we have come to expect from the Obscure—or *skoteinos*, the nickname Heraclitus earned in antiquity.[166]

There is indeed a tension between who we are and who we could be, but in the Heraclitean account we are this tension. Contradictory? Yes. As contradictory as a frozen fire. For we too are chiasmus. Grasping ourselves as such, we do not resolve any tension—for that would indeed be our death, just as the resolution of tension in bow or lyre would be theirs— but rather we enhance it. This enhancement is wisdom. Not reconciling contradiction but maintaining both it and reconciliation in chiasmus, the wise are analogous to brightly burning fire, which does not become exclusively need or satiety, but instead increasingly both in equal measure. Knowing ourselves, thinking soundly, which is to say chiastically, we recognize ourselves as this very chiasmus. The wise, by achieving this height of self-knowledge, grasp themselves as cosmic logos, divine chiasmus, becoming god.

Chapter 3

Parmenides and Pythagoreans

Pure reason is the goal of both Parmenides and the Pythagoreans, although they conceive it differently. This chapter aims to appreciate their conceptions of reason alongside their correlative notions of the divine, our selves, and how we should live. Beginning with Parmenides, we shall see how he develops his rival version over against the style of reason found in the aphorisms of Heraclitus. Forbidding as contradictory all change, becoming, and passage of time, this purification of reason will prove to be of paramount importance for the subsequent tradition of Greek philosophy. Plato adopts it, fusing it with an ethical program of purification and divinization he found in the Pythagoreans. After scrutinizing the logical subtleties of Parmenides' argument in this chapter's first half, we shall turn in its second to the complex evidence for Pythagoreanism in the century before Plato.

3.1 Mystagogical Logic

Parmenides is usually celebrated as the Greek pioneer of logic and ontology. He is less often remembered for couching his deductive arguments in the hexameter verse characteristic of epic poetry, let alone for introducing these arguments with a narrative proem that flouts their severe strictures on speaking, thinking, and being. In this narrative, a young man (*kouros*) recounts his journey to the house of a goddess.[1] This is a strange tale whose every detail hints at some obscure symbolic significance. We shall decode its main symbols eventually, but only after we have taken several steps along the same road ourselves, analyzing the equally strange deductive arguments it introduces. For only with an understanding of these arguments' radical conclusion about thinking and being can we appreciate the full meaning of the spiritual journey both described and enacted by Parmenides' poem.

Here is how his *kouros* tells it. Pulled in a chariot by wise mares as far as he aspired to go, he first traveled every stage of the goddess's road (*hodos*), a road accessible to knowing-mortals. The mares pulled his chariot so swiftly that its axle (*axōn*) blazed, shrilling like a musical pipe (*syrinx*). Daughters (*kourai*) of the Sun next emerged from the House of Night, thrusting aside their veils, and escorting his chariot to the gates of the roads of Night and Day. Justice guarded these gates, but these immortal escorts persuaded her with blandishments to open them. The gates swung on posts in their sockets ("posts" translates the plural of *axōn*, while "sockets" translates the plural of *syrinx*), and their opening created a vacant gap (*chasm*) through which the chariot then moved. Finally entering the House of Night, the *kouros* then tells how he was welcomed warmly by an unnamed goddess (simply, *thea*). Taking his right hand in hers, she instructed him that neither motion, diversity, nor gaps can exist; indeed, they cannot be described in speech or contemplated in thought. All is static, homogeneous, and whole, despite the appearances of motion, diversity, and fragmentation that accompanied his journey. So far, though, he understands none of her strictures. The goddess thus says to him, and by implication to us: "There is need for you to learn all things, both the unshaken heart [*atremes ētor*] of persuasive Truth and the opinions of mortals, in which there is no true reliance."[2]

After this proem, Parmenides' poem was divided into two sections: Truth (*alētheia*), and Mortal Opinion (*doxa*). Most of what survives of Parmenides' text are verses from Truth. Although there were many more verses in Mortal Opinion, few remain, and we shall speculate little about them, instead focusing on the unshaken heart of persuasive Truth, which trades the young man's narrative imagery for the deductive rigor of the goddess. In this spirit, she argues first that there are two roads (*hodoi*) of inquiry, although she adds later a third road which merges them. Along the first, she says, lies the thought "that (it) is, and that it is not possible for (it) not to be"; along the second, "that (it) is not and that it is necessary for (it) not to be."[3] The second road she calls "completely unlearnable," for reasons we shall consider in a moment. As for the first road, scholars have found it far from easy to learn.[4] The Greek verb may stand alone, leaving the subject unexpressed, and so allowing her to say simply *esti*: (it) is. Among the many questions raised by this peculiar claim—that (it) is and that it is not possible for (it) not to be—is the identity of the unexpressed subject. What, in other words, is *it*? Two answers have divided commentators.[5] According to the first, it is what-is; in a word, being.[6] According to the second answer, it is what-can-be-thought-or-spoken; in other words, the proper object of thought and speech.[7]

The first reading of the goddess's main premise makes it the earliest version of the principle of non-contradiction: whatever is cannot not be.[8] If this reading is correct, the first road of inquiry claims that what-is is, and that it is not possible for being not to be. Some commentators have complained that this reading reduces at least the first half of her main premise, if not all of it, to a tautology. But this complaint overlooks the fact that the statement of tautologies can be useful whenever they have been ignored and unwittingly contradicted.[9] Parmenides seems to have believed that not only his predecessors, but all "mortals, knowing nothing, two-headed,"[10] contradict this tautology all the time. The most flagrant contradiction would lie along the second road of inquiry. For if the subject of its verbs is also what-is, or being, it asserts that what-is is not and that it is necessary for being not to be. Her new principle stands astride this road as an obstacle—denying passage to any contradiction—so it is no wonder this road must be completely impassable, unlearnable.

Few of us are tempted to travel such a road, but we two-headed mortals nonetheless follow a third road that heedlessly merges the second with the first. "Equally deaf and blind," says the goddess, we are "hordes without judgment, for whom both to be and not to be are judged the same and not the same, and the path of all is backward turning (*palintropos*)."[11] Our deepest error, it seems, is that we tolerate contradiction. We judge being and not-being to be different, or not the same, insofar as we distinguish the first and second roads, forswearing such flagrant contradictions as that what-is is not or that it is necessary for being not to be. Yet we also judge being and not-being the same whenever we travel the third road, which turns out to be the road of time. For in this critique of deaf and blind mortals who permit contradiction, many commentators have seen Heraclitus as the target. "Not comprehending," he wrote in one aphorism, "they hear like the deaf";[12] in another, he added that "eyes and ears are poor witnesses for men, if their souls do not understand the language."[13] This language was the logos, as we saw in Chapter 2, which described paradoxes and sometimes outright contradictions. Among the many we examined, Parmenides takes aim here at the paradigms of unity in opposition. "They do not comprehend how a thing agrees at variance with itself," wrote Heraclitus; "it is a backward-turning (*palintropos*) harmonia, like that of the bow and the lyre."[14]

Some scholars have contested this remarkable verbal parallel, but they cannot easily reject the dozens of others Daniel Graham has shown scattered throughout the surviving fragments of Parmenides' poem.[15] Cumulatively, these clues argue that Heraclitean thinking is the target of his goddess. Chapter 2 named this style of thinking "chiasmus," argued that it was most appropriate to a temporal world, and concluded that its paradoxical principle stood at the summit of Heraclitean philosophy: "wholes and not wholes, convergent divergent, consonant dissonant, from all things one and from one all things."[16] Against the principle of chiasmus, then, Parmenides marshals a rival, the principle of non-contradiction. For although few mortals adopt Heraclitus's principle, most of us credit the temporal flow that it describes and exemplifies. By criticizing the style of thinking most appropriate to time, Parmenides is thereby criticizing most of us. We two-headed mortals believe that there are fragments as well as wholes, diversity as well as unity, movement from one to the other and back again. All three will be criticized soon by the goddess. Above all, however, her argument aims to dispel the illusion of time. Transcending this illusion, traveling her divine road, knowing-mortals may be welcomed into her House. Transcending time, in other words, mortality shall put on immortality.

To promote this transcendence, she exposes the contradictions immanent not only in time, motion, and change, but also in fragmentation, diversity, and imperfection. Briefly, she argues that each requires non-being, which her principle has forbidden: non-being cannot be.[17] Beginning with change, for instance, she argues that with it something new must come-into-being (out of non-being) and something old must perish (into non-being).[18] But because non-being cannot be, neither can coming-to-be nor perishing. Both require non-being, and change requires both; change, then, cannot be. Focusing on coming-to-be, the goddess says "I will not permit you to say or to think <that it grew> from what is not; for it is not to be said or thought that it is not."[19] It is not to be said or thought that it is not, according to her principle, because "what-is is not" is a contradiction. The same considerations apply to passing away, or perishing: the goddess will not permit us to say or to think that anything perishes into what is not, for that too would be a contradiction forbidden by her principle. Personifying this principle as the same gatekeeper who allowed her mortal initiate to enter her immortal dwelling, she says "Justice has permitted it neither to come to be nor to perish."[20] The being she describes is thus unchanging.[21]

In the discussion of time and change in Chapter 2, we saw how they involve simultaneous coming-to-be and perishing, need and satiety, absence and presence.[22] Every moment in time, therefore, must both be and not be. Believing in such moments, traveling down the third road where "to be and not to be are judged the same and not the same," mortals are not surprisingly two-headed, as the goddess complains. By formulating the first version of the principle of non-contradiction, then, Parmenides has made explicit this conflict between it and time. Other mortal opinions fall quickly in successive conflicts with the same opponent. Motion is a sort of change, but according to the principle of non-contradiction there is nowhere for what-is to go—nowhere, that is, where what-is is not (already). Similarly, the other forbidden attributes (fragmentation, plurality, and imperfection) would each require non-being to interrupt the continuity of being. All three, consequently, are as contradictory as change, motion, and time. "Being ungenerated," the goddess says of pure being, "it is also imperishable, whole and of a single kind, unshaken [*atremes*] and perfect."[23] Using pure reason, in other words, she has demonstrated that diversity, plurality, and the passage of time are illusions: "Nor was it ever, nor will it be, since it is now, all together, one, continuous."[24]

So the first reading of the goddess's central premise ("that it [what-is] is, and that it is not possible for it [being] not to be") yields substantive philosophical conclusions. More than simply substantive, these conclusions are as radical as any in the history of philosophy: being is whole, one, and perfect, as well as changeless, motionless, and timeless. Yet a second reading of this same premise—according to which *it* is the possible object of thought and speech—has nonetheless attracted proponents. This reading not only appears to yield similar conclusions, but also seems to echo the goddess's own words: "that which is there to be spoken and thought of," she says, "must be."[25] Speech and thought require successful reference, according to this reading; to refer successfully, a word or thought must point out something existent. "For you could not know what-is-not," she says, "nor could you point it out."[26]

But why is it that you cannot point out what-is-not? Is it a problem of reference, the problem of negative existentials, the problem discussed by Bertrand Russell?[27] Philosophers in his tradition are often disposed to think so. Even if they are right, though, there is nevertheless a more fundamental problem beneath this one. You cannot point out what-is-not because what-is-not cannot be; it is forbidden by the principle of non-contradiction. You cannot point out the present king of France, for example, because he does not exist. But can you not think or speak of him? It would seem so, since you are thinking of him right now. Or are you? Such thought and speech is in fact no more possible than are thought and speech of change and motion, future and past, fragmentation and plurality. In each case there is a problem of reference, to be sure, but the more fundamental problem is one of contradiction, the contradiction imported by everything but what-is, being. For just as change was impossible according to the first reading because it required non-being, an impossibility, so too according the second: it is unthinkable and unspeakable because doing so requires thinking or speaking of non-being—both of which are impossible. If this second reading of Parmenides' main premise were correct, then, it would yield the same conclusions as the first, only now transposed onto the plane of thought and speech.

The same transposition can be accomplished for all the other contradictions produced by non-being. They are each unthinkable and unspeakable because they each require thinking or saying that what-is is

not, and "it is not to be thought or said that it is not."[28] Were we to follow
the second reading, then, we should nonetheless agree that there can be
only one object of thought and speech. This is the same being alone
permitted by the first reading. "From where I am to begin," says the goddess,
as if intending this and other ambiguities to become equivalent in the end,
"to there shall I come back again."[29]

3.2 Being Oneself

Following these austere strictures, who is left to think or speak of being?
Parmenides—or at least his goddess—has at least tried to do so, in the very
argument in question. But has either succeeded? For our part, we cannot
think or say that they have. They cannot have thought or spoken in time,
for example, because the passage of time, from non-being into non-being,
is unthinkable and unspeakable; neither past nor future can be. Nor can we
think or say that either Parmenides or his goddess has changed in any way;
we can think and speak only of the changeless. Finally, we cannot think or
say anything that requires either to be an individual, divided from whatever
else is. We must think and speak only of *it*: undivided, homogeneous, perfect and static being. Indeed, lest Parmenides—or anyone else who attempts
to think or speak of it—rupture its perfect unity, he must *be* it. According to
his goddess's main premise, however we read it, the ontologist must be
identical with being. Or, equivalently, being must be an ontologist. It makes
no difference, apparently, to her. "Thinking and being," she says, "are the
same."[30]

   This fragment (the third in Diels-Kranz) has polarized commentators,
provoking a debate as much philological as philosophical. The two
contesting interpretations, as A. A. Long has conveniently named them, are
the mind/being identity reading, on the one hand, and the mind/being
non-identity reading, on the other. The first began with Neoplatonists
(Plotinus and Proclus) and a Church Father (Clement). Together, in fact,
they are the only sources for this controversial fragment.[31] After Hegel, who
admired Neoplatonism, German scholars preferred this reading.[32] With A.
H. Coxon, then, we may call it also the traditional reading.[33] Even though it
has been challenged since the early twentieth century (first by E. Zeller), it
has recently found some champions.[34] David Sedley, for instance, has
claimed that the translation upon which the traditional reading is based,
the translation we have adopted in the quotation above, is "the only natural
reading of the Greek."[35] Whether it is natural or not, this reading provides

a solution to the problem introduced by the prosecution of Parmenides' argument to its extreme. Only by collapsing thinking and being, in the manner this reading promotes, can he preserve both the unity of being and a place for himself as ontologist.

Shrinking from the precocious idealism this reading attributes to an early Greek philosopher,[36] some scholars have favored a second reading of fr. 3: the mind/being non-identity reading. "The same thing is for thinking and for being," goes a translation of the fragment that is more favorable to this reading; "it is the same thing that can be thought and can be," goes another.[37] In the first translation, both Greek infinitives have been rendered into English as datives (*for* thinking, and *for* being).[38] In the second, the Greek infinitive *noein*, although active, has been converted to the passive voice (*be* thought). The conversion of an infinitive from active to passive is not "linguistically impossible," as Long has conceded;[39] nor is the dative use of the infinitive unprecedented. Coxon argues, in fact, that it is a common philosophical idiom after a conjugated form of *einai*, which fr. 3 exhibits.[40] Each of the Parmenidean passages in which Coxon thinks he sees this idiom,[41] however, may be translated more naturally with the infinitives rendered not as datives but as nominative subjects.[42]

Here, for instance, is fr. 8.34 as translated by Gallop, a proponent of the mind/being non-identity reading, and thus of the dative rendering of *noein*: "the same thing is for thinking and [is] that there is thought."[43] The result is unintelligible. Better is the same verse as translated by Long, a proponent of the mind/being identity reading, and thus of the nominative rendering of *noein*: "thinking and that which prompts thought are the same."[44] Thinking and its prompt are the same, according to this reading, because being prompts thought; and this is so, as fr. 3 seems to say most explicitly, because thinking and being are the same. Combining fr. 3 and fr. 8.34, in fact, we get the prophetic result that thinking is thinking of thinking.[45]

To those still skeptical of this reading, however, let us consider three additional arguments in its favor. The first comes originally from Gregory Vlastos.[46] According to it, even if the mind/being identity reading is not granted, and being is supposed for the moment to be distinct from thinking, thought must nonetheless exist. Otherwise, as we have seen, there is no ontological room for Parmenides' argument—or for any argument at all. But being is not "divided, since it all is alike."[47] Being, as we have seen, is homogeneous. "If thought is any part of being," Vlastos concludes, "all being must be thought." By dexterously presuming the hypothetical truth of the mind/body non-identity reading, then, Vlastos's argument manages to support instead its traditional rival, the mind/being identity reading.

Typical of scholars' hesitation to accept this argument, and the idealist train of thought it underwrites, is W. K. C. Guthrie's objection. "Fortunately we possess practically the whole Way of Truth," he writes, "and can say with some confidence that Parmenides nowhere states this train of thought."[48] This objection begs the question against the mind/being identity reading, however, because Vlastos's argument aims to show that Parmenides did state this train of thought, most explicitly in fr. 3.

As a second argument in favor of this train of thought, the very ambiguity that originally provoked the rivalry between it and the mind/being non-identity reading—the uncertain subject, or *it*, of the goddess's main premise—ultimately supports idealism. For if thinking and being are the same, as this reading would have it, then we should expect the *it* to be ambiguous between being and the object of thought.[49] If being is thinking, after all, the proper object of its thought, which is being, must also be itself: thinking. Thinking, according to this reading, is thinking of thinking. If this is correct, the gap between being and the object of thought closes completely: both are thinking.[50]

As a third and final argument in favor of the mind/being identity reading, Long highlights both the assumptions of Parmenides' predecessors about the cosmos and the assumptions of his successors about him. Let us begin with these successors. As most historians of early Greek philosophy concede, Empedocles and Anaxagoras "attempt to give phenomena a rational explanation which does not conflict with Parmenides' proof that 'what is' can never begin nor cease to be."[51] Their partial commitment to Parmenides' argument makes them indirect sources for its interpretation. Empedocles, for instance, fashioned a cosmos that was "a rounded sphere, exulting in its circular solitude."[52] He also called his elements "gods."[53] Anaxagoras exalted *nous*, or thought, as the instigator of motion in his cosmos.[54] Each successor differed in his own way from Parmenides when it came to the total stasis of his austere monism, "but, these differences apart," asks Long, "could Anaxagoras and Empedocles have regarded themselves as relatively Parmenidean (as they clearly did) if they took his Being, in contrast with their own, to be devoid of mind and life?"[55]

If the allegiance of these pluralists be questioned,[56] Long adduces one of Parmenides' own successors, Melissus, who also seems to have read him as a proponent of thinking being.[57] Melissus denies that it—what-is, the One—feels pain. "A thing feeling pain could not always be," he writes, "nor would what is healthy be able to feel pain."[58] It is not clear from these claims whether Melissus believes the One to be something healthy, or whether instead he believes it is "absurd to think that what is could be either healthy or in pain," as McKirahan writes.[59] If the former interpretation is correct, as Long assumes, Melissus wrote as though his One were a sentient being. Long thinks later testimony confirms this interpretation by reporting that Melissus believed "the One and the all are god."[60] But even if the One were divine, as it seems to have been, its divinity could have removed it altogether from the realm of health and pain, not just secured it from the flaw of pain alone.

In any case, by animating the cosmos, and making it divine, Melissus would not have been alone among early Greek philosophers.[61] The Milesians argued as if the cosmos were animate: Thales may have said that "all things are full of gods,"[62] and Anaximenes reportedly declared that "air is a god."[63] Xenophanes, moreover, made one god direct his cosmos, if he did not also believe, as later authors report, not only "that the whole is one, and that god is bound up with all things," but further that "he is spherical, impassible, unchanging, and rational."[64] After Xenophanes, Heraclitus divinized the cosmos as *logos*, giving us a share of it, as we saw in Chapter 2, just as Parmenides equates our thinking with being.[65] This was the philosophical milieu in which he developed his austere monism, a milieu that took for granted the ubiquitous presence of divine intelligence. We should not be surprised, therefore, that "according to Parmenides," as Aëtius later wrote, "the changeless and perfect spherical being [is god]."[66] Whether or not this god is spherical—"like the bulk of a well-rounded ball,"[67] as his goddess describes being—we should not balk at Long's conclusion that it "constitutes cognition or true thinking," so that "we are being invited," just as Heraclitus invited us, "to learn to think correctly by assimilating our minds to the knowledge and thought which pertain to truth as such."[68]

Assimilating our minds to Truth, in sum, we recognize that our thinking is already identical to divine being. As such, we find ourselves to be unchanging, unmoving, timeless, whole, perfect, and one. By contrast, the temporal world—the world of diversity, imperfection, fragmentation, change, and motion—has been exposed as an illusion. So too, then, has our death, which requires time and non-being to be. To dispel this most fearsome illusion, we have learned, we need only regiment our thinking according to the goddess's new principle. Purging thought of all contradiction, we abandon the road traveled by two-headed mortals. On the one hand, they confuse being and not-being, thinking them the same and not the same; crediting the time that would permit themselves to change, they fear the death that would bring their being into not-being. On the other hand, we knowing-mortals think only of being, which is to say, our own thinking; recognizing ourselves as eternal and immortal, we thereby conquer the illusions of time and death. Knowing-mortals, we travel the road to immortality. This is the road of the goddess.

3.3 Going Under

"The man who knows" appears to have been a Greek expression for an initiate into a cult.[69] Parmenides' *kouros* travels a road accessible to an *eidota phōta*: a "knowing mortal," a "man of understanding," or a "man who knows."[70] He would thus seem to be an initiate into the cult of the goddess whose road he travels. This is not to say that he understands her teaching fully, otherwise he would have no need to receive her instruction. But he does seem to have been granted this privilege by virtue of some previous initiation; he travels to her House, that is, to consummate a journey already begun. Peter Kingsley has discovered clues throughout the proem suggesting that this initiation resembled incubation, the Greek spiritual practice of lying silently in one of "the dark places of wisdom" (the title of his book on the proem), awaiting the epiphany of a tutelary divinity.[71] In Parmenides' proem, this divinity is called simply the goddess (*thea*), but Kingsley shows that she is Persephone, bride of Hades, queen of the dead.

The names of underworld divinities were not usually mentioned by pious and fearful Greeks,[72] but their visual art speaks loudly and hopefully enough to communicate the identity and purpose of this one. Vase paintings excavated from southern Italy, the region of Parmenides' Elea, show Persephone accompanied by Justice (*Dikē*) and welcoming a *kouros* into the underworld with a clasp of her right hand.[73] Sometimes the *kouros* depicted is Orpheus, whose favorable reception in the underworld allowed him to retrieve Eurydice, even if he failed to return her above.[74] Other times the *kouros* is Heracles, whose mythic travels included not only southern Italy, where he founded several cities that were later ruled by Pythagoreans, but also a trip to the underworld, whence he retrieved Theseus and Pirithoüs.[75] Diodorus Siculus describes this scene, saying that Perspehone welcomed Heracles "like a brother."[76] Her warm greeting, but especially her offer of her right hand, signals that she will permit him to return from her House.[77] In other words, she grants him victory over death, thereby making him a symbol of immortality. When the identical goddess greets the *kouros* of Parmenides likewise, offering him her right hand, she is making him the same promise.

To reach that promise, as we saw, this *kouros* had to pass through the chasm of gates guarded by Justice, and then only with the help of his escorts, the immortal maidens, the *kourai*.[78] Also called daughters of the Sun, it is tempting to consider them strangers to the House of Night. Yet Greek myths housed their father in the underworld at night. In the evening he sinks below the horizon, after all, and in the morning he rises from the opposite horizon.[79] The mythological placement of celestial fire in the underworld—so alien to our modern astronomy, yet so obvious to the ancient imagination—linked it with volcanic fire, especially the volcanic fire of southern Italy and Sicily. According to the logic of this association, there is no going up to the heavens and immortality without first going down and receiving permission from the queen of the dead.[80] Empedocles, for example, already considered himself an immortal god while he lived, but some reports claim that he ended his sojourn among humans by leaping into Mt Etna. His final ascent, it would seem, required a plunge into the fires of the underworld. We shall consider this mythic logic in more detail once we turn to the Pythagoreans in the following sections of this chapter. For now, we should mention how it helps explain the immortalization of Heracles, whose journey to the underworld was a necessary stage of his divinization. Only after he had been purified of his poisonous body by his funeral pyre, moreover, could he rise to join the Olympians.

Depictions of Heracles' purifying immolation show him rising as a *kouros*.[81] The *kouros* was less a young man, Kingsley argues, than someone with a special connection to the divine, and particularly the divinities of the underworld.[82] The unnamed *kouros* standing before an unnamed goddess, he writes, is "a well-known scenario in the mysteries of initiation."[83] Significantly, other components of these mysteries seem to appear in Parmenides' proem, although none can be determined with any degree of certainty. Something is likely symbolized, for instance, by the double appearance of the *syrinx*. Kingsley suggests that the hissing of this pipe evoked the ritual snakes sacred to Apollo and his son, Asclepius.[84] Both were gods of healing, with consequent powers over death, and both had attendant cults who practiced incubation. Typically depicted as a *kouros*, moreover, Apollo supervised the exalted roles of physician and prophet, as well as poet and political leader.[85] As we have seen, Parmenides was a poet, expressing his logical and ontological revolution in verse. No one doubts, additionally, that he was a legislator whose laws for Elea outlived him by five-hundred years, making him the founding hero of the city.[86] Was he also a physician and prophet?

He was, according to Kingsley, who argues that he was in fact an *iatromantis*, a healer whose power derived from a broader and divine inspiration.[87] If this is correct, Parmenides would likely have been a priest of Apollo. Several inscriptions have been excavated from Elea testifying to its cult of Apollo the Healer, Apollo Oulios.[88] One of these reads: *Ouliadēs* ("Son of Oulios"), *Iatromantis, Apollo.*[89] We do not know the subject of this dedication, nor can we determine with any certainty that it was Parmenides, but a similar inscription has been found at the same site, this one naming the philosopher by a variant spelling that is arguably more authentic: *Parmeneides son of*

Pyres Ouliadēs Physikos.[90] As a *Physikos*, this man would likely have been a physician as well as a natural philosopher, two roles often fused in the archaic period,[91] but especially by an *Ouliadēs*. As such, this man was not only the natural son of Pyres, but also a spiritual son of Oulios. In other words, he was a priest of Apollo. Assured that these two roles were played by our Parmenides, who was consequently an *iatromantis*, Kingsley believes that the other inscription was likewise dedicated to him.

Whether or not Parmenides was the subject of this cultic inscription, the repetitive verses of his proem, which have led some scholars to dismiss him as a mediocre poet, could have been intended as a cultic incantation, or at least an imitation of one, the sort of verses we should expect from a priest of Apollo.[92] Such a priest would have been a physician and prophet as well as a poet and political leader—four roles Empedocles claimed for himself—for he would have been devoted to the god of healing and oracles, the god of lyre and bow.[93] Self-knowledge was also Apollo's province, as we discussed in our chapter on Heraclitus, and self-knowledge is exactly what the goddess offers in Parmenides' Truth.[94] As we have seen, the goddess teaches that thinking is the same as being. Consequently, the self that thinks this thought—whether it is Parmenides, his goddess, or you—is but thinking of its own thinking. Because there cannot be any gap of non-being in this thinking being, this self, there cannot be separate selves. Parmenides, his goddess, and you are all subsumed in this one, homogeneous, and timeless thinking being. This is the immortal self recognized by Parmenides, his goddess, and any other initiate of her mysterious Truth.

Perhaps, as Kingsley argues, this initiation involved incubation, incantation, and the hissing of the *syrinx*. But perhaps, whether as a complementary or exclusive alternative, the mystagogical clues of the proem allude to a new sort of initiation. In other words, Parmenides may have appropriated the symbols of traditional mystagogy in order to chart another road to the same destination: immortality. Guarding the gates of the roads of Night and Day, as we have seen, is Justice (*Dikē*). Unless this goddess unlocks her gates, the Parmenidean *kouros* cannot enter the House of Night to learn from the goddess that he is timeless thinking being, to be liberated by her from the illusion of death. Yet this is not the only appearance of Justice in the poem. She is mentioned again, much later, permitting being "neither to come to be nor to perish."[95] Each, we concluded, is forbidden as contradictory. If this is correct, Justice would be a personification of the principle of non-contradiction. Guarding the gateway to immortality, in short, would be Parmenides' new principle. Acknowledging it, his *kouros* is already a knowing mortal, an initiate. "It was not an evil destiny that sent you forth to travel," says the goddess to him, "but Right and Justice."[96]

This initiation of the *kouros* has brought him along the road of the goddess, through the gates of her House, and into her presence. She will now teach him the heart of persuasive Truth, but she begins her instruction with the principle he apparently already acknowledges: "that it is and that it is not possible for it not to be." Merely acknowledging this principle, however, falls far short of recognizing its dramatic consequences. Avoiding all contradiction, the *kouros* must accept that neither future nor past exists, that change and motion are impossible, as are birth and death, fragmentation and diversity. He must ultimately accept that all is one, being is thinking, and he is its eternal contemplation. Anyone who acknowledges the principle of non-contradiction as the firmest principle of all, then, will in the manner of this *kouros* stand before Parmenides' goddess as an initiate of her cult, the cult he inaugurates with his poem. She promises immortality to anyone willing to follow this logos to its eternal conclusion. Should we?

To follow this logos faithfully, we knowing-mortals must forswear the road of two-headed mortals, those "knowing nothing," "for whom both to be and not to be are judged the same and not the same."[97] It would appear that this contradictory road is none other than the road of Mortal Opinion (*doxa*). For after surveying the non-contradictory road, her "reliable account," she invites the *kouros* to turn to the *doxa*, calling it "the deceitful ordering of my words."[98] As such, many commentators have wondered why she bothers describing it at all.[99] Why, moreover, did she apparently devote more verses to it than she did to the Truth?[100] Some of these verses advanced genuine discoveries about the heavens, others described theories of reproduction and the constituents of the changing world perceived through our senses.[101] Why did Parmenides invest so much ingenuity in an account of the appearances that only two-headed mortals could believe? Why, in other words, does his goddess lead her *kouros* down a road she has already exposed as contradictory?

At the very least, her initiate will desire some explanation of the journey that brought him to her—with its appearances of motion, time, and diversity, not to mention the giant gap opened by Justice between the gates she guards. All of these appearances prove contradictory; none can be; yet every one appears to him on his way. Similarly, as we imagine his journey, as we reason through the abstract instruction of his goddess, motion, time, and diversity appear to us. In fact, everything forbidden by the Truth appears to us throughout our reading of Parmenides' poem. In its Mortal Opinion, then, the goddess diagnoses our shared error: "they made up their minds to name two forms, of which it is not right to name one—in this they have gone astray."[102] These two forms, she adds, are the contraries "light and night,"[103] so that anyone who affirms both must affirm an inconsistent world.[104]

Too little of the Mortal Opinion has survived to secure any interpretation of it and its relation to the rest of Parmenides' poem. But if this interpretation is correct, if the goddess sought to explain our appearances upon the basis of admittedly inconsistent principles, then she traced our contradictory appearances back to a fundamental error, an original sin against the principle of non-contradiction. This is the kind of account she forecasts when she turns to the "deceptive ordering of my words," saying that she will present "all the ordering as it appears, so that no mortal opinion may ever overtake you."[105] Fortified by an account of how error arises, her followers will be less easily tricked by inconsistent principles. Thus fortified, they will resemble the *kouros*, who had to pass through the gates of the roads of Night and Day, leaving behind the form of light, before he could enter the House of Night alone. If we are to follow his journey, Parmenides seems to be saying, we too must abandon inconsistent principles, purifying our thought of all contradiction. The only pure thought, he would have us believe, is thinking being itself.

But a congenital illness still infects his heart of persuasive Truth. His goddess teaches that all is one and homogeneous, without any gaps; but if so, there cannot be any distinction between appearance and reality. She recognizes this at the end of the proem, saying that "the things that appear must genuinely be, being always, indeed, all things."[106] Ironically, though, this valid recognition invalidates her whole lesson. For if the distinction between appearance and reality collapses, what need is there of her instruction? She cannot disabuse us of our illusions, after all, unless there are illusions of which we can be disabused. Yet the weakness at the heart of her argument is still stronger. Even if there were a sustainable distinction between illusion and truth, so that we could err, we could not be instructed, so that we could improve. To be instructed, we must be capable of change; the goddess instructs, however, that all change is impossible! Likewise forbidden, needless to say, is becoming immortal. Least of all can we recognize ourselves as immortal, after having falsely believed that we were mortal. Such a change would require two contradictions: an initial but impossible distinction between mortal opinion and truth, followed by a later and nonetheless impossible movement from one to the other. What is the point of teaching, in short, if there is nothing to teach and we cannot learn?

Assuming the cultic context of Parmenides' poem, we could put the same critique this way: what is to be gained by joining his cult, if it were possible for anyone to change and do so? Its central tenet is the principle of non-contradiction, and although none has drawn consequences from this principle as radically as its first exponent did, many have nonetheless joined him in making it "the firmest principle of all." Next and most important after Parmenides himself was Plato, who blended austere Eleatic logic with a program of purification and divinization he inherited from the Pythagoreans.[107] This inheritance was direct, as we shall see in Chapter 4, but it may also have been indirect, if we trust the ancient testimony that Parmenides' teacher was Ameinias, a Pythagorean, as well as the other evidence Kingsley has unearthed linking the founder of logic to this myste-rious cult. In other words, their ethical and religious program may be sym-bolized by Parmenides' proem.[108] The Pythagoreans were more obviously cultic, and more explicitly preoccupied with becoming divine, than any of their Greek predecessors. As Aristotle's student, Aristoxenus, wrote in his account of them: "Every distinction they lay down as to what should be done or not done aims at communion with the divine."[109] To understand the effort of subsequent Greek philosophers to achieve this communion, then, we must now turn to the Pythagoreans.

3.4 Ordered Cosmos

Little is known about Pythagoras himself, and the religious devotion he inspired in followers throughout antiquity has made it difficult to separate fact from fiction in their accounts of him. Yet most agree that he was born on Samos (near the Ionian coast) sometime in the middle of the sixth century B.C.E., and that in approximately 530 he established a colony of followers in Croton, on the coast of southern Italy.[110] This society persisted at least a century; the school of thought it initiated continued through much, if not all, of antiquity.[111] "The Pythagorean tradition admits of a wide range of philosophical ideas and interests," warns Carl Huffman, "and we should be wary of assuming a rigid set of philosophical dogmas accepted by all Pythagoreans."[112] What united them, it seems, was a way of life. Speaking not of Pythagoreanism exclusively but of ancient philosophical schools more generally, Pierre Hadot has concluded that they were each united by "the choice of a certain way of life and existential option which demands from the individual a total change of lifestyle, a conversion of one's entire being."[113] Before examining the conversion expected of Pythagoreans, we should note, again with Hadot, that "this existential option, in turn, implies a certain vision of the world."[114] Let us try, first, to reconstruct the vision of the world—a dualistic vision—shared by most Pythagoreans.

We must first be wary of confusing the so-called Neopythagoreanism of Roman times, which produced most of the extant accounts, with the pristine Pythagoreanism of the sixth and fifth centuries B.C.E.[115] Walter Burkert has convinced most scholars that the version of Pythagorean philosophy preserved in later antiquity was the product of Plato and his school.[116] We may avoid this difficult controversy by limiting our sources to those who either preceded Plato or would have been aware of any Platonic distortions of the tradition. Two authors will prove especially helpful: Philolaus of Croton (ca. 470–390), who was the only pre-Platonic Pythagorean to publish their doctrines, and Aristotle, who knew Plato well enough to distinguish pre-Platonic Pythagoreanism from his own teacher's appropriations and elaborations of it.[117]

The Pythagoreans are now most widely known by the theorem which bears their name. However, the "Pythagorean" theorem was discovered by the Babylonians a millennium or more before the birth of Pythagoras.[118] Borrowing from the East their knowledge of harmonics and astronomy as well as mathematics, the Pythagoreans introduced into Greece the arithmetic regularity of plucked strings and the geometric patterns of orbiting stars.[119] In harmonics, for example, they took strings of different materials and showed that they could always produce the same chords so long as they maintained the same ratios of their lengths: 1:2, for instance, sounded a note and the same note an octave lower; 2:3 and 3:4 sounded the perfect fifth and the perfect fourth respectively.[120] This fact suggested that qualities, like sound, could be reduced to quantities, and that mathematics revealed the secret order of the cosmos. As a symbol of this order, the Pythagoreans revered the *tetractys* (fourness) *of the decad*, an equilateral triangle of sides four units long. By arranging ten pebbles as a triangle, placing one at its apex, two in the second row, three in the third, and four in the fourth, they symbolized the harmonic ratios: 1:2:3:4.[121] Of all the special meanings which they assigned to numbers,[122] the cosmic significance they devoted to four and ten appears most readily understandable.

According to some accounts, Pythagoras was the first to use *kosmos* to speak of the heavens.[123] Whoever used it first, the word signified both order and ornament, an ambiguity from which we derive "cosmetic" as well as "cosmos." It was natural for the Greek philosophers who made *kosmos* the object of their inquiry to conceive the universe as both ordered and beautiful. The Pythagoreans specifically believed this *kosmos* to express a *harmonia*.[124] The extent of this belief becomes more intelligible once it is recognized that *harmonia* not only came to mean "harmony," as we know it from music, but also preserved its original meaning: joint, fitting together, or composition.[125] The Pythagoreans believed that the spheres of the heavenly bodies sounded a musical harmony corresponding to the mathematical ratios of their composition.

They assumed there were ten such bodies, thinking "the number ten is something perfect and encompasses the entire nature of numbers,"[126] apparently because of their reverence for the tetractys. The precise identity of all ten is unclear, as is the status of cosmic fire among them.[127] What is clear about fire, in particular, is that Philolaus placed it both at the boundary of the cosmos and at its center, apparently drawing on the association between the celestial and chthonic deities mentioned in section 3.3.[128] This boundary fire was indisputably the stars; the central fire may accordingly have been in the underworld.[129] Pythagorean inhabitants of volcanic Sicily and southern Italy were well situated to observe such fire. Wherever exactly they placed it, they believed it was orbited by the other heavenly bodies harmoniously—which is to say, with both mathematical regularity and musical beauty.[130] Their legends claimed that only Pythagoras himself could hear this music. Though it surrounds us all, we notice it no more than does a blacksmith the habitual noises of his shop.[131]

Less fancifully, they believed that everything, both in the heavens and below, exhibited mathematical ratios. "All things that are known have number," wrote Philolaus, "for without this nothing whatever could possibly be thought of or known."[132] Numerical form, in other words, is necessary for intelligibility. Whether or not the Pythagoreans also considered it sufficient for existence, and what it would mean if they did, is a matter of controversy. Aristotle reports that they believed "the whole heaven (*ouranos*) . . . is numbers."[133] Because they equated *ouranos* and *kosmos*, this was to say that they believed the cosmos to be numbers. In the same vein, writes Aristotle, they believed "number was the substance of all things,"[134] and that "sensible substances are formed out of it."[135] Huffman rejects Aristotle's testimony on this point, especially when it comes to the specific equation of the number one and the substance of the central fire.[136] It is "impossible to imagine that he [Philolaus] confused the arithmetical unit with the central fire," he writes, "for if he did, his arithmetical unit is more than a bare monad with position; it is also fiery and orbited by ten bodies."[137] As odd as this equation may seem to us, Kahn sees no reason to doubt Aristotle's report of it.[138] It does agree with Philolaus's own statement that "the first thing fitted together, *the one in the center of the sphere*, is called the hearth."[139]

More generally, if Aristotle's report is correct, and number really was for the Pythagoreans the substance of all things, they believed numerical form to be what he called the *archē*, or principle, of the cosmos. This technical term is one component of Aristotle's philosophy that will help us to appreciate the novelty of Pythagoreanism, another is his account of the four causes: material, formal, efficient, and final.[140] By this account, for example, the form or shape of a house is easily distinguished as a cause not only from the house's matter (its wood and nails), but also from both its efficient and its final cause. The efficient is a builder—or, more specifically, what it is that makes a builder a builder: his craft (*technē*) of building.[141] At the very least, the final cause is shelter. This four-fold scheme rarely applies to Aristotle's predecessors as neatly as he thought, but since he is one of our two principal sources for early Pythagoreanism, familiarity with it helps us to recognize any distortions it may have introduced into his reports.[142]

Beginning with the Milesians in the sixth century, Aristotle saw most of the early Greek philosophers isolating some one thing to be "that of which all existing things are composed and that out of which they originally came into being."[143] Their principles were at first purely material, according to him, although each was animate in some way. Anaximenes, for instance, said that his air rules the whole cosmos, "just as our soul, being air, holds us together and controls us."[144] Not long after the Milesians, Xenophanes made earth and water the generative material principles of the cosmos,[145] but also exalted one god over everything, granting him dominion by the power of his thought alone.[146] As early as the sixth century, then, Greek philosophy became acquainted with the notion of a distinct efficient cause, even if Aristotle would not recognize its appearance until the late fifth century, with Anaxagoras's mind or thought (*nous*).[147]

In the beginning, wrote Anaxagoras, "all things were together."[148] Nothing was apart from this primal cosmic mixture except *nous*, which remained pure, and began its rotation of the cosmos in order to "set in order all things." By this providential rotation, Anaxagoras effectively equipped the one god of Xenophanes with a mechanism of movement, imagining *nous* as a cosmic centrifuge.[149] Nothing was apart from this primal cosmic mixture except *nous* (thought). It remained pure and then began rotating the cosmos in order to "set in order all things." With this rotation, Anaxagoras effectively equipped the one god of Xenophanes with a mechanism of movement—centrifugal force.[150] Plato would later appropriate Anaxagoras's pure *nous*, making it heed the final cause of the cosmos.[151] This final cause was his Form of the Good, a Form of the abstract Forms that were Plato's formal causes, but not entirely his innovation. For even if Huffman is right that the Pythagoreans believed numerical form only to order things which exist independently (rather than constituting their substance, as Aristotle reports), their use of number nonetheless introduces formal causes into Greek philosophy.[152]

The Pythagoreans showed that harmonies were not to be explained by appeal to the matter of plucked strings but instead to the ratios—that is, to the numerical form—of these strings. In anticipation of Plato, however, we should notice that the Pythagoreans also seem to have reified their numbers. The first integer, recall, was the one in the center of the sphere, the central fire. Yet it is not the only one. "There are many ones in the cosmos," writes Kahn, "but the *first* one is the central fire."[153] Plato's Forms will lead a similarly double life. There are many instances of beauty in the world, but the first beauty, so to speak, is that of the Form of Beauty. Like Platonic Forms, Kahn concludes, Pythagorean numbers are "both universals and privileged particulars."[154] In his later years, Plato would also adopt the most important of the Pythagoreans' numerological distinctions.[155] For they considered each number to be one of two types: *apeiron* or *peperasmenon*—indefinite or defined; alternately, as most translators prefer, unlimited or limited.[156]

According to Huffman, this obscure distinction, rather than number itself, was primary in Philolaus's system.[157] After all, he began *On Nature*, the book in which he scandalously divulged Pythagorean doctrines, with this sentence: "Nature in the cosmos was composed out of unlimiteds [*apeirōn*] and limiters; both the cosmos as a whole and everything in it."[158] Kahn has explained this obscure distinction by recalling the Pythagoreans' use of pebbles to generate numbers, introducing space or void between them. "The same process that generates the numbers," the Pythagoreans may have reasoned, "will generate geometrical solids and the visible heavens."[159] Though obscure, this claim helps make sense of one still more obscure. Aristotle wrote that the Pythagoreans imagined "the world inhaling also the void which distinguishes the natures of things, as if it were what separates and distinguishes the terms of a series."[160] Perhaps, then, the central fire, the one at the hearth of the cosmos, inhaled the void, the way fire must inhale air, and thus generated the other numbers, which is to say, the cosmos.

Recalling the Pythagoreans' musical investigations, F. M. Cornford offered another way of understanding the distinction between limit and unlimited. He suggested that the Pythagoreans took the unlimited continuum of sound made by strings of indefinite lengths and imposed limit on it by fretting them according to definite ratios. This is how they produced the harmonies already described. In doing so, "the unlimited is no longer an orderless continuum; it is confined within an order, a *cosmos*, by the imposition of Limit."[161] There were many unlimiteds according to the Pythagoreans, not simply the one *apeiron* of Anaximander. Limiting their unlimiteds—or defining their indefinites—the Pythagoreans not only posited two sets of principles, they moralized them. Thus Aristotle: "evil belongs to the unlimited, as the Pythagoreans conjectured, and good to the limited."[162] In so doing, they introduced into Greek philosophy a cosmic and moral dualism that emerges more fully in another report of Aristotle. "Others of this same

school," he wrote, "declare that there are ten principles (*archai*), arranged
in parallel columns . . .

limit	unlimited
odd	even
one	plurality
right	left
male	female
at rest	moving
straight	bent
light	darkness
good	evil
square	oblong"[163]

We cannot be sure of the list's rationale. The selection of opposites and
their arrangement have puzzled commentators, beginning with Aristotle
himself.[164] No scholar since has successfully explained the whole list,
although progress has certainly been made to explain some of the opposing
pairs.[165] The simplest such example is the opposition of square and oblong.
Because Pythagorean numbers were concrete arrangements of pebbles, or
figures, the number 2 was considered oblong: two pebbles form a rectangle
(of dimensions 1×2); by contrast, the number 4 was a square (2×2).[166] The
ratio of its sides was therefore 2/2, or 1. In fact, square numbers always
exhibited the ratio of 1: 2/2, 3/3, 4/4, etc. Limited in this way, their ratios
differed from those of the oblong numbers, which exhibited unlimitedly
many ratios: 1/2, 2/3, 3/4, etc. In one stroke, then, we see a connection
between *square*, *limit*, and *one*, all of which are ranked together with *good* in
the first column of the Pythagorean table of opposition; correlatively, we
see the connection between *oblong*, *unlimited*, and *plurality*, which are ranked
together with *evil* in the second.[167]

No early text illuminates the Pythagoreans' reason for assigning light and
darkness to their respective columns, but Cornford offers a plausible hypothesis: "Light is the medium of truth and knowledge; it reveals the knowable
aspect of Nature—the forms, surfaces, limits of objects that are confounded
in the unlimited darkness of night."[168] For the Pythagoreans, then, as harmony is good, so too is light; and as cacophony is bad, so too darkness.
Simultaneously, it would appear, they introduced into Greek philosophy the
canonical contrast between light and darkness, and with it an ethics that
enjoined specific actions that promoted light and eschewed darkness.[169]
The importance of this particular contrast to the thought of Plato cannot be

overestimated, and we shall examine it when we come to him. Now we should consider the correspondence between this Pythagorean contrast and the dualism of Zoroastrianism. Once we set out eastward to explain Greek philosophical dualism, however, we shall find ourselves going farther than Persia. Crossing the Hindu Kush, we shall reach a plausible source of Greek philosophical monism as well. This route follows that of Alexander the Great, whose teacher was Aristotle, whose teacher in turn was Plato. Let us travel this same route, hoping that when we return from our expedition we shall better understand Plato's conquest of Heraclitus. Understanding the history of this conquest will enable us to see more clearly the simmering strife of its rival territories, monism and dualism.

3.5 One or Many

"Ormazd was on high in omniscience and goodness," begins the Zoroastrian cosmogony, or *Bundahišn*, "for boundless time He was ever in the light."[170] Against this good god was ranged Ahriman, the evil, who "was abased in slowness of knowledge," and "darkness is his place."[171] Although this sharp contrast between good and evil, light and darkness, corresponds neatly to the cosmological dualism of the Pythagoreans, difficult problems of chronology interrupt any confident assertion of influence. The so-called *Greater Bundahišn* dates from the late ninth century C.E., more than a millennium after the early Pythagoreans we have been discussing. But as P. O. Skjærvø writes, these late texts "encapsulate the orally transmitted knowledge of the priests of that time and so contain material that reaches far back into the history of Zoroastrianism."[172] More specifically, as M. L. West observes, the *Bundahišn* is a commentary "on the *Dāmdāt Nask*, one of the lost portions of the *Avesta*, presumably dating from the Achaemenid period," which began a generation before Pythagoras formed his society.[173]

Other scholars trace the *Avesta*, and thus Zoroastrianism's cosmogonic dualism, much further back.[174] Even though it is the oldest text of this ancient religion, it was not written down until the sixth century C.E. It records a long oral tradition, however, and studies of its dialect argue a much earlier date of composition. Skjærvø concludes that "on the basis of linguistic considerations it is possible to assign its oldest parts to the second half of the second millennium B.C.E. and the later parts to the first half of the first millennium."[175] Not all scholars agree with this use of linguistic considerations to date either the *Avesta* or the life of Zarathustra (whom the Greeks called "Zoroaster"). S. A. Nigosian, for example, thinks they are unreliable and that therefore "the tradition of placing Zoroaster at about the seventh to sixth centuries B.C.E. may have to be allowed to stand."[176] Whatever the merits of these linguistic dating methods, and whether or not the Greek tradition of dating Zoroaster to the seventh or sixth centuries is correct, all scholars—including those of antiquity—agree that Zoroastrianism arose early enough to have influenced Pythagoreanism. In the Roman era, several authors went so far as to claim that Pythagoras himself studied under Zoroaster, or at least the Persian Magi.[177] This story goes back to Aristotle's student, Aristoxenus,[178] who apparently wrote that "Pythagoras went to Babylon and learnt from Zaratas that Light and Darkness were the male and female principles from which the world was created."[179] If the tradition were baseless, as Guthrie observes, "at least it is evidence that a resemblance between the Greek and Persian systems was remarked by the fourth century."[180]

Their resemblance is not limited to a cosmos divided between good and evil, light and darkness. Skjærvø distinguishes Zoroastrianism's *two* dualisms: the *cosmogonic* dualism we have been discussing ("two primordial entities: the one good, the other bad"), and another, *cosmic*, dualism ("the world of thought and that of living beings").[181] These two divisions are linked by the fact that both worlds were created as battlegrounds for the war between the two primordial entities, their minions, and the humans who must choose sides.[182] The Zoroastrians chose the side of the good and imagined themselves fighting on his behalf by the correct performance of rituals designed to keep the evil at bay. According to the logic of these rituals, "the world of thought contains 'models' (*ratus*) for all things in the world of living beings," and in the daily sacrifice "these 'models' in the world of thought are re-assembled and arranged by means of their representatives in the world of living beings in order to produce a ritual microcosmic model that will then contribute to the regeneration of the ordered macrocosm."[183] These 'models' resemble in some ways Pythagorean numbers. The one of the central fire was a sort of model for the many inferior ones,[184] and Pythagorean rituals, invoking the tetractys, symbol of cosmic order, very likely aimed to promote a similar regeneration in agreement with their own cosmological dualism.[185]

Zoroastrian rituals were as ubiquitous as the cosmic battle. By the medieval period, observes J. K. Choksy, "every action came to be regarded as either opposing the Evil Spirit or aiding him, for it was dictated that all acts and deeds were either meritorious works or sins, with there being no neutral functions."[186] But even in antiquity, Zoroastrians sought to achieve in mundane life "purity of thought (*humata*), word (*hukta*), and deed (*huvarashta*)."[187] Although espousing no world-denying asceticism,[188] because our world was supposed to be home to the forces of light as well as the forces of darkness,[189] the *Vidēvdāt* prescribed many rules for avoiding pollution.[190] Most important were those concerning the disposal of corpses.[191] Nearly as important was avoiding certain bodily substances when they became separated from the body and so 'died': "skin, saliva, breath, cut nails and hair, blood, semen, the products of menstruation, urine, and feces."[192] Contact with each had to be avoided as carefully as contact with a corpse. "After hair was cut and nails were pared," for instance, "they were taken separately to a desolate spot at least ten paces from human beings, twenty paces from fire, thirty paces from water," in order not to defile these sacred elements.[193]

From just this sort of ritual Pythagoreanism may have inherited its own peculiar prohibitions, some of which were recorded by Aristotle in his *On the Pythagoreans.*[194] "Don't . . . stand upon your nail-and-hair-trimmings," went one of these prohibitions.[195] Of course, the Pythagoreans and the Zoroastrians have not been the only groups to share taboos against bodily products; every culture finds one or another threatening and "dirty." In her book on the subject, Mary Douglas presented the purity rules of biblical Jews and of Indian Brahmins,[196] among other groups, concluding that "there is no such thing as dirt; no single item is dirty apart from a particular system of classification in which it does not fit."[197] Dirt, in other words, is disorder,[198] and order is restored by purification.[199] Moreover, writes Douglas, "order implies restriction; from all possible materials a limited selection has been made and from all possible relations a limited set has been used."[200] Purification should be a matter of limiting the unlimited, since "disorder by implication is unlimited, no pattern has been realized in it, but its potential for patterning is indefinite."[201] Although she neglects to mention them, no group could more neatly epitomize Douglas's theory than the Pythagoreans, for whom the cosmological dualism of unlimited and limit serves as the perfect background against which the soul is purified, as we shall see in the following section, by mathematical study and self-restraint.

In the meantime, let us consider two additional Pythagorean prohibitions: "don't wipe up a mess with a torch, don't commit a nuisance towards the sun."[202] These peculiar taboos become more understandable when we assume an Iranian influence. To the Zoroastrians, after all, "fire, represented especially by the sun, is regarded as a symbol of divine purity."[203] *Vidēvdāt* 8 says that a fire fed with fragrant sandalwood will slay thousands of demons, and yet it is vulnerable to defilement by contact with garbage.[204] *Yasna* 36 invokes fire, both the fire here below and that of the sun, as "the most beautiful form of forms."[205] Not only would Zoroastrians have avoided wiping up a mess with a torch, their "religious practice dictates that it [fire] should always be kept thirty paces away from carrion, fifteen paces from the polluting gaze of menstruating women, and three paces from excrement."[206] Protecting both fire and himself from impurities, then, the Zoroastrian waged daily skirmishes in a great cosmic battle. "In every sphere and in every situation demanding a decision between two opposites," as we have seen, "human beings have to make a choice between these two principles."[207] The ultimate reward for those who have sided with the good principle— Ohrmazd, or, as he was originally known, Ahura Mazda—is eternity in his divine company. "The souls of the just," reads the *Vidēvdāt*, "proceed to the golden thrones of Ahura Mazda."[208]

Besides the Pythagorean resemblances to Zoroastrianism we have noticed so far—their moralized cosmological dualism, their contrast between light and darkness, their belief in abstract models for the material world, and some of their taboos—we have yet to discuss a final resemblance: the importance they both accorded to purity of thought. We shall examine this resemblance in the following section, however, after arguing that the credibility of the hypothesis of a Zoroastrian influence on Pythagoreanism is based not solely on these resemblances, but also on the growing contact between Greeks and Persians.

Since the 'Orientalizing' period of the seventh century B.C.E., Greeks had been adopting artistic styles from the Near East and Egypt, showing their wide diffusion not only as artists but also as merchants, mercenaries, and craftsmen.[209] This diffusion brought them into contact with the mythology and astronomy of the older civilizations. Thales' prediction of the eclipse in 585 B.C.E., for example, has traditionally been used to mark the beginning of Greek philosophy.[210] But Thales stood on the shoulders of giants, owing his astronomical success at least in part to the ancient records of Babylon.[211] Besides their astronomical data, he may also have borrowed from the Babylonians their idea of water as a cosmic principle. "When Apsû primeval . . . mingled their waters together":[212] so begins the Babylonian cosmogonic poem, *Enuma Elish*, "with a description of the watery chaos that preceded the formation of the universe."[213] Whatever his sources, Thales shows no trace of Zoroastrianism. The Persians would not conquer Babylon until 537, by which time Thales was very likely dead. But before that, in 546, they controlled many of the Greeks of Asia Minor.[214] There is good reason, then, to believe that Zoroastrianism would find its way into Greek thought shortly afterwards.

Aside from their fundamental similarities, the Pythagoreans differed from Persian—and likewise traditional Greek—religion on at least two important points. First of all, they posited not personal gods but the impersonal opposites of limit and unlimited. This difference was typical of Greek philosophy, even from its earliest period, when Milesian philosophers largely rejected the anthropomorphism of Homer and Hesiod, fashioning instead a cosmos ruled by impersonal substances and forces. The Pythagoreans' spirit of abstraction argues an affiliation with Miletus as much as with Iran. But in a second respect the Pythagoreans differed from all three—from Zoroastrianism, the epic poets, and also the Milesians. They taught the transmigration of souls, a doctrine which they likely drew from still farther East.[215] In time we shall come to transmigration—otherwise known as reincarnation (between species), or by its Greek name, *metempsychōsis*—but not before noticing earlier correspondences between Greek philosophy and the East that make the case for westward influence more plausible.

We have already mentioned Thales' use of Near-Eastern astronomy for his prediction of an eclipse, and of its mythology for his abstraction of a cosmic principle. His successor in Miletus, Anaximander, seems to have borrowed the Iranian astronomy which "placed the stars nearest the earth, then the moon, then the sun."[216] But when it came to a cosmic principle, he proposed one still more abstract than water. This indefinite he described as "deathless and indestructible," declaring it "to contain all things and steer all things."[217] All these things—the many, as they would be called—"perish into the things out of which they come to be, according to necessity, for they pay the penalty and retribution to each other for their injustice in accordance with the ordering of time."[218] In order to find precedents for these doctrines, as West has also argued, we must go beyond Mesopotamia, to India, where monism rather than dualism dominated cosmological thought.[219]

"As a unity only is It to be looked upon," *Brahman*, the principle of the cosmos, "this indemonstrable, enduring Being."[220] So reads one of the earliest Upaniṣads, the Bṛhadāraṇyaka, which most scholars date to the eighth or seventh centuries B.C.E., placing it well before the emergence of Greek philosophy.[221] From other Upaniṣads we learn that their cosmic principle, like Anaximander's, "is not born, nor dies."[222] Yet this is only the most generic of their resemblances. More specifically, *Brahman* is "the One embracer of the universe,"[223] the "One controller."[224] Indeed, says the Bṛhadāraṇyaka again, it is without qualities and wholly indefinite (*neti, neti*—not this, not that).[225] Like Anaximander's indefinite, moreover, it exacts retribution from whoever succumbs to the illusion of independent qualities and existence. For "there is on earth no diversity," and "he gets death after death, who perceives here seeming diversity."[226] With diversity an illusion, and unity their only reality, the Upaniṣads are preoccupied with the problem of reconciling real unity with the appearance of change and diversity—the so-called problem of the one and the many.[227] This problem was also a concern, as we have seen, of early Greek philosophers.

Yet this similarity between early Greek and early Indian philosophy is but one of the many catalogued by Thomas McEvilley; nor has he been the only scholar to do so.[228] West has shown that Thales was not the last of the Presocratics to absorb religious ideas from the East, especially from Persia and India. After presenting unmistakable parallels between the Heraclitean and Upaniṣadic cycle of the elements, for instance, he remarks "that the *Bṛhadāranyaka Upaniṣad* alone throws more light on what Heraclitus was talking about than all the remains of the other Presocratics together," although "it is a long walk from Ephesus to India."[229] To explain this influence, however, we need not imagine anyone making such a trek, for McEvilley has also enumerated far more plausible routes of transmission.[230] Their ventures eastward would not likely have brought the Greeks so far as India, but it would have brought them into intermediate territories.

In the mid-sixth century, the Persians began to unify these territories, eventually bringing both Greeks and Indians under one rule. Herodotus relates the story of Scylax, from his home region of Caria, who not only navigated the Indus river for Darius in 517, but later wrote a widely read book about his voyage.[231] Several years earlier, Darius came to power and commissioned the Behistun inscription, which listed the territories he had inherited. One of these was Gandhāra, whose capital, Taxila, was likely where the author of the *Chāndogya Upaniṣad*, Uddālaka, trained.[232] Darius's empire thus encompassed, at its eastern edge, a center of Upaniṣadic study, and, at its western, the cradle of Greek philosophy—the coast of Asia Minor. This region included not only Miletus, but also Xenophanes' Colophon, Heraclitus's Ephesus, Anaxagoras's Clazomenae, and Pythagoras's Samos. By his influence on the affairs of this island, in particular, Darius demonstrated a salient example of the sort of "diffusion event that could have brought Indian traditions through the Persian court and into the center of a Greek philosophical school with lightning-like speed."[233]

Darius would later send there as ruler, complete with Persian retinue, a certain Syloson, who was the brother of Polycrates, the former tyrant of the island who had been killed by a Persian satrap in 520.[234] This influx of Persians to his native island would not have affected Pythagoras directly; he had emigrated in 530 to escape the tyranny of Polycrates.[235] But when the tyrant was killed, Darius summoned his famed personal physician, Democedes of Croton, to the Persian court, where he kept him under house arrest to treat the royal family.[236] After curing the Queen of an ailment, Democedes was allowed to participate in a Persian reconnaissance mission around Greece and southern Italy, where he escaped and returned to his hometown. Physicians were often indistinguishable from philosophers in antiquity, as we have observed, and this was especially true of the Pythagoreans. Therefore it would not have been unusual if Democedes had spoken with them when he returned, or perhaps joined their society.[237] He could have transmitted to them medical ideas he may have learned from Gandhāran physicians who were likewise detained in the Persian court.[238] "A seemingly Indian physiology which Plato knew," writes McEvilley, "was also known to Pythagoreans."[239]

We should add this salient route of transmission between India and Greece to others that included imperial displacements of whole populations,[240] conscription of subjects into royal building projects,[241] and finally, in the heart of Persian court itself, spectacles such as the one recorded by Herodotus, when Darius was supposed to have confronted the Greeks with the funeral practices of Indians, and *vice versa*, for the amusement of seeing the disgust of both.[242] In addition to such official encounters, it is possible, though not likely, that mendicant Indian seers made it to Greece themselves. Aristoxenus believed that an Indian yogi had come to Athens to visit Socrates.[243] According to the *Bṛhadāraṇyaka Upaniṣad*, after all, upon recognizing that one's inmost self (*ātman*) is but a drop in the ocean of the cosmic principle (*Brahman*), "one becomes an ascetic."[244] Desiring only this self "as their home," it adds, "mendicants wander forth."[245] Ordered to travel abroad, then, yogis may have brought asceticism into Greece itself, or at least into neighboring territories.

By one route or another, however, early Greek philosophers seem to have learned of Indian cosmology and psychology, rather than the other way round. Focusing on the doctrine of reincarnation shared by the Indians and the Pythagoreans, McEvilley shows how "in Greece this doctrine seems to have appeared in the seventh or sixth century with little or no sign of development,"[246] in works with other Eastern elements, and remained culturally isolated from the dominant religion of the epic poets. The Indian version, by contrast, "seems to have crystallized in the seventh century, after a series of developmental stages involving the progressive synthesis of a number of elements from different sources."[247] This synthesis produced the following tripartite structure: reincarnation (*saṃsāra*), according to merit (*karma*), bringing ultimate escape (*mokṣa*) from the cycle of birth and death.

For good conduct in this life, after death we may find ourselves in the womb of an upper-caste mother; for bad, in "the womb of a dog, or the womb of a swine."[248] With supreme merit—which is a matter of thought and purity—a seer may escape rebirth altogether: "he, however, who has understanding, who is mindful and ever pure, reaches the goal, from which he is born no more."[249] Specifically, he achieves this goal, *mokṣa*, by recognizing that diversity is illusion, for "there is on earth no diversity," and "he gets death after death, who perceives here seeming diversity."[250] By recognizing this illusion as such, a seer sees finally that *ātman* is *Brahman*. But this recognition comes only after having exercised "restraint of the breath, withdrawal of the senses, meditation, concentration, contemplation, absorption."[251] This six-fold technique, or *yoga*, aims to achieve a purification of thought. "With effort he should cleanse it," namely thought, for "if thus on *Brahman* it were fixed, who would not be released from bond?"[252] Thinking purely of the principle of the cosmos, in other words, brings liberation from the prison of embodiment. Thinking purely, in short, one becomes divine: "even the gods cannot prevent his becoming thus, for he becomes their very self."[253]

With its rejection of diversity in favor of unity, and with its injunction to purify thought, this rough outline of the Upaniṣads bears remarkable resemblances to our earlier interpretation of Parmenides. As we shall see in the following section, it also matches the eschatology of the Pythagoreans. India has therefore seemed the most plausible source of these doctrines.[254] "That an Ionian of the sixth century," writes Burkert, "should assimilate elements of Babylonian mathematics, Iranian religion, and even Indian metempsychosis doctrine is intrinsically possible."[255] More recently, scholars have become more confident of this pedigree. "The only religious tradition in which the doctrine of transmigration is at home from a very early period is that of India in pre-Buddhist times," writes Kahn, so "we can at least see that the . . . legend of Pythagoras's journey to India in search of the wisdom of the East may very well contain a grain of allegorical truth."[256] However, the case for Indian influence upon the Pythagoreans rests not simply upon their adoption of the doctrine of transmigration, but also upon its precisely similar tripartite structure. As McEvilley has noticed: *saṃsāra* becomes *metempsychōsis*; *karma* becomes *katharsis*; and *mokṣa* becomes *lusis*.[257]

3.6 Ordered Self

In the earliest extant report about Pythagoras, Xenophanes famously said that he had interceded on behalf of a beaten puppy with these words: "Stop, don't beat him, since it is the soul of a man, a friend of mine, which I recognized when I heard it crying."[258] This belief in transmigration linked the cosmological dualism of the Pythagoreans with their psychological dualism. By aligning one's soul with the good side of the cosmic divide, and by practicing purification (*katharsis*), one could ensure a better incarnation in one's next life. "What seems especially Pythagorean," writes Louis

Moulinier, "is the application of the word *katharsis*, which is usually reserved for corporeal things, to the psychological realm."[259] The goal of this purification was not just a better incarnation, but an escape (*lusis*) from the tedious cycle of embodiment altogether. For "the soul has been yoked to the body as a punishment," wrote Philolaus, "it is buried in it as though in a tomb."[260] To escape the body, paradoxically, was to escape death.

A Byzantine encyclopedia of ancient lore, the *Suda*, claims that it was Pherecydes of Syros (sixth century B.C.E.) who introduced the doctrine of reincarnation into Greece.[261] His father's name, Babys, "belongs to a group . . . which are certainly of Asiatic origin,"[262] and this is only one of several puzzle-pieces assembled by West to argue that Pherecydes imported into Greece Iranian and Indian doctrines, not the least of which was reincarnation.[263] Later biographers made him the teacher of Pythagoras,[264] and some modern scholars believe the story.[265] Already in the fifth century, a Pythagorean named Ion of Chios wrote that Pherecydes, "even in death has a delightful life for his soul, if indeed Pythagoras was truly wise about all things."[266] Open to several interpretations,[267] this passage likely means that Pherecydes had been good in this life, and therefore received a delightful afterlife because that is the reward of the good—just as Pythagoras taught. This appears to have been the eschatology of the fifth-century Pythagoreans, as well as of Pythagoras himself: the soul transmigrates according to the merits or demerits it has achieved in its former life.

This doctrine surfaces in the work of two fifth-century poets who wrote on Sicily, near enough to the Pythagorean colonies of southern Italy to have been familiar with their doctrines.[268] The first of them was Pindar (518–438). Though not himself a Pythagorean, while on Sicily he wrote an ode for the Olympic victory of Theron of Akragas in 476. This poem, the second Olympian Ode, begins with a reference to Heracles, "and maintains the general theme of the hero right through to its mystical passage,"[269] in which Pindar elaborates an eschatological myth that includes multiple reincarnations, punishments, and (for those who have kept their oaths) eternal "company with the honored gods."[270] In another poem, lost but for a fragment quoted by Plato, Pindar has Persephone reward the souls of the dead according to the atonement they have tendered her in life. Scholarly reconstruction of the myth from later Orphic sources makes the original sin of all humans our creation. Born from the ashes of wicked Titans—whom Zeus had smitten with his thunderbolt after they had eaten Dionysus, his divine son by Persephone—we inherited the mixture of evil and good present in these ashes.[271] The aim of Orphic cult would naturally have been the purification of the one from the other. Should we overcome our ancestral debt by this purification, Pindar has Persephone reward us with a better life in our next incarnation.[272]

A more elaborate Pythagorean eschatology can be found in the writings of a second poet of the fifth century, Empedocles (ca. 492–32), a resident of Akragas who may have studied among the Pythagoreans.[273] Eulogizing Pythagoras, apparently, he called him "a man of immense knowledge, who had obtained the greatest wealth of mind."[274] Indeed, he added, this man could remember his past incarnations, and thus "easily saw each and every thing in ten or twenty generations."[275] Claiming the same clairvoyance for himself, Empedocles said that he had already been a girl, a bush, a bird, and a fish—though perhaps not in that order.[276] He imagined a hierarchy of animals and plants in which souls were reincarnated according to their merits. As he told it, the best animal to become was a lion; the best plant, a laurel.[277]

Best of all incarnations was that of a human. Only so, presumably, could one act to purify oneself, and assiduous purification would bring the ultimate reward: life beyond the cycle of reincarnation. One of the gradual developments in Indian eschatology described by McEvilley is the replacement of an early version, according to which the soul progresses through all the species randomly (thereby recognizing that *ātman* is *Brahman*—roughly, that self is world—by dint of longsuffering experience), with a later version that includes early escape for those humans who recognize this by dint of contemplation.[278] Like the Pythagoreans who espoused transmigration, Empedocles seems to have described a version of the later sort. Without any extant record of indigenous development, this version seems to have arrived in Greece already formed.

In order to understand Empedocles' own particular adaptation of transmigration we must first explain his dualistic cosmology, which seems to owe more to Persia than to India. Two forces compete for supremacy in his cosmos, Love and Strife, which mix and separate its stuff in alternating cycles.[279] "If we said that Empedocles in a sense both mentions, and is the first to mention, the bad and the good as principles," wrote Aristotle, "we should perhaps be right."[280] This paradigm of early Greek dualism also epitomizes the philosophical spirit that sought divinization through purification of thought. Empedocles imagined a stage in his cosmic cycle, the stage in which Love dominates, when everything is intermingled and the cosmos forms one giant sphere. This sphere is "merely a mind, holy and unutterable, rushing with rapid thought over the whole world."[281] Although the individual soul was originally unified with this intelligent sphere of Love, Strife has separated it, imprisoning it in a body.[282] Here it is doomed for a certain time to wander the earth—no less than "thrice ten thousand seasons"[283]—preserving a divided allegiance.[284] While incarcerated and in exile it may act to promote either the Strife that cursed it or the Love from which it originally sprang.[285] "Two fates or spirits take over and govern each of us when we are born."[286] We must choose between them.

Not surprisingly, Empedocles enjoins his readers to attend to Love in their thought.[287] Those who do so, as if recalling the Zoroastrian motto quoted earlier, "think friendly thoughts and perform deeds of peace."[288] Such deeds preclude eating meat and having sex. "The bodies of the animals we eat," he believed, "are the dwelling places of punished souls."[289] To eat them would therefore be murder, possibly patricide or matricide.[290] As for sex, it favors Strife rather than Love, ironically, because it coöperates in the construction of more human bodies in which souls may be imprisoned.[291] Pitched between Love and Strife, then, the reincarnated soul participates daily in a cosmic contest. To favor Love is to seek purification— for which reason the practical side of Empedocles' poetry was known as *Katharmoi*.[292] These "purifications" are matters not just of action, but also of thought. By thinking divine thoughts, the convert to Love imitates the pure thought that reigns when the cosmos is one giant sphere. "Happy is he," Empedocles thus wrote, "who has gained the wealth of divine thoughts."[293]

Beyond mortal happiness, Empedocles promised divinization. Those humans who had lived nobly, as "prophets and poets and physicians and political leaders" (incidentally, Empedocles' own professions, and perhaps also those of Parmenides, as we saw earlier), "arise as gods, highest in honour."[294] Having lived piously and justly, having fully purified their souls, they escape the cycle of rebirth and possess happiness for eternity, "at the same hearth and table as the other immortals, relieved of mortal pains, tireless."[295] By several accounts, Empedocles may have symbolized his own such purification and divinization by casting himself into Mount Etna. Examining this peculiar story, which has generated ridicule since antiquity, Kingsley has decoded its complex synthesis of Pythagorean eschatology and cosmology.[296] The volcano, for example, offered the ritual significance of purification by fire; it also offered a gateway to the fiery heavens above, connected as they were to the fiery underworld below.[297] Empedocles seems to have anticipated his purifying death by claiming escape from the cycles of reincarnation while alive: "I go about you an immortal god, no longer mortal."[298]

His Pythagorean eschatology reproduced the tripartite structure of the Indian doctrine—*metempsychōsis* upon death, *katharsis* in increasingly noble human lives, and *lusis* after one's final incarnation as a prophet, poet, physician, or political leader. As such, it marked a sharp departure from the eschatology of the Homeric epics. For example, the Homeric soul (or "shade," *psychē*) emerges as something distinct only after death, never entering another body, persisting only as something insubstantial and miserable in Hades.[299] Achilles would famously rather "slave on earth for another man—some dirt-poor tenant farmer who scrapes to keep alive—than rule down here over all the breathless dead."[300] Inverting Achilles' lament, then, the Pythagoreans preferred to this life another—either the chance to purify oneself further in another bodily existence, or better, an escape from mortal bodies altogether. It appears odd, at first, that Pythagoreans often practiced medicine,[301] the art which aims to make our time in mortal bodies both longer and more comfortable. Empedocles, for instance, promised to teach "all the potions which there are as a defence against evils and old age."[302] Yet also, he wrote, "you shall bring from Hades the strength of a man who has died."[303] Mastery over old age was a part of his mastery over death, it would seem, and both threatened Homeric religion, which reserved true immortality for the gods.[304] Indeed, immortality was for traditional Greek religion synonymous with divinity.[305] Not even heroes were permitted more than the persistence of their name on earth and their shade in Hades. No heroes, that is, except Heracles and Dionysus.[306]

Their apotheoses helped humans imagine the same for themselves, and so it is not surprising that "the idea of imitating or identifying with Dionysus in later times often tended to go hand in hand with the idea of imitating Heracles."[307] For his part, Heracles earned a seat on Olympus thanks to his extraordinary deeds, or 'labors,' and became, as Burkert writes, "a model for the common man who may hope that after a life of drudgery, and through that very life, he too may enter into the company of the gods."[308] Empedocles seemed to realize this hope, since three of his purported deeds recapitulated Heracles' labors: diversion of a river for the sake of cleansing,[309] retrieval of someone's soul from the underworld,[310] and immortalization through fire.[311] Heracles had a traditional place in Greek mythology; Empedocles and the other Pythagoreans were newcomers. The arrival of these philosophical 'heroes' challenged old precepts: "Nothing in excess," declared the temple of Delphi; "do not, my soul, strive for the life of the immortals," wrote Pindar.[312] A mortal could never expect to imitate Heracles' super-human accomplishments, but could perhaps wish for his retrieval of the soul from Hades, just as he was supposed to have retrieved Alcestis.[313] Consequently, "Pythagoreans are presented as practicing the 'imitation of Heracles' from the very beginning of Pythagoreanism in the West."[314] Heracles died on a funeral pyre and then, purified, entered the company of the gods. Empedocles' immortal leap into Etna was not expected of the Pythagoreans, but by joining their company, or at least by beginning their ascetic preparation for pure thought, an initiate could strive less dramatically for the same end.[315]

The cult of Dionysus encouraged similar hope, promising immortality and divinity to its initiates. From burial sites throughout the Greek-speaking world, including southern Italy, archaeologists have exhumed gold plates that read "from a man becoming a god," and, more mysteriously, "I am a kid who has rushed for the milk."[316] As Kingsley has observed, young goats were associated with Dionysus, "specifically in the context of suckling milk."[317] Moreover, this allusion was preceded by another: "I have made straight for the breast of Her Mistress, queen of the underworld." As we saw in our discussion of Parmenides' proem, this queen was Persephone, and the coincidence of her with Dionysus in an eschatological context evokes Orphic mythology.[318] Before the initiate could rush for the milk of the underworld, Bacchic festivals in this life were means of purification and divinization, making votary and god one.[319] Perhaps it is not so surprising, then, to learn that a work called *Bacchae* has been attributed to Philolaus, or that Archytas the Pythagorean "refers in his writings to details from Dionysiac ritual."[320]

Nor were Bacchic festivals and Pythagorean societies the only alternatives available to fifth-century Greeks seeking intimacy with the divine. The Eleusinian mysteries seem to have made similar promises.[321] So too did the Orphics, who are difficult to distinguish from the Pythagoreans, in some ways; in other ways, from the worshipers of Dionysus.[322] In Euripides' *Hippolytus*, for instance, Theseus scorns his son's newfangled Orphic piety with words that reveal four features at odds with the Homeric religion represented by the traditional hero: immortality, chastity, dietary restrictions, and literacy. "So you're a companion of the gods," Theseus spits sarcastically, "someone special?" First of all, the initiates of the cults claimed the company of the gods: immortality at least, if not also unity with the divine. Secondly, chastity was one way that they distinguished themselves from others, a means of purification. "So you're chaste," adds Theseus, "and pure of evil?" Hippolytus advertises his sexual purity in the portentous words of his opening speech.[323] Another means of purification was dietary restriction, especially vegetarianism. "Peddle your vegetables," concludes Theseus, "and revere the smoke of your voluminous books."[324] The Orphics seem to have been readers as well as vegetarians.[325] Central to Homeric religion, by contrast, were animal sacrifice and ordered public festivals that preserved the oral tradition of bards.

"The characteristic appeal to books is indicative of a revolution," observes Burkert; "the new form of transmission introduces a new form of authority to which the individual, provided that he can read, has direct access without collective mediation."[326] This revolution made Orphic religion and Pythagorean philosophy indistinguishable—to us, but also to ancient writers of the period. For example, Ion of Chios said that "Pythagoras composed some things and attributed them to Orpheus."[327] Herodotus wrote that the prohibition against burial in woolen clothing "accords with the Orphic and Bacchic rites, as they are called (though they are actually Egyptian and Pythagorean)."[328] Ion's claim argues an assimilation of Pythagoreanism and Orphism; Herodotus's, a conflation of both with the cult of Dionysus.[329] That contemporaneous authors could confuse them offers some consolation to the frustrated scholar.[330] More importantly, it reveals the similarity of Pythagorean philosophy to the doctrines of archaic salvation cults.[331] No such confusion was made with the other philosophies of the period, nor was such a confusion possible. Heraclitus, as we saw, sought immersion in this world rather than escape from it.

Even though the Pythagoreans shared with the salvation cults their ultimate goal, escape, their route to this goal seems to have been quite different. Whereas Eleusis promised immortality to those who had been initiated and had seen the holy objects, and whereas the Bacchics tasted unity with the divine in the midst of their revels, the Pythagoreans—and perhaps also the Orphics—favored small congregations whose asceticism was aimed at a purification of thought. Although the Zoroastrians also made the purification of thought one aim of their rituals and taboos, asceticism was foreign to them. If ascetic practices such as chastity,[332] vegetarianism,[333] and the apparently related prohibition of bean-eating,[334] were imported, they must be traced to another source. Since the doctrine of transmigration seems to stand behind them, at least in the case of Empedocles, they likely had the same provenance—namely, India. Whether or not these particular ascetic practices should be traced outside the Greek world, though, the ascetic impulse is nonetheless at home in the Pythagoreans' adapted variety of dualism. After all, asceticism is self-restraint, or self-limitation, and Pythagoreans venerated limit over against the unlimited. Cosmology matched ethical practice; dualism warranted a way of life.

Alongside limit went harmony, it seems, first of lyre strings and later of the revolving heavenly spheres. Musical and astronomical study were further means by which Pythagoreans sought to align themselves with the good over against the evil. Ascetic restraint purified the body while inquiry purified the soul. Each imposed limit on the unlimited, but the soul's study of the cosmos, in particular, assimilated the one to the other. The correspondence between cosmos and soul "very likely goes back in some sense and to some degree to Bronze Age Mesopotamia where the trail of the macrocosm/

microcosm correspondence leads."[335] The Milesians take it for granted. Anaximenes, for instance, asserted that an infinite air ordered the cosmos just as breath orders our body.[336] He also believed that the soul shares in the divinity of the cosmos itself, since "air is a god."[337] Although Philolaus did not divinize air, he did write that the cosmos "drew in from the unlimited time, breath, and void which in each case distinguishes the place of each thing."[338] As obscure as this doctrine appears, the idea seems to be that time, breath, and void are unlimited continua—like lyre strings—which, when limited by the imposition of boundaries from without, become discrete quantities. No extant fragment connects this doctrine with the breath of the human body, yet one does say that we resemble the quantified cosmos by virtue of our mathematical reason. For "mathematical reason," wrote Philolaus, "inasmuch as it considers the nature of the universe, has a certain affinity to it (for like is naturally apprehended by like)."[339] In other words, our mathematical abilities show an affinity between our soul and the divine cosmos. By practicing mathematics in addition to self-restraint, it seems, the Pythagoreans sought to develop and augment this affinity.[340]

They thereby fomented a revolution that was simultaneously religious and philosophical. In philosophy, they justified a peculiar way of life. In religion, they disregarded the indigenous precept to think mortal thoughts and instead enjoined their initiates to become divine through pure thought of the divine.[341] This revolution seems to have synthesized the contributions of several older traditions of philosophy and religion. From Miletus—and still further, from Babylon—they seem to have inherited their mathematics and astronomy; from India, their tripartite eschatology. And yet the cosmologies of these traditions were equally monistic: the Milesians sought one *archē*; the *Bṛhadāraṇyaka Upaniṣad* declared of *Brahman*: "as a unity only is It to be looked upon."[342] With diversity an illusion, and unity their only reality, the Milesians and the Upaniṣads were equally preoccupied with the so-called problem of the one and the many, the problem with which we concluded our accounts of both Heraclitus and Parmenides.[343] If Pythagoreans were less concerned with this problem, it may have been because they integrated elements of these monistic traditions into a dualistic cosmology adapted from Iran. Conceptually unstable as it may have been, this synthesis and the program of purification it enjoined— according to which the soul, and especially its reason, was to eschew the body, and through repeated incarnations decide for limit against the unlimited, good against evil, light against darkness—would promise union with the divine, and achieve the allegiance of the most influential of Greek philosophers, Plato.

Chapter 4

Plato

Awaiting his execution for impiety and corrupting the youth, Socrates continued to do the very thing that had made him a scapegoat to the angry and humiliated Athenians—he philosophized. How better to prepare for death? How else to prepare for divinity? "No one may join the company of the gods," he says, "who has not practiced philosophy and is not completely pure when he departs from life."[1] Death alone frees us totally from the senses and pleasures of the body, he claims, but in the meantime philosophy purifies: it liberates the soul, and especially its reason, from a bodily prison.[2] This Platonic picture of philosophy appears dualistic in at least two ways. Not only does it divide soul from body, it divides the cosmos as we perceive it through our senses from the cosmos as we know it by our reason. Along with this picture goes the practical demand that we eschew our bodies and everything that they produce in us: sensations, imagination, appetites, and emotions. Favoring pure reason in their stead, Plato promises us the consolation of divinity.

Shortly before receiving his own consolation, according to the short autobiography Plato writes for him in *Phaedo*, Socrates recounts his youthful enthusiasm for "that wisdom which they call natural science," the philosophies of his monist predecessors.[3] The first of them was Thales of Miletus.[4] He seems to have supposed that all the changes of the cosmos were but variations of one substance, water.[5] Next after him, in the same city, Anaximander likewise claimed that there was one substrate of all change and diversity, but rejected anything so definite as water, favoring simply "the indefinite" (*to apeiron*).[6] Also from Miletus, Anaximenes returned to a definite substance, air, arguing that it ruled the cosmos just as breath—which the early Greeks conflated with *psychē*—rules our bodies.[7] He explained the mutation of his principle into the many things of the cosmos by adding the mechanism of condensation and rarefaction.[8] Despite the brilliance of this innovation, it supplied only the conditions in which a substrate changes from one thing into another. As far as we can tell, none of the Milesians explained *why* this happens.

Although Socrates does not name all the philosophers he studied in his youth, he does say that his enthusiasm for them faded once he realized their silence about the *real* cause of anything: "what was the *best* way for it to be."[9] Besides the Milesians, and the philosophers we treated in earlier chapters of this volume, he may have considered the Atomists, Leucippus and Democritus, whose cosmos was an amoral collision of atoms in a void. More dramatically than with the other predecessors, then, there could be no best way for such a cosmos to be.[10] Against this background, Socrates' interest in philosophy was apparently rekindled when he heard someone reading from a book of Anaxagoras which claimed that *nous* (mind, thought, or reason) directs and causes everything.[11] "I was delighted with this cause," he says, "and it seemed to me good that *nous* should be the cause of all. I thought that if this were so the directing *nous* would direct everything and arrange each thing in the way that was best."[12]

In other words, Socrates initially thought that Anaxagoras had supplied his cosmos with efficacious value—specifically, what Aristotle would later distinguish as a *final* cause: an ultimate goal, the best good.[13] He read Anaxagoras's writings quickly, eager to learn about this best good which *nous* seemed aimed to effect. His hope was soon dashed, however, once he recognized that Anaxagoras's *nous* was not directing anything toward the best; in fact, he came to believe it played no role whatsoever in explanation.[14] Had he asked Anaxagoras about his predicament—"Why am I in this cell?"—the answer would not have been that *nous* is directing him and everything in the cosmos towards the best. The answer he instead imagines receiving is a parody of materialist monism: "the reason that I am sitting here is because my body consists of bones and sinews, because the bones are hard and are separated by joints, that the sinews are such as to contract and relax," and so on.[15]

To be fair to Anaxagoras, he might have given *nous* more of a role than Socrates allows. His bones and sinews could have been arranged in this way by its rotation of the cosmos.[16] Be that as it may, Anaxagoras never explained *why* the cosmos was rotated by *nous* in this particular way rather than another. His answer remained a material one, or at most an efficient one—to anticipate again Aristotle's distinction among causes—and Plato's Socrates thereby considered it limited. Limited, but not irrelevant. After all, the material cause supplies the necessary conditions of an event; the final cause, its sufficient condition. Socrates compares his philosophical predecessors to "people groping in the dark," for they sought only the necessary conditions, not the sufficient condition, which he calls the real cause. "Imagine not being able to distinguish," Plato writes, "the real cause from that without which the cause would not be able to act as cause."[17] Successors to the Milesians may have supplied explanations of why the cosmos changed—by adding a *theos* (Xenophanes), a *logos* (Heraclitus), or a *nous* (Anaxagoras)—but their additions only pushed Socrates' question one step further back. Why, it remained to be explained, did these principles act? Why, he wonders, is it best for anything to be the way it is, let alone to change into something else?

Why, to return to the question Socrates imagines posing to Anaxagoras, is he *here*, sitting in this prison cell? The question is not idle. In *Crito*, a dialogue whose narrative precedes that of *Phaedo*, a disciple and devoted friend of Socrates has begged him to slip past the conniving warden.[18] But Socrates refuses, arguing notoriously that he is bound to obey the laws, no less when the jury has applied them unjustly. These laws have safeguarded him his whole life, and by his lifelong presence in Athens he has tacitly agreed to follow them, whatever they might require of him.[19] Thus, to ask "Why am I here?" in *Phaedo* is to return to this reasoning of *Crito* and ask again, "Why is it best for me to be here, accepting death, even affirming it?" In *Phaedo*, then, the question transcends its political meaning and assumes a cosmological significance. The answer assembled by Plato's Socrates in this and other dialogues, as we shall see in this chapter, betrays a commitment to the Pythagorean program of purification and divinization elicited in the previous one. More than any of these other dialogues, *Phaedo* communicates this allegiance, beginning with several of its dramatic clues.

The location, for example, is Phlius, a center of Pythagoreanism in Plato's lifetime. As the dialogue begins, moreover, a certain Echecrates entices Phaedo to recount Socrates' death-bed conversation about the immortality of the soul, a central Pythagorean doctrine. Echecrates was himself a student of the foremost Pythagorean of the fifth century, the philosopher who is our main source for early Pythagorean cosmology, Philolaus.[20] He also taught Socrates' two main interlocutors in this dialogue, Simmias and Cebes.[21] Beyond these Pythagorean characters, location, and topic, the dialogue advances cosmological and psychological dualism, relating them by an ethical program of purification and divinization. After having exposed the origins of this program in Chapter 3, our aim in the present one is to explore Plato's attempt to synthesize this program's disparate elements into a coherent whole held together by the principle of non-contradiction he inherited from Parmenides.[22]

4.1 Consistently Pure

Aristophanes portrayed Socrates as a student of things beneath the earth and in the heavens,[23] which is to say as a *physikos,* or student of nature, like so many of the predecessors Plato shows him criticizing in *Phaedo*. This portrait offered plenty of opportunity for ridicule. After all, legend had it that the first *physikos*, Thales, "was gazing upwards while doing astronomy," and was so oblivious of his situation that "he fell into a well";[24] and so, as Aristophanes' Socrates stood gaping at the night sky, "a speckled gecko on the roof shat right on his head."[25] Anaximenes posited condensation and rarefaction as the mechanism by which air changed into other elements; to Aristophanes' Socrates this mechanism explains only the farts of a gnat.[26] Anaxagoras had *nous* rotate the cosmos in order to effect its separation into distinct things; in *Clouds* this rotation becomes the comical "whirling of the Celestial Basin."[27] Of all the *physikoi* ridiculed by Aristophanes, Diogenes of Apollonia has the most in common with this portrait of Socrates. "That which possesses intelligence," he taught, "is what people call air, and all humans are governed by it and it rules all things."[28] "The heavenly Clouds," says Aristophanes' Socrates, "grace us with our intellect."[29] Consequently, he prefers to spend his time suspended in a basket: "hanging up my mind and mixing the minute particles of my thought into the air which it resembles."[30] According to Aristophanes' Socrates, it would seem, suspension purifies thought.

But this Socrates is a condensation not only of the *physikoi*, but also of the Pythagoreans, not to mention the Sophists, who were largely silent on the fundamental constituents of the cosmos. We need not consider his Sophistry,[31] but we cannot neglect his Pythagoreanism. Adept in musical theory, he asks Strepsiades to tell him "which measure is more aesthetically pleasing, the three-quarter beat or the four-quarter beat."[32] More importantly, he shows himself to be no stranger to the mystery cults. "Don't worry," he reassures Strepsiades as he prostrates him upon a sacred couch, crowns him with a wreath, sprinkles him with meal, and then recites over him an invocation of the Clouds—"it's just part of the initiation rites."[33] Moreover, when Strepsiades asks one of Socrates' students to clarify an obscure reference, the student says of the physical doctrines under debate in Socrates' school: "Only students may be told such things. It's the sacred law."[34] Such secrecy was the hallmark not only of the mystery cults, but also of the Pythagoreans. As legend had it, in fact, Hippasus suffered expulsion from the society, or perhaps divine retribution in the form of a shipwreck, once he had divulged Pythagorean secrets.[35] Aristophanes' Socrates thus seems as much a Pythagorean as a *physikos* or a Sophist.

Plato's Socrates appears rather different—at first glance. "If anyone says that he learned something from me or heard something in private that all the others didn't also hear," he pleads during his defense, "you may be sure he isn't telling the truth."[36] This challenge comes in the midst of his protest that he is not a teacher, as alleged in the unofficial charges, the slander which he must refute before coming to the official indictment.[37] Specifically, then, he is not a teacher like the Pythagoreans because everything he says he says publicly. He is not a teacher like the *physikoi*, moreover, because their subject is one that he knows "neither a lot nor a little but nothing at all about."[38] And he is not a teacher like the Sophists, finally, because he asks no fee, invites no students, and freely admits his ignorance of the subject some of them pretend to teach: virtue.[39]

In the end, Plato's Socrates is not a teacher of any sort: he proposes no doctrines, only questions.[40] These questions are part of his notorious technique of "cross-examination," the *elenchos*, which he has used as comfortably for years in the interrogation of politicians, artists, and artisans about the marketplace as he uses it now in the courtroom-refutation of Meletus. To submit to the Socratic *elenchos* required exposing to scrutiny one's every thought about the most important matters, especially the virtues. Its goal was the harmonization of these thoughts. "Which of these propositions should we abandon, Protagoras?" he asks the famous Sophist, after exposing a contradiction in his thought. "The two statements are dissonant," he adds, "they are not in harmony with one another."[41] Socrates submitted himself as thoroughly to this examination as he submitted his interlocutors. "It's better to have my lyre or a chorus that I might lead out of tune and dissonant," he says to one of them, "than to be out of harmony with myself, to contradict myself."[42] This effort to purge all contradiction makes the Platonic Socrates sound like Parmenides. With his analogies between music and thought, overtones of Pythagoreanism first become audible.

Like the Pythagoreans, Socrates considered the harmonization of thought his divine mission. Asked whether anyone were wiser than Socrates, Apollo's oracle had answered that no one was. He was wisest who knew nothing grand, distinguishing himself from others only by the recognition of his ignorance. Human wisdom was of little account, as Socrates interpreted the oracle: it amounted to no more than this humble recognition.[43] To convey his divine message to the Athenians, he subjected their cherished beliefs to the *elenchos*, purifying them of pretensions and dissonant contradictions.[44] Cornford observed the connection of "the idea of the Socratic *elenchos* with the idea of *purification*."[45] Plato himself wrote that "the *elenchos* is the principal and most important kind of *katharsis*."[46] As for his divine mandate to perform this *elenchos* upon himself and his fellow citizens, Socrates would never doubt it. "The god stationed me here," he claimed at his trial, "to live practicing philosophy, examining myself and others."[47]

Remaining within the Pythagorean tradition, then, Socrates advanced philosophy as the means of purification and even salvation—of the city, but more particularly of the soul. Urging his fellow citizens to eschew wealth, honor, and the care of their bodies, he advised them instead to take care that "your soul (*psychē*) may be in the best possible condition."[48] We have difficulty now, in the wake of the Pythagorean revolution he helped advance, to appreciate the novelty of Socrates' advice. But in a culture still indebted to the Homeric epics, in which *psychē* was a miserable shade, pursuit of its best condition must have appeared strange.[49] Socrates nonetheless went to his death pursuing it, enjoining its pursuit, and believing that it could be achieved by obedience to Apollo and the demands of the *elenchos*.

Plato appears to have recognized shortcomings in the latter, if not both. As for obedience to the gods in general, he too would enjoin proper reverence of them.[50] Indeed, should his injunction be disobeyed in the utopia he describes in *Laws*, the meet penalty is death.[51] Plato's reverence also included respect for oracles, and he would fashion several divine myths of his own.[52] Yet his vision for the philosophical life would carry it beyond Socrates' posture of humble submission. In *Republic*, for instance, philosophers are to be not only "god-fearing," but also as "godlike as human beings can be."[53] Following the Pythagoreans in this respect above all, Plato abandons the traditional precept to think mortal thoughts. His philosophers must transcend the Socratic recognition that "human wisdom is worth little or nothing."[54]

What about the *elenchos*? Interrogating his interlocutors about the virtues, Socrates illuminated their implicit commitments and thereby exposed their contradictions. His method alone, however, could not decide which of their contradictory beliefs should be surrendered, which (if either) maintained. Socrates may have recommended consistency, but it seemed that the *elenchos* alone could determine no truth. In *Gorgias*, in fact, Plato has him all but recognize this shortcoming. Speaking of his conclusions that it is better to suffer wrong than to do it, and that once caught it is better to pay the penalty than to escape unpunished—two conclusions that have survived his interrogation unrefuted—he nonetheless says, "I don't *know* how these things are, but no one I've ever met, as in this case, can say anything else without being ridiculous."[55] The *elenchos* excludes absurdity by ensuring consistency; in order to yield knowledge, it would seem, its practitioner had to supplement it with dogma, whether in the form of oracular conviction, traditional belief, or fabricated myth.

Plato elsewhere recognizes the danger of mistaking such unexamined dogma and then conforming everything else to it.[56] He dramatizes this danger by confronting Socrates with two spirited rivals—Callicles in

Gorgias, and Thrasymachus in *Republic*—who claim that traditional beliefs about justice are but the products of power politics. "The people who institute our laws are the weak and the many," fulminates Callicles, "and they assign praise and blame with themselves and their own advantage in mind."[57] Thrasymachus adds defiantly: "justice is nothing other than the advantage of the stronger."[58] Despite some differences, their critiques correspond to this extent at least: traditional beliefs about justice have been shaped by political and rhetorical manipulation. They are, as we might say now, false ideologies.[59]

If the *elenchos* draws upon traditional beliefs about justice and the other virtues, then, it cannot refute this critique without begging the question against it.[60] If philosophers are to find truth outside ideology, if they are to find purification and salvation by thought, the *elenchos* and its pursuit of consistency must somehow transcend ideology. To remedy just these shortcomings, it would appear, Plato returns to Pythagorean topics and a more rigorous use of the Parmenidean principle of non-contradiction. In *Meno,* for example, the discussion turns to mathematics, and not just to mathematics, but to a special case of the Pythagorean theorem.[61] Socrates interrogates this time not a politician, artist, or artisan, but a slave. Without any previous education in geometry, Meno's slave seems to learn the true dimensions of an eight-foot square, overcoming his prejudice that these dimensions were simply double those of a four-foot one. Socrates' questions have been instrumental in the slave's success: first they expose the contradiction of his false claim to knowledge, and then eventually they lead him to recognize the correct answer.

Naturally it seems to us that the slave has *learned* and that Socrates has been his teacher. But our prejudices about knowledge prove no less mistaken than the slave's about mathematics. He cannot have learned the dimensions of the square, it turns out, because learning has been precluded by the so-called Meno paradox: we can never find what we seek to know unless we already know what we seek—otherwise we would seek in vain, never recognizing our object even were we to find it. Whether someone knows something or not, he cannot learn it: "he cannot search for what he knows—since he knows it, there is no need to search—nor for what he does not know, for he does not know what to look for."[62] But if learning is impossible, how has the slave deduced the eight-foot square's dimensions? Plato's peculiar answer to this question distinguishes *Meno,* and the other dialogues we shall now discuss, from the dialogues that appear to present a more historically accurate Socrates.

4.2 Pure Thought

According to Aristotle, the historical Socrates asked questions but did not pretend to know the answers himself,[63] sought universal definitions of the virtues but was unconcerned with nature as a whole,[64] and did not hypostatize these definitions the way Plato would soon do.[65] Aristotle's report of Socrates resembles the portrait of him found in Xenophon's dialogues.[66] In the group of Platonic dialogues thus labeled "Socratic," Socrates often interrogates someone who claims to understand a virtue until he reduces him to perplexity. Characteristically, in this group, he offers no answers of his own, nor does he widen the investigation to incorporate the whole cosmos. In a second group of dialogues, by contrast, he does, advancing positive doctrines—including doctrines of epistemology, ontology, psychology, and eschatology, which are most relevant to our inquiry. In the latest group, finally, in which the character of Socrates recedes, Plato refines, reformulates, or perhaps even rejects these doctrines. The Platonic corpus is therefore commonly divided into three groups.[67]

Meno and most of the dialogues we shall presently discuss come from the second,[68] where Plato weaves into the Socratic persona some of the Presocratic philosophies we have mentioned.[69] Besides the Parmenidean doctrine of pure being, most prominent of all of these threads is Pythagoreanism, with its denigration of body and exaltation of soul, its quest for divinity through purification, and finally its cathartic method: pure thought. For Plato, this thought is first of music, later of mathematics, next of immaterial form, and finally of the Form of Forms—the Good. Before rising to those heights, however, we must still answer the question raised by *Meno*: if learning is impossible, how has the slave deduced the eight-foot square's dimensions? By itself, Socrates' *elenchos* has not taught him mathematical truth, nor truth of any other sort, it would seem. This method served only to expose inconsistencies in the answers he had given. But with help from it as a mnemonic device—that is to say, with a number of leading questions that begin to look suspiciously like instruction—anyone can recollect knowledge already possessed but forgotten.[70] Famously, then, the slave has not *learned* the square's dimensions, he has *recollected* them.[71]

As his lifelong master attests, however, he has never been educated in mathematics. He could not have acquired his knowledge in this life; he must have acquired it earlier.[72] Plato has Socrates introduce this solution upon the authority of unnamed priests and priestesses, but also, significantly, by invoking Pindar. In fact, he quotes the very fragment of Pindar's poetry we examined when we discussed Pythagorean eschatology in Chapter 3.[73] "As the soul is immortal, has been born often and has seen all things here and in the underworld," Socrates concludes, "there is nothing which it has not yet learned."[74] Having learned everything in his past lives, "nothing prevents a man after recalling one thing only—a process men call learning—discovering everything else for himself."[75] But a crucial point has been ignored. The Meno paradox should have rendered learning in former lives as impossible as it is in this one. Indeed, an infinite number of incarnations should have added nothing to the wisdom of a soul doomed to seek either what it knows and cannot learn, or what it does not know and cannot find.

As if to answer this objection, Plato in *Phaedrus* embellishes his eschatological epistemology by imagining a pure soul, unencumbered by a body, moving in a divine realm where it perceives directly "what is truly real."[76] The Meno paradox required of learning a search. Direct perception obviates it: what we wish to know lies right before us. Denied this direct perception while still embodied here below, however, we must labor in indirect perception, using sensible things for "recollection of the things our soul saw when it was traveling with god."[77] What we saw while traveling with god will be explained shortly. For now we should notice that our means of recollection are not only the *elenchos*, as in *Meno*, but also the sensible world itself—or at least those parts of it that reflect the true reality. "When he sees the beauty we have down here," says Plato of the noblest type of soul, he "is reminded of true beauty."[78]

According to this myth, before its conjunction with a body each human soul at least glimpsed what is truly real, whether true beauty or the true form of anything else known by us. Indeed, our glimpses of these forms distinguished our souls from those of animals; never having directly perceived forms, animals cannot recollect them, and are doomed to ignorance.[79] Conversely, our direct perception has permitted us knowledge. But not every human soul was in the best possible condition when it perceived true reality; our levels of knowledge vary as a result of these conditions. Confidently including himself among those—the philosophical souls— who were in the best possible condition, Socrates says of true reality, "we saw it in pure light because we were pure ourselves."[80] Plato thus treats philosophy as a cult that purifies its devotees for "that blessed and spectacular vision . . . the mystery that we may rightly call the most blessed of all."[81] By philosophizing, therefore, we become perfect enough to perceive directly the true forms, the "sacred revealed objects that were perfect, and simple, and unshakeable and blissful."[82] Unmistakable here is the language of mystery cults such as that of Eleusis, and throughout the dialogue we find the language of ecstatic rites such as Bacchic frenzy.[83] The account of philosophy as purification recalls the more intellectual tradition of Pythagoreanism.

This Platonic debt to the Pythagoreans emerges still clearer from *Phaedo*. Besides the dramatic hints of Pythagoreanism in this dialogue, we find music and mathematics featured prominently among the philosophical examples. Simmias, for instance, suggests that "the soul is a kind of harmony," a harmony of the body's elements.[84] If so, it cannot be immortal: it disappears once the body decays and its elements become discordant. Socrates rejects this hypothesis because it is incompatible with the epistemology of recollection. After all, if recollection is to occur, as in the case of Meno's slave, the soul must have existed before the body. Musical harmony cannot exist before its instrument; neither, then, could the soul if it were a harmony of the body.[85] Yet recollection is not simply taken for granted in *Phaedo*. Plato has Socrates defend it as vigorously here as he did in *Meno*, and his argument once again exploits a mathematical concept: equality.[86]

We reason about it, and speak of it, although our bodily senses never perceive perfect equality. They do perceive many things we judge to be (imperfectly) equal: things that are equal only in some respects, or from some perspectives; and then only fleetingly, or rather not at all, for they are perpetually subject to the time that makes each thing unequal even to itself. But perfect equality cannot be unequal in any way. Consequently, we cannot have acquired our knowledge of it by perception of the many (imperfectly) equal things here in time. None of them is sufficiently equal to be a standard of equality, and yet such a standard is required for comparison whenever we judge two things to be (imperfectly) equal. For how else could we judge anything to be equal, let alone imperfectly so, except by comparison with something we know to be perfectly equal? We must have access right now to something without any mixture of inequality, something *purely* equal, something outside of time. This is none other than the Equal itself.

But "our present argument is no more about the Equal," adds Socrates, "than about the Beautiful itself, the Good itself, the Just, the Pious and, as I say, about all those things to which we can attach the word 'itself.' "[87] Of all these "Forms"—as they have come to be known in English, thanks to Cicero's translation (*forma*, "beauty") into Latin—Plato describes Beauty in most detail.[88] The dialogue devoted to it is *Symposium*, and, as in *Phaedrus*, the language is that of sacred rites. In his capacity as mystagogue, *Erōs* leads us to Beauty, "the final and highest mystery."[89] Plato informs us that "it always *is* and neither comes to be nor passes away, neither waxes nor wanes."[90] Such a description recalls Parmenides, who, as we have seen, argued that being is one, ungenerated, and imperishable, "nor was it ever, nor will it be, since it is now, all together, one, continuous."[91] Plato similarly removes Beauty from the contradictory temporal world described by Heraclitus—where everything is a unity in opposition, something whose only stability is change.[92] Beauty, he writes, is not "beautiful this way and ugly that way, nor beautiful at one time and ugly at another, nor beautiful in relation to one thing and ugly in relation to another."[93] Like Equality and all the other Forms, it would seem, Beauty must satisfy the principle of non-contradiction. Only so could it be an object of knowledge, the perfect and eternal paradigm we dimly access whenever we judge anything here in time to be (imperfectly) beautiful.

4.3　Purging Contradiction

Plato's most explicit statement of the principle of non-contradiction appears in *Republic*. "It is clear that the same thing cannot do or undergo opposites," says Socrates; "not, at any rate, in the same respect, in relation to the same thing, at the same time."[94] At this point in the text, book four, it functions as the first premise in an argument about the composition of the soul. We shall examine this argument closely at the end of this chapter, seeing how it allows Socrates to infer from the fact that a soul undergoes opposite desires the conclusion that it must have different parts.[95] After introducing this principle to analyze the soul into parts—including the rational part which is the exercise of this very principle—he marshals it again to characterize those in whom this rational part rules: the "philosophers," lovers of wisdom or knowledge. But, he asks, what is knowledge? Like ignorance and belief, from which it differs in important ways, it is a power. But what kind of power is it, and how does it differ from these subordinate powers?

Different powers have different objects, he begins, and do different things with these different objects.[96] Knowledge has for its object "what is," whereas ignorance has instead "what is not."[97] These two powers, with their two objects, should recall for us the first two ways of inquiry described by Parmenides' goddess: the way of being, on the one hand, and the way of non-being, on the other.[98] The first and only permissible way, as we saw, respected her new principle, the principle of non-contradiction; the second flouted it—non-being cannot be—and was accordingly deemed "unlearnable." Yet Parmenides' goddess warned also against a third way, "on which mortals, knowing nothing, two-headed, wander."[99] Traveling this third way, "they are carried on equally deaf and blind, amazed, hordes without judgment, for whom both to be and not to be are judged the same and not the same."[100] This way was for those who mixed being and non-being, those who flouted the principle of non-contradiction, those who were senseless because ironically they credited the senses and the changing realm of time reported by them. This way was traveled by Heraclitus, which was why Parmenides called it "backward turning" (*palintropos*), ridiculing his symbols of unity in opposition and harmonia, the bow and lyre.[101]

Like Parmenides before him, Plato takes aim less at Heraclitus than at all "the lovers of listening and seeing,"[102] which is to say all those who credit the senses and time—in short, anyone "who believes in beautiful things but does not believe in the beautiful itself."[103] For according to Socrates an (imperfectly) beautiful thing "partakes in both being and not being,"[104] and every beautiful thing in time suffers this contradiction at each moment.[105] Everything here in time, therefore, is "a wandering, in-between object grasped by the in-between power."[106] This in-between power is belief. Flouting the principle of non-contradiction at every moment, its objects "are ambiguous, and one cannot understand them as fixedly being or fixedly not being, or as both, or as neither."[107] The lovers of listening and seeing deny the existence of Forms, putting their trust instead in these ambiguous and contradictory objects, thereby earning from Socrates the name "philo-doxers" (lovers of belief). They cannot love wisdom because any object of knowledge—according to Plato now, as much as to Parmenides earlier, and likewise to Aristotle later—must be unambiguous, pure of contradiction. The objects of the philodoxers' inferior cognitive power, by contrast, are ambiguous and contradictory.

Apparently more liberal than Parmenides, who permitted only one thing to be thus pure—the one, homogeneous, and static being—Plato permits many: the Forms.[108] Like Parmenides, he requires that each be purely what it is, a being without any mixture of non-being.[109] Pure of all such contradiction, then, it must be outside of time.[110] In *Phaedo*, Socrates stresses the eternity of "the Equal itself, the Beautiful itself, each thing in itself, the real,"[111] calling them all "divine, deathless, intelligible, uniform, indissoluble."[112] Similarly, in *Symposium*, he describes the Form of Beauty as "absolute, pure, unmixed, not polluted by human flesh or colors or any other great nonsense of mortality."[113] The terms of this description of Form match those attributed in *Phaedrus* to the sacred revealed objects. Each was said to be perfect, and simple, and unshakeable and blissful, but also "without color and without shape and without solidity, a being that really is

what it is, the subject of all true knowledge."[114] If there is to be any stability
in the cosmos, but especially in our knowledge of it, then there must be
these Forms.[115] They must be purely what they are, without mixture of
anything else, without becoming anything else, without any of the movement, color, shape, solidity, or "pollution" from the "nonsense" of the
changing material world. In short, they must be non-contradictory.

By separating Forms from matter—the one stable and pure, the other
changing and impure—Plato draws a starker cosmological distinction
than did his Pythagorean predecessors. He thereby also synthesizes the
philosophies of other Presocratic predecessors, making Parmenides the
philosopher of real being, Heraclitus the philosopher of illusory coming-
to-be. This is nowhere more evident than in a passage of *Sophist*, where the
main character, the Eleatic Visitor, questions a representative of "the friends
of the Forms." "You people distinguish coming-to-be and being," he asks,
"and say that they are separate?" The question could very well be addressed
to Plato himself. "And you say that by our bodies and through perception
we have dealings with coming-to-be," he continues, "but we deal with
real being by our souls and through reasoning." Summarizing nicely the
philosophy we ourselves have been discussing, he concludes: "You say that
being always stays the same and in the same state, but coming-to-be varies
from one time to another."[116] This dichotomy matches a story from Diogenes
Laertius about Plato's education. After the death of Socrates, he studied
with a Parmenidean, Hermogenes, and his Heraclitean brother, Cratylus.[117]
Both appear as Socrates' interlocutors in *Cratylus,* where Cratylus's
Heracliteanism, if not Hermogenes' Eleaticism, is evident.[118] Whether or
not Plato studied these opposed philosophies under quarreling brothers—
a story too charming to be credited, were there not evidence for it in
Aristotle—he does take their rivalry very seriously.[119]

Indeed, the philosophical battle between them, which flares most hotly
in *Theaetetus*,[120] forges the basic distinction of Plato's ontology: Form versus
matter, being versus coming-to-be. Privileging the former for its consistency,
Plato nonetheless adopted both in *Republic*, although naturally he had to
modify each. Departing from Parmenides' austere monism, which failed
to account for the deceptive appearances his own goddess denounces,[121]
Plato allows not only the existence of many Forms—as many as are needed
to account for the many things known—but also a role for becoming.
Unlike Heraclitus, Plato considers the perpetual flux and contradiction of
time as a mere shadow of eternity.[122] Without any reference to eternal
Forms, he thinks, life in time would be fraught with intolerable problems.
"It isn't even reasonable to say that there is such a thing as knowledge," he

writes in *Cratylus*, "if all things are passing and none remain."[123] As he adds in *Theaetetus*, a whole new language would be required by this hypothesis; otherwise every utterance would prove equally correct.[124]

Going still further than his critics, it should be noted, Cratylus saw the futility of speech in a world where meanings too were unstable. Accordingly, wrote Aristotle, he "did not think it right to say anything but only moved his finger."[125] But if all opposites were to flow together, and mix, so too would Form and matter, collapsing the distinction Plato is so intent upon preserving between consistency and contradiction. Reserving Heraclitean flux and opposition for the material realm reported by our senses, while multiplying Parmenidean unities according to the epistemic needs of our reason, he next introduces an intermediary between being and coming-to-be: the Pythagorean soul.

4.4 Purifying Oneself

"When the soul investigates by itself," writes Plato in *Phaedo*, "it passes into the realm of what is pure, ever existing, immortal and unchanging, and being akin to this, it always stays with it whenever it is by itself and can do so."[126] The Forms are pure, as we have seen, because they suffer no contradiction; they are "by themselves," as Plato defines them.[127] So, for example, the Form of Equality is equal and never has any inequality about it. By remaining outside of time—separate from material particulars, which share contradictory properties because of their temporal change—it remains purely equal. The soul, by comparison, is impure to the extent that it is not "by itself," but mixed with anything contradictory, especially the body. It becomes pure, or more nearly so, when it "investigates by itself"; in other words, when it forswears the body, separating itself from the material realm of mixture and impurity, identifying itself instead with the purely consistent realm of Form.

As in Pythagoreanism and the mystery cults alike, so in Plato, "it is not permitted to the impure to attain the pure."[128] In order to think of pure Forms, the soul must transcend the body. Citing the "language of the mysteries," but also recalling Philolaus, Plato deems the body a prison, not to mention an evil infection, an inebriating contamination, and a source of discord.[129] For, as matter, it is "most like that which is human, mortal, multiform, unintelligible, soluble, and never consistently the same." By contrast the soul, as we have seen, is "most like the divine, deathless, intelligible, uniform, indissoluble, always the same as itself."[130] In its rational exercise of consistent thought, thinking purely of Form, it abandons the contradictory illusions of changing material particulars presented to it by the senses, identifying instead with the unchanging being accessible to its reason. *Phaedo* is thus the *locus classicus* not only of soul-body dualism, but also of the Pythagorean effort to purify the one of the other. *Katharsis* and its cognates occur thirty-three times in the dialogue—more than once for every two pages of the Stephanus edition.[131]

The ultimate bodily transcendence is death. Although Socrates has hitherto heeded Philolaus's prohibition of suicide, once his death is required by law, and his *daimōn* makes no protest, he welcomes it.[132] Incarcerated in a body, but forbidden to escape it by our own hand, Plato offers us an interim but fleeting transcendence through contemplation of Form. Philosophy becomes a training for death.[133] Above all other studies, it eschews the senses and "bids the soul to gather itself together by itself, to trust only itself and whatever reality, existing by itself, the soul itself understands."[134] Above all other studies, more precisely, philosophy enjoins the activity of pure reason, thinking pure of contradiction. Only in total isolation from the material body, Plato implies, can we achieve the ultimate purification: assimilation to the objects of pure thought, the Forms.

He experiments with several images of this assimilation; ironically, as we shall see, all of them are bodily. The first of them casts reason's assimilation of Form as sexual intercourse, the second as eating, the third as sight. After discussing the first two in enough detail to appreciate their ironic role as explanations, we shall focus primarily on the third. For sight is the image that Plato anticipates in the other two, the one he develops most fully, and yet also the one that plays the most ambivalent role in his thought.

In *Symposium*, Plato describes the ascent of a lover from the many beautiful things, including beautiful bodies, to the Form of Beauty.[135] Along the way, the lover passes through the "beauty of knowledge," and becomes a lover of learning, a philosopher. "The real lover of learning naturally strives for what is," he writes in *Republic*, and so "he does not linger over each of the many things that are believed to be."[136] Like any lover, the philosopher longs to be with his beloved. Finally in its presence, he looks on it not with the eye of the body, but with the eye of his soul: reason. "Do you think it would be a poor life for a human being," once he has arrived before the Form of Beauty, "to look there and to behold it by that which he ought?"[137] The philosophical lover, however, will not satisfy his passion with this beatific vision. He is frustrated until "he *grasps* what the nature of each thing itself is with the element of his soul that is fitted to grasp a thing of this sort because of its kinship with it."[138] Already akin to Forms because of its reason, the soul becomes more so by mixing with them, by having "intercourse with what really is."[139] The union is not fruitless. Once he "has begotten understanding and truth, he knows, truly lives, is nourished, and—at that point, but not before—is relieved from his labor pains."[140] Metaphorically speaking, reason enjoys sex with Form. The progeny are true virtue, understanding, and truth.[141] United with the pure, Plato therefore implies, the philosopher is purified of vice and ignorance, two conditions he elsewhere calls the worst impurities afflicting the soul.[142]

As a second means of the soul's purifying assimilation of Form, Plato imagines the contemplation of Form as ingestion. With a double irony, he also marshals the model in order to favor intellectual over bodily pleasures.[143] According to it, bodily pleasure involves being filled with matter, and thus with a mixture of what-is and what-is-not, being and non-being, whereas intellectual pleasure is being filled with what-purely-is: Form. The pleasures of the table, for instance, consist of being filled with food. But food ceases to be food once it has been digested. Because it exists in time, moreover, at any given moment it is both itself and not-itself, both food and not-food.[144] Based upon the ingestion of impure mixtures, the pleasures of the table are themselves impure. The pleasures of ingesting Forms, however, are pure—as pure as the eternal Forms themselves.[145] The Form of Equality is purely equal, as we saw, just as the Form of Beauty is purely beautiful. Respects, perspectives, and times make no difference to them. Nourished with Form, Plato thereby implies, the soul assumes the purity of its nourishment. We become what we eat. Or rather, our reasoning souls become what they think. Eating, like sex, is mingling and union.

The third metaphor for the soul's assimilation of formal purity, sight, is less intimate, and yet ultimately more important to the logic of Plato's program of purification. As he concludes this analogy between thinking and eating, the language of sight surfaces in his complaint about people who pursue only bodily pleasures. Oblivious of the Formal realm, "never looking up at it," they are "never filled with what really is," and so live "never tasting any stable or pure pleasure."[146] The pair of reason and sight feature more prominently in the use of the same model in *Phaedrus*. "A god's mind is nourished by intelligence and pure knowledge," he writes there, "as is the mind of any soul that is concerned to take in what is appropriate to it, and so it is delighted to be seeing what is real and watching what is true, feeding on all this and feeling wonderful."[147] Only the philosopher's soul rises to the intellectual heights from which it may join the gods and "gaze upon what is outside heaven," namely the Forms.[148] Although they are without color, shape, and solidity, they are nonetheless visible, but "only to reason [*nous*]."[149]

"Philosophy," Plato tells us in *Phaedo*, "persuades the soul to withdraw from the senses in so far as it is not compelled to use them,"[150] and the sense

of sight does not escape his censure: "investigation through the eyes is full
of deceit."[151] Elsewhere, however, Plato writes that "our sight has indeed
proved to be a source of supreme benefit to us," a gift of the god.[152]
We should not be surprised by this importance of sight, especially to the
assimilation of Form, not only because it has emerged in both of the images
we have just examined (sex and eating), but also because a connection
between sight and the Forms has already been forged by Plato's Greek. His
favored terms for "Form" are *eidos* and *idea*, words which are derivatives of
eidō, a verb which means primarily "to see," but also, in the perfect tense,
"to know." For Plato, then, sight appears to play an ambivalent role. His
ambivalence may be traced back, first, to his Pythagorean predecessors,
who esteemed the stars and yet scorned the bodily prison housing the eyes
with which we see them.[153]

But their ambivalence we have traced still further back, arguing that they
synthesized from India, on one hand, an ascetic contempt for the body,[154]
and from Iran, on the other, the reverence of fire, sun, and the light
produced by both.[155] This light distinguishes parts within an otherwise
indefinite darkness, grants limit to the unlimited, form to the formless; the
Pythagoreans consequently ranked it with the good.[156] To Plato as much as
to them, the celestial lights have special significance, dividing the dark
heavens with their light but also with their numerical regularity. "Our
ability to see the periods of day-and-night, of months and years, of
equinoxes and solstices," he writes, "has led to the invention of number,
and has given us the idea of time and opened the path to inquiry into the
universe."[157] Sight has a divine purpose, accordingly, for "these pursuits, in
turn, have given us philosophy, a gift from the gods to the mortal race whose
value neither has been nor ever will be surpassed."[158]

4.5 Divine Light

At once both a propaedeutic to reason and a bodily capacity, sight stands on
the border, so to speak, of Plato's fundamental distinction—much like the
sun which makes it possible. Between the visible (which both is and is-not)
and the intelligible ("what purely is")[159] stands the sun.[160] For just as we see
material particulars thanks to the rays of the sun, he claims, so too do we
understand Forms thanks to the enlightenment produced by another Form,
that of the Good. And just as the sun sustains visible things in being, by
nourishing the plants and indirectly the animals as well, so too the Form of
the Good sustains the other Forms. "The Good is not being [*ousia*]," says

Plato, but "superior to it in rank and power."[161] Likewise superior in *its* realm, the sun is not only, like all the other planets and stars, a god,[162] but "an offspring of the Good and most like it."[163] Although visible, the sun rises to the border of the invisible and intelligible thanks to its divine parentage.

By raising the sun to this sublime level, Plato is subtly drawing on an ancient religious tradition that exalted the sun as a god. The Greeks knew they shared this tradition not only with Persia but also with Egypt,[164] and in typical fashion they expressed their own reverence in poetry. The Homeric epics, for instance, consider the sun the god of sacred oaths; Hesiod, the exposer of crime. Aeschylus says that its light is blessed; Sophocles, that it beholds and nurtures all.[165] In *Oedipus Tyrannus*, for instance, where symbols of light and dark play evident roles, the chorus calls Helios "foremost of the gods."[166] Above all these Greek authors, writes James Notopoulos, "the poet par excellence of the sun and light is Pindar, Plato's favorite."[167] "A dream of a shadow is man," he writes, "but whenever Zeus-given brightness comes, a shining light rests upon men, a gentle life."[168]

While Plato follows Pindar in his esteem for light, as in his doctrine of reincarnation, for his theory of sight he follows the other poet associated with Sicily and Pythagoreanism—Empedocles.[169] In Empedocles' general view of perception, like perceives like: "by earth we see earth, by water water, by ether divine ether, and by fire destructive fire."[170] Calling this ether divine, Empedocles remains faithful to the religious veneration of the sun and its light. But he also requires us to possess an inner source of ethereal light. Just as a burning lamp produces light by its internal fire, in our eyes, too, "the ancient fire, guarded in the membranes and fine tissues, lies in ambush in the round pupil."[171] Retaining the aqueous humor, these fine tissues nevertheless "let the fire pass through inasmuch as it is finer-textured."[172] This theory survived into the Renaissance—"He seemed to find his way without his eyes," says Ophelia of Hamlet, "for out o" doors he went without their helps, / and to the last bended their light on me"—largely because Plato adopted it in *Timaeus*, the dialogue that exercised preëminent philosophical influence in Western Europe for much of the Middle Ages.[173]

"The eyes," Plato tells us there, "were the first of the organs to be fashioned by the gods, to conduct light."[174] And as in Empedocles, the light they conduct is in part their own. Before adding that "like makes contact with like,"[175] then, Plato describes how "the pure fire inside us, cousin to that fire, they made to flow through the eyes."[176] Intent on preserving its purity, these gods "made the eyes—the eye as a whole but its middle in particular—close-textured, smooth, and dense, to enable them to keep out all the other coarser stuff, and let that kind of fire pass through pure by itself."[177] The eyes must therefore possess a light that is already pure. For in order to assimilate the light of the ethereal heights, they must share a similar purity. The heavenly gods, the stars of the firmament, have been made "mostly out of fire, to be the brightest and fairest to the eye."[178] Purer still is the sun—for Plato, the Pythagoreans, and the Zoroastrians. In order to see this purity, our eyes must shine with a spark of it. Lest this spark be dimmed by looking downward, where it will be mixed with dark earth, Plato enjoins us to look upward, rarefying it by the further assimilation of divine ether. Providently, his subordinate gods have made this a little easier, placing our eyes in the head, the uppermost part of our body. There the organs of sight join their spiritual counterpart: reason.

Partitioning human anatomy as carefully as the philosopher-kings zone their city,[179] the gods next ensured that "they had built an isthmus as boundary between the head and the chest by situating a neck between them to keep them apart."[180] The chest and flesh below house ambition and appetite, which always threaten civil war in the soul. If the first wins such a war, and begins to rule a soul with anger, this soul risks being reincarnated as a four-footed animal, because it will be "drawn more closely to the ground."[181] If appetite wins, the soul risks reincarnation as a snake, sinking still lower, and "crawling along the ground."[182] When reason remains supreme, it combines with sight to elevate the philosopher, both in body and soul. While reason gains mastery over him, he begins in the present life to assume a more upright posture.[183] This "most sovereign part of our soul," another divine gift, "raises us up away from the earth and toward what is akin to us in heaven."[184]

Combining sight and reason, astronomy becomes a means of elevation, a process that purifies both. The heavens revolve in a circle—or at least they appear to do so—and Plato, like most Greek philosophers, honored the circle above all other shapes.[185] Once we have come to know the celestial revolutions and to calculate their cycles, Plato writes, "we should stabilize the straying revolutions within ourselves by imitating the completely unstraying revolutions of the god."[186] Cosmological observations have salubrious effects on the soul, thanks to the regular cycles observed. "This kind of motion," writes Plato in *Laws*, "bears the closest possible affinity and likeness to the cyclical movement of reason."[187] Fixed by its center, circular motion is "regular, uniform, always at the same point in space."[188] Like reason itself, this motion is "determined by a single plan and procedure."[189] Similarly, in *Timaeus* we learn that gods fashion mortals by imbuing their bodies with "the orbits of immortal soul."[190] Disturbed from birth by the passions and sensations to which flesh is heir, however, not until bodily growth declines do "the soul's orbits regain their composure."[191] Only then do they begin "to conform to the configuration each of the circles takes in its natural course."[192] At this point, observation of the celestial revolutions hastens the conformity and makes reason more rational; in other words, it purifies it.

In concert with harmonics,[193] its Pythagorean sister-science, astronomy directs reason upwards, toward the celestial lights, the "gods."[194] And yet this redirection must not be merely literal. After all, astronomical ratios are "connected to body," because their subjects "are visible things."[195] In fact, he ridicules satisfaction with the visible heights accessible to astronomy when superior but invisible heights may be achieved by dialectic.[196] "No one will dispute our claim," he writes, "by arguing that there is another road of inquiry that tries to acquire a systematic and wholly general grasp of what each thing itself is."[197] Even the geometry-of-solids-in-motion, which Plato envisions as an astronomy purified of all visibles,[198] would still leave some of its basic concepts unexamined. It would never ask, for example, whether Parmenides and Zeno were right and motion impossible. Dialectic alone investigates such questions. It alone dispenses with hypotheses, as Plato writes, and "journeys to the first principle [*archē*] itself."[199] By returning us to the *archē*, he returns us to the question with which Greek philosophy began. Plato's *archē*, as it turns out, is the final revelation, the most sacred object, of his philosophical cult.

4.6 Dialectical Ascent

Following Plato's famous allegory of the cave, mathematics, harmonics, and astronomy lift us, the "cave-dwellers," out of the darkness of our "prison,"[200] an incarceration that recalls the bodily prison of not only *Phaedo* but, originally, Philolaus.[201] As the liberated ascend, they pass the wall behind which puppeteers have been parading statues in front of a fire—statues that cast the shadows they had taken for realties before their liberation.[202] Cornford noticed the correspondence of this and the other stages of their ascent with the initiation rites of mystery cults, such as that of Eleusis, which involved torch-lit darkness and climaxed with the revelation of a sacred statue.[203] Remembering also the passage of *Phaedrus* that compares the spiritual ascent into the realm of Forms with a similar revelation—the passage in which the soul is also said to be imprisoned in a body like "an oyster in its shell"—we cannot overlook Plato's appropriation of cultic imagery, whether it be of Eleusis, the Orphics, or the Pythagoreans.[204]

Just as these cults sought union with the divine, Plato soon promises a sort of divinity to his initiates.

Their reason has been purified, but this eye of the soul is no more sufficient for intellectual sight than is the bodily eye for ordinary sight. No matter how clear and pure it is, if it is to see, it must be "turned around from darkness to light."[205] Dialectic effects the conversion. Mathematics, harmony, and astronomy begin by drawing "cave-dwellers" out of their prison, but only with dialectic will they contemplate first the objects illuminated above, and then ultimately the source of their illumination.[206] In the allegory, when someone emerges from the cave, once he has adjusted to the brilliant light, he sees "shadows most easily, then images of men and other things in water, then the things themselves."[207] Therefore, just as his ascent from the cave involved stages—first recognizing the images projected on the wall as such, and then seeing the projectionists' models as mere artifacts—so too does he proceed in stages when he arrives in the upper air. Of *Republic*'s three most famous images—the Sun, the Divided Line, and the Cave—the second marks these stages most clearly.[208]

Beginning with the Sun's distinction between two realms, and so "a line divided into two unequal sections," Plato asks us next to "divide each section—that of the visible kind and that of the intelligible—in the same proportion as the line."[209] The significance of these proportions has eluded commentators,[210] but all are agreed that four subsections result and that each represents not only a stage of the cave-dweller's epistemic ascent, but also the increasingly real objects which he apprehends as he ascends. Apprehension of the first main section, the visible, happens with two inferior cognitive powers: imagination (*eikasia*) and belief or faith (*doxa* or *pistis*), the former devoted to apprehending images, the latter to their originals: physical objects, or material particulars.[211] Apprehension of the second main section, the intelligible, happens with two superior cognitive powers: discursive thought (*dianoia*) and thinking (*noēsis*).[212] Distinguishing these two superior powers proves more difficult.

"Using as images the things that were imitated before," Plato's *dianoia* "is forced to base its inquiry on hypotheses, proceeding not to a first principle [*archē*], but to a conclusion."[213] In this way, as Plato observes, geometers rely on images of squares and diagonals in their proofs about them—for instance, their proofs that the diagonal is incommensurable with the side of the square—although "they make their arguments with a view to the square itself and the diagonal itself."[214] The "square itself" and "diagonal itself" are, as we have seen, Plato's ways of speaking of the Forms of square and diagonal, and Forms are his *archai*. Without direct access to them, *dianoia* uses images of these intelligible Forms to make hypotheses about them. These images cannot be diagrams, whether drawn in sand or on wax tablets, for such images are within the purview of the lowest epistemic power, *eikasia*. Instead, the images used by *dianoia* seem to be words or concepts, of the sort geometers hypothesize in order to produce conclusions. Its association with images of any sort distinguishes it from the ultimate epistemic stage, *noēsis*, which dispenses with images, and indeed with all representations.[215]

"A non-representationalist account of knowledge," writes Lloyd Gerson, "holds that knowledge is a state in part constituted by the knowable, not merely caused by it."[216] Such a state is not readily understood by us in the wake of the modern scientific revolution, which prompted philosophers to return to the representationalist epistemologies of the Epicureans and Stoics.[217] According to them, roughly speaking, the mind is like a mirror, whose knowledge is an image or representation of reality. To non-representationalists such as Plato, by contrast, the mind is more like a sponge, whose knowledge is an assimilation or reception of reality.[218] Aristotle and Plotinus later offered variants of this alternate epistemology, which we may call an epistemology of assimilation, reception, and ultimately identification.[219] "Thinking" *(to noein)* writes Aristotle, "must be capable of receiving form."[220] This reception of form makes thinking—the highest cognitive power for Aristotle—partially constituted by the knowable, the way a sponge is partially constituted by the water it has absorbed. Aristotle goes so far as to say that "what thinks and what is thought are identical,"[221] advancing the Pythagorean epistemology according to which like is known by like.

As with so many other Pythagorean elements, this epistemology seems to appear in *Phaedo*. It makes explicit the suppressed premise of this dialogue's so-called Affinity argument,[222] according to which the soul must be immortal because the Forms it knows are so: like can be known only by like. An identification epistemology, with its assimilation of known by knower, would also explain why knowledge, and especially philosophical knowledge, is supposed to purify.[223] For when a philosopher knows a Form, according to this epistemology, he must somehow become identified with it. If he is not annihilated by this identification, he should assume the Form's properties. Insofar as Forms are pure of contradiction, he ought likewise to be purified. Should the ideal philosopher know the Form of the Good, the supreme Form, his purification would be total—especially if, as we shall see, this Form is the rational order of the cosmos. Consistent with the epistemology of the Divided Line, however, this ultimate identification must remain ineffable: description would taint non-representational knowledge with words and concepts (which are a sort of image or representation of their referents). Hence there is method in Plato's mystical madness. Were you to reach its summit, he writes accordingly, "you would no longer see an image of what we are describing, but the truth itself."[224]

Short of this revelation, Plato must resort to images. The ones he chooses to illustrate the direct apprehension of Forms, as we have seen, describe identification with them in bodily terms. Sex unites in a way that makes the boundary between lovers difficult to draw; digestion incorporates food so thoroughly that it altogether erases the boundary between eaten and eater. The last of Plato's images for knowledge of Forms is, as we saw, doubly ironic. In order to illustrate a relation that is free of images, he adduces the faculty of imagery: vision. Although it downplays total identification, this image exploits not only the religious echoes noted earlier, but also, more importantly, the fact that vision can take in its object instantaneously as a unity. Forms, after all, are paradigmatic unities. Of the Form of Beauty, Plato says "it is always one in form [*monoeides*]."[225] But beyond their individual unity, it seems, all the Forms are united in a super unity, a Form of Forms, the Form of the Good. For this Form is the "unhypothetical and the first principle [*archē*] of everything."[226] Indeed, as we have seen, it "illuminates" the other Forms so that they may be "seen," despite the fact that they too are *archai*, real beings and genuine objects of knowledge. "Not only do the objects of knowledge owe their being known to the Good," Plato writes, "but their existence and being are also due to it."[227]

4.7 One over Many

The Form of the Good presents at least three problems. First of all, the additional unification of things that are always one in form "seems otiose."[228] After all, Plato has described Forms as being "themselves by themselves."[229] Why make these paradigmatic unities parts of a super unity? Secondly, and more seriously, if this super unity has the individual Forms as parts, how can it remain always one in form, for it too is a Form? And finally, how can the individual Forms remain grounds of both being and knowability, as noted earlier, while also depending for their own being and knowability upon the Form of the Good? If we are to understand Plato's Forms at all, then, we must try to understand this obscure source of intelligible light. We must try, analogously, to behold "the sun—not reflections of it in water or some alien place, but the sun just by itself in its own place."[230]

Socrates himself trembles before such a task: "I'm afraid that I won't be up to it and that I'll disgrace myself and look ridiculous by trying."[231] Recent scholars have shown less trepidation. John Cooper, for example, suggests that the Good is rational order: mathematics—which otherwise appears to be ethically neutral—helps lead philosophers to it.[232] Plato himself says that "the excellence of each thing is something which is organized and has order."[233] The Good is something like the excellence of the whole cosmos; it should therefore be a supreme organization and order. Indeed, if we recall the anthropological conclusions of Douglas from the previous chapter—according to which disorder is impure and evil; order, pure and good—we should expect a benevolent god to bring about a supreme cosmic order.[234] And this is precisely what happens in the cosmogonic story of *Timaeus.* "The god wanted everything to be good and nothing to be bad so far as that was possible," begins this story, "and so he took all that was visible . . . and brought it from a state of disorder to one of order, because he believed that order was in every way better than disorder."[235]

Assuming that the Good is indeed a supreme order, encompassing the other Forms, Gerson has offered two reasons why Plato would have adopted such a view, one historical and the other more philosophical. First of all, Plato may unify his many Forms so as to join the quest for ultimate unity that animated the Milesians. "That the ultimate principles of reality should be an infinity of Forms," adds Gerson, "must have seemed to the mathematically minded Plato intellectually intolerable."[236] In other words, despite his separation of Form from matter, despite his pervasive allegiance to the Pythagorean dualists, and even despite his eventual agreement with the Zoroastrians that there was a malevolent god at war with the benevolent one just mentioned,[237] Plato also had a hankering for unity. The roots of this ambivalence go deep into the soil of Asia, as we discussed in the previous chapter.[238] To complement this history, let us consider the philosophical reasons Plato unified the individual Forms by one super Form, that of the Good.

For if these many individual Forms remain altogether independent of one another, suggests Gerson, "if, say, the Form of Five and the Form of Odd are separate, there is no explanation within the theory of Forms of why instances of the former are always accompanied by instances of the latter."[239] The Form of the Good—as rational order—becomes, in the terms of more recent philosophy, "an ontological mirror of analyticity,"[240] a feature of reality that explains why some truths are necessary. But this Form cannot be merely an arrangement of all the other Forms, lest it lose the unity characteristic of a Form.[241] It must somehow remain simple while it integrates the individual Forms, grounding their being and knowability. Gerson suggests that the Form of the Good meets these apparently impossible requirements by being "*virtually* all of the other Forms."[242] In itself, that is to say, the Good is a simple unity; as known, however, it appears multiple.[243]

Although this suggestion maintains the unity of the Form of Forms, it appears to do so by compromising the independence of the individual

Forms. How can they remain grounds of both being and knowability, while also depending for their own being and knowability upon the Good? If Gerson's suggestion is right, it would seem, they do not so remain: the individual Forms lose their independence. But perhaps this loss can be justified by other examples of virtuality. "A function is virtually all of its arguments," for instance, in the sense that a function grounds the being and knowability of its arguments insofar as they are arguments. [244] Other examples follow rapidly, some more controversial than others: "white light is virtually all the colors of the rainbow," "a properly functioning calculator contains virtually all the answers to the mathematical questions that its rules allow it to be asked," and "the artist is virtually all of his creations."[245] These examples succeed only if the being and knowability of the latter are due to the former. For according to Plato, "the objects of knowledge owe their being known to the Good," and "their existence and being are also due to it."[246] The Form of the Good is superior in rank and power to the other Forms because it is independent of them, while they depend on it.[247]

While fruitful, Gerson's suggestion does not appear to explain one important feature of the Good. Plato likely did join the Presocratic quest for the *archē* of the cosmos, and a Form of the Good that is all the Forms virtually has supplied a better candidate than any of its predecessors. But Plato also had Socrates complain in *Phaedo* that of all the Presocratics not even Anaxagoras, who made *nous* its *archē*, could provide the cosmos with a purpose.[248] C. D. C. Reeve has shed light on this role of the Good by noticing how it provides an ultimate purpose to Plato's conception of craft (*technē*). Each particular craft aims at some particular good—as medicine, for example, aims at the good of bodies.[249] Moreover, one craft often uses the products of another, so that the crafts as a whole form a sort of hierarchy. Now, in Plato's view, users alone have knowledge of "the *aretē* (virtue or excellence), the goodness and correctness of each manufactured item, living creature, and activity,"[250] whereas producers have no better than true belief on such matters. Everything—whether it be an artifact, action, or organism—has a natural purpose or use, according to Plato, so virtue and the rest are "related to nothing but the use for which each is made or naturally developed."[251] In the completely teleological cosmos he envisions, finally, these individual purposes somehow serve one architectonic, cosmic purpose.

"Only the god knows whether it is true," adds Plato, with a humility often overlooked; "but this is how these phenomena seem to me."[252] And how do they seem? All explanation must be in terms of Form—this much he thinks he has proven.[253] That all Forms have been ordered according to the best, though, remains for him a matter of hope. This teleological faith finds its most concise expression in Aristotle, who represents all crafts and inquiries as forming a natural hierarchy aiming at the good, with what he calls "first philosophy" at the top.[254] For Plato, only philosophers have been trained in the one craft, dialectic, that aims to discern this benign rational order.[255] But, as he knew, only statesmen have the power needed to ensure that this craft is effective in the world.[256] In *Republic*, famously, he unites the two.[257] The ideal philosopher, the philosopher-king, uses the results of the other crafts and orchestrates them in imitation of the cosmic order he has seen, digested, and "known."[258]

Having thus achieved a synopsis of all knowledge, the hallmark of an authentic dialectician,[259] the philosopher-king perceives the rational order of the entire cosmos. Recall that at the ultimate stage of the Divided Line this perception of Form was supposed to be immediate, unmediated by representations, whether images or words. Beyond discursive thinking (*dianoia*), then, the philosopher achieves direct perception, non-representational thought (*noēsis*), of the most fully real. This most fully real is the Good, all the Forms virtually. Even if it itself cannot be known, once the ideal philosopher has lifted the eye of his soul (reason) toward the radiant truth shed by it, his intellectual vision should be purified of all images. He will use "pure thought alone . . . to track down each reality pure and by itself."[260] And if he sees the perfect harmony of these Forms, "he imitates them and tries to become as like them as he can."[261] Purified to this extent, finally, "the philosopher, by consorting with what is orderly and divine, becomes as divine and orderly as a human being can."[262]

4.8 Becoming Divine

Whether Plato's philosopher becomes a full-fledged divinity is at best unclear. Usually he is careful to specify that the philosopher becomes divine only "to the extent that human nature can partake of immortality,"[263] so that he will possess "what Homer too called divine and godly when it occurred among human beings."[264] Such passages suggest that Plato intends "divine" as an epithet of superlative praise. In other passages, though, he exalts philosopher-kings beyond human status, although he does not fully divinize them. Those who have finished their tenure of service to the city, he says in one such passage, "will depart for the Isles of the Blessed and dwell there."[265] After they are gone, "the city will publicly establish memorials and sacrifices to them as *daimones*, if the Pythia agrees."[266] If she disagrees, they will be honored simply as "divine and happy people."[267]

His glorification of philosophers in *Phaedo* comes closer to divinization, where the soul of the voluptuary "can have no part in the company of the divine,"[268] because it has been riveted to the body by its pleasures, not to mention its pains, whereas that of the philosopher can "spend the rest of time with the gods."[269] Even if they do not become gods, by spending eternity among gods they become immortals; to traditional Greek religion, this was sufficient for a claim to divinity.[270]

The eschatological myth that follows describes more exactly the blessed life that philosophers will enjoy in such company.[271] Besides communicating with the gods in speech, they will breathe pure ether, and see the "sun and moon and stars as they are."[272] Plato imagines divinization as a consummation of ethereal purity and celestial light. "That area is so bright," however, "and the eyes of most people's souls can't bear to look at what's divine."[273] Naturally, then, admission must be restricted to those who can bear it, those whose life of pure thought has divested their thinking of images—inasmuch as this is possible for embodied persons—and prepared the eye of their soul for the brilliance and rarity of the place. The inadequate vision of the many whom these philosophical initiates leave behind recalls not only the dazzled emergence of the future philosopher-kings from the cave into sunlight, but also the longstanding mythological tradition according to which unaided humans were unable to look directly upon the glory of Zeus.[274]

In the ascension myth of *Phaedrus*, similarly, Plato allows that when some people die, their "soul becomes a companion to a god."[275] But in the tedious cycle of rebirth, only "if it is able to do this every time," only if the weight of bodily concerns never again draws it back down to earth, will it remain among the stars and "always be safe."[276] For the Pythagoreans, the soul transmigrated according to its merits.[277] So long as it strove for purity in each of its incarnations—whatever that might mean to a bird or a bush—it ascended with each one. Finally purified of all bodily taint, the soul would reach the level of divinity, there remaining forever safe from the danger of renewed pollution. Plato adopted this eschatology more or less in its entirety.[278] Thus, the soul of the man who had striven for goodness throughout his life, "would at the end return to his dwelling place in his companion star."[279] Installing pure souls in the pure ether of the heavens, Plato enriches his educational stargazing with additional moral and religious significance. It is no wonder that astronomy stands near the summit of his program of purification and divinization.

We have already seen how this program advances that of the Pythagoreans. Beginning with their mathematics, harmonics, and astronomy, Plato not only adds dialectic to their curriculum, but also explains its supremacy with an unprecedented breadth and depth, synthesizing the insights, arguments, and methods of so many predecessors, monists and dualists alike. The most important components of this synthesis are his innovations in epistemology, ontology, and psychology. We have discussed the first two fields in some detail, but have mentioned the third only in passing. As far as psychology is concerned, we have seen how Plato adopts the Pythagorean division of the soul and body. We have also seen how he begins to distinguish within it a special part, reason, which identifies itself with Forms in the process of purification and divinization. We have yet to see, however, the way in which he justifies this distinction, let alone how he divides the soul still further into three parts. Although this innovation also incorporates the thoughts of predecessors—Anaxagoras's *nous*; Parmenides' principle of non-contradiction—the psychological division it codifies is among the most novel and enduring contributions of Plato's philosophy. Let us turn to exposing it and the integral role it plays in his program of purification and divinization.

4.9 Divided Soul

In antiquity *Phaedo* acquired the appropriate subtitle *On the Soul.* Just before Socrates is to die—a fact which heightens the pathos of the discussion—Plato has him argue that the soul is immortal. Destruction, he claims, is nothing but the dissolution of a composite into its parts. Hence the soul cannot be destroyed: it is an undivided unity, a partless simple. In fact it must be so inasmuch as it is like "the things that always remain the same and in the same state,"[280] namely, the Forms. Only among them does the soul feel at home; once with them, "it ceases to stray and remains in the same state as it is in touch with things of the same kind."[281] These things are invisible and so "can only be grasped by the reasoning power of the mind."[282] Yet this reasoning power cannot be a separate part of the soul: the soul must remain simple in order to be indestructible and immortal. In *Phaedo*, then, the soul seems to be identified with reason. Appetites and ambitions are supposed to be products of embodiment.[283] *Phaedo*'s brand of psychological dualism seems therefore to be between rational soul, on the one hand, and body, on the other.

Such dualism presupposes that the body can indeed produce other human motives, the irrational or non-rational ones. In *Phaedrus*, though, Plato allows only the soul such production, because "this self-mover is also

the source [*archē*] and spring of motion in everything else that moves."[284]
This doctrine of motion is no passing fancy, but the crucial premise in
Plato's campaign against materialism and atheism, a campaign he wages
most openly in *Laws*. According to its argument—which anticipates
Aristotle's more famous one for god as the unmoved mover—immaterial
soul is superior to material body, as mover to moved; soul must likewise be
superior, as god, to the whole material cosmos.[285] If the soul alone produces
motion, including its own, the body is inert and incapable of producing
rival motives. "Desire is not a matter of the body," he writes in *Philebus*.[286]
"Every impulse, desire, and the rule over the whole animal," he adds, "is the
domain of the soul."[287]

Granting the soul powers beyond the rational ones that are its exclusive
possession in *Phaedo*, in *Phaedrus* Plato represents reason colorfully as a
charioteer who must keep his chariot on a true course by directing two
powerful horses. One of these horses is white, "needs no whip, and is guided
by verbal commands alone."[288] That is, when it decides to follow the driver
rather than impetuously disobeying. The other horse is black, sometimes
disregards the whip, "leaps violently forward and does everything to
frustrate its yokemate and its charioteer."[289] The first is a spirited element in
the soul; the second, an appetitive—as we learn from parallel treatments of
the soul in two other dialogues. In the ninth book of *Republic*, for example,
Plato also represents the soul as tripartite, first likening reason to a little
human being, then fusing this homunculus with both a lion and a many-
headed beast, the mythical hydra.[290] As we learn from the less metaphorical
psychology of the same dialogue's fourth book, the lion represents a narcissistic element in the soul that produces ambition and then anger when it is
frustrated, while the hydra represents our many appetites, including sexual
passion. This precise partition of the soul is confirmed still further by
Timaeus, in which each element inhabits a separate region of the body:
reason, the head; ambition, the chest; appetite, the gut.[291]

In all three dialogues, then, Plato appears to abandon the dualism of
Phaedo, where a simple soul opposed its bodily prison. Despite appearances,
however, the crux of this dualism remains. Yes, *Phaedo* understood the soul
as pure reason, whereas these other dialogues offer a more sophisticated
psychology, according to which the soul is complex. Yet the crucial rivalry
between reason and the irrational persists, and they are still distinguished
by their divergent respect for the principle of non-contradiction.

In *Republic*, this principle serves as the first premise of a psychological
argument.[292] "The same thing cannot do or undergo opposite things," Plato
writes; "not, at any rate, in the same respect, in relation to the same thing,

at the same time."[293] Assuming the truth of this premise—which we shall henceforth call the principle of consistency—if we find opposites done or undergone in the same respect, in relation to the same thing, at the same time, we can conclude that they must be done or undergone not by one thing but instead by two or more things. This is how the sentence that follows the premise anticipates the strategy of the following argument that divides the soul. "So," Socrates claims, "if we ever find that happening here, we will know that we are not dealing with one and the same thing, but with many."[294] Thus, if we find the soul doing or undergoing opposites in the same respect, in relation to the same thing, at the same time, we will know that we are dealing not with a proper unity, but instead with a collection of many things, however unified it may appear.

This argument for a divided soul will only be as strong as its first premise, the principle of consistency, and so Socrates tests it straightaway against two challenges, each based upon a readily imaginable physical object.[295] In the first, he imagines "a man standing still but moving his hands and head."[296] The same man appears to be doing opposites (standing still and moving), at the same time (let us call this certain moment "now"). To be precise, he appears to be doing these opposites in the same respect (rectilinear motion), in relation to the same thing (a certain point in space, which we shall simply call "here").[297] Despites appearances, though, this is not a counter-example to the principle. "If anyone should say," according to Socrates, "that the same man is at the same time at rest and in motion we should not, I take it, regard that as the right way of expressing it, but rather that a part of him is at rest and a part in motion."[298] Properly speaking, that is, we should not say the one man is the subject of these opposites. Instead, his torso is the proper subject of one of them (motionless), while his head and hands are the proper subject of the other (moving).

This maneuver seems insufficient, however, to handle a second, more difficult example. Socrates imagines that "our interlocutor should carry the jest still further with the subtlety that tops at any rate stand still as a whole at the same time that they are in motion."[299] The same spinning tops appear to be doing opposites (standing still and moving), in relation to the same thing (here), at the same time (now), but not in the same respect.[300] "We would say that there was a straight line and a circumference in them," adds Socrates, "and that in respect of the straight line they are standing still since they do not incline to either side, but in respect of the circumference they move in a circle."[301] In other words, with respect to rectilinear motion, the top is standing still, but with respect to circular motion, it is moving.[302] As a result, it is no more a counter-example to the principle of consistency than was the first example, of the moving and static man. That said, the principle handles the two cases differently.

In this second case, after all, the principle shows that apparent opposites are not genuinely opposed, for they are different kinds of motion (rectilinear and circular). In the second case, then, the apparent subject (the top) may remain the genuine one and whole without violating the principle. But the principle handles differently the first case, that of the man. Here there were genuine opposites: opposing rectilinear motions, in relation to the same thing, at the same time. Consequently, the principle determines that these opposites cannot belong to the one apparent subject, but must instead belong to others, the genuine subjects. Speaking properly, in this case, we should say that the torso stands still, while the head and hands move. This is likewise how Plato would have us speak of the soul: although it appears to be one thing, the genuine opposites it appears to do or undergo must—if the principle of consistency is true—be done or undergone not by the whole but instead by parts of it.

As humans, we often experience conflicting motives in relation to the same thing, at the same time, and in the same respect. Too often, of course, we follow the worst of them. The Greeks called this phenomenon *akrasia*, and Plato first raised the philosophical problem posed by it in *Protagoras* and *Meno*.[303] In both of these dialogues, Socrates' so-called intellectualism— his belief that knowledge is both necessary and sufficient for virtue— required him to argue that *akrasia* is impossible, so that it is impossible to do anything other than what one judges to be best.[304] In *Republic*, Plato seems to avoid this conclusion by invoking Parmenides' principle. Whenever we both want to do something and at the same time do not want to do it, different parts of our soul are in conflict. Sometimes a rational part wins this contest, and we do what we think best. Other times we go against our better judgment because an irrational part is victorious. The soul is not really one thing doing or undergoing opposites, then, but instead a collection of many disparate things.

To be sure, the soul appears unified to someone who cannot penetrate below its surface, but so too would a cage imprisoning hydra, lion, and homunculus if it were somehow covered over. After Socrates has asked us to imagine the soul as this menagerie, he enjoins us to "fashion around the outside the image of one of them, that of the human being, so that to any- one who cannot see what is inside, but sees only the outer shell, it will look like a single creature, a human being."[305] Whenever we think of the soul as one thing, we have been fooled by its outer shell, the body. By contrast, anyone who is not fooled by appearances, anyone who can see what is inside, anyone who is a true psychologist—which is to say a philosopher—sees that the soul is many things, not one. According to the image, we are not really the whole soul but instead just one of its parts. This one part, our self, turns out to be reason. Trapping it in the cage of a human body with two beasts, appetite and ambition, the complex psychology of *Republic* thus preserves the crux of *Phaedo*: philosophy liberates us from our bodily prison, allowing us to become who we are, pure reason. In each case, the argument to this conclusion relies on the principle of consistency. Properly understood, in fact, this conclusion shows us that we are nothing but this very principle.

After proposing and defending this first premise of his argument, Plato describes an example of a soul in conflict: a man whose disease and suffering make him thirsty, but whose rational calculation of what is best—perhaps heeding the prescription of a Hippocratic physician—motivates him not to drink.[306] Pushed toward a drink by the one motive, pulled back by the other, such a man is like the archer who pushes away a bow with one hand, but draws its string with the other.[307] (The analogy is Plato's, but it seems to recall deliberately the Heraclitean bow. Whereas Heraclitus used the bow as an example of the conflict that constitutes each one thing, Plato uses it to show the incompatibility of conflict with unity.)[308] The archer's conflicting motions are possible only because he has at least two parts to his body, two hands. The conflicting motives of the thirsty man are possible, correlatively, only because he too has at least two parts to his soul. He may know what is best, thanks to the calculation of his rational part, but another part of his soul makes no such calculation, relying instead on immediate appearance.[309] This other part can gain mastery over reason, leading the soul to act against its judgment.

Plato calls this oblivious part "the irrational and appetitive element," saying that with it the soul "feels passion, hungers, thirsts, and is stirred by other appetites."[310] Accordingly it is the rebellious horse, following the charioteer's commands only when persuaded by his whip. It is also the hydra, a beast "with a ring of tame and savage heads that it can grow and change at will."[311] These heads are the particular appetites that dwell within the appetitive part, growing and changing without pattern,[312] unless one of them gains supremacy over the others and has regimented them according to its own agenda.[313] Some will come into being from nothing, while others will disappear altogether. Characterized in this way, they begin to resemble the aim of their devotion: the Heraclitean realm of visible, material objects. These unstable mixtures of being and non-being offer impure pleasures, as we have seen.[314] By exploiting the cognitive weakness of the bodily senses, by relying on contradictory appearances and images, they lure the soul into seeking all its satisfaction with them.[315] When the appetitive element gains mastery in the soul, it orients the whole soul down toward these dark impurities. Hunched and enslaved, the soul remains heedless of the invisible yet brilliant rational order that it can neither perceive nor comprehend.[316]

To see this order, a soul must possess a "rationally calculating element."[317] In its calculations this element seeks not just a theoretical, let alone a merely eschatological, acquaintance with rational order. Its ultimate goal is a purifying assimilation in this life as well as the next. This order is none other than the Good, so that such purification cannot leave the soul's practical life unchanged. When reason gains mastery of someone and he consorts with the greatest of Forms, "only then will it become possible for him to give birth not to images of virtue (because he's in touch with no images), but to true virtue."[318] Making goodness the goal as much of his action as of his thought, his reason concerns itself with "what is beneficial for one and all."[319] The pleasure produced is not only pure, but the purest: Forms are pure being, but the Good is superior to them all in rank and power.[320] Whenever there is conflict between pure reason and the other parts within the soul, "it is better for everyone to be ruled by divine reason."[321]

This conflict between reason, on the one hand, and the irrational parts of the soul, on the other, is evident likewise in *Timaeus*, which recounts the origin not only of the cosmos, but also of the human soul. Plato there imagines the subordinate gods creating it in two steps. "Having taken the immortal origin of the soul," they first encased it in a round body (the head). Within the rest of the body, the trunk, "they built another kind of soul as well, the mortal kind."[322] This mortal soul receives another division, into ambition and appetite, making the embodied soul tripartite, and so concordant with the psychological accounts of *Republic* and *Phaedrus*. But in origin, at least, the human soul is bipartite: immortal and divine reason above, mortal and merely human soul below. Upon death, accordingly, these two souls will separate again. The subsequent fate of the mortal soul is unclear, except that it will fall away from the immortal like so many barnacles from the sea-god Glaucus.

4.10 Consistent Self

A divinity in truth, writes Plato, Glaucus nevertheless has his radiance dimmed here below by "the shells, seaweeds, and rocks," that "have grown into him."[323] So likewise for our divine reason. In this terrestrial life its natural radiance is dimmed by the appetite and ambition that, thanks to its embodiment, encrust it. Epistemically, this means that it must think discursively, using representations. Plato's presentation of these very images—of Glaucus, along with all the other indelible images of *Republic*—exemplifies embodied thought. "The effort to employ images to convey the truth about images themselves and what they represent," writes Gerson, "is the embodied philosopher's burden."[324] Dialectic seeks to purify the philosopher, however, by pushing him to think without such images, without words or concepts. Philosophy, according to Plato, encourages him to eschew *dianoia* in favor of non-representational *noēsis*, a direct assimilation to the Forms, and ultimately to their rational order. As we have seen, this order is the Form of Forms, the Form that is all Forms virtually, the Form of the Good.[325] The goal of philosophy may therefore be characterized as the assimilation of the philosopher's thinking to this Good: the perfect purification of his thought.

What the thinking soul "is like when it has become pure," writes Plato, we cannot perceive by the senses; "that we can adequately see only by means of rational calculation."[326] While embodied, our rational calculation remains mired in representations which keep us from "seeing" anything directly. But by thinking ever more consistently, we may at least identify ourselves with the activity of reason rather than with the activities of the soul's inferior parts, those parts generated by reason's imprisonment in body. "The more one engages in what Plato considers to be non-bodily activity," writes Gerson, "the more one is inclined to recognize that one is an entity other than a body."[327] The human being, after all, is a hybrid. Although our embodiment has fused our reason with ambition and appetite, not to mention a body, Plato seems to think that reason is nonetheless what we *really* are. This, at least, seems to be the message of the images we have considered: in one, reason is depicted as the human being among beasts;[328] in another, it is the human charioteer directing horses.[329] But these are merely images. Is there an argument to this effect? Two may be reconstructed from the dialogues we have examined.

A first one comes from *Republic* alone, where the principle of consistency appears explicitly as the first premise of the argument for a tripartite soul, but is already assumed by Socrates' first argument of the dialogue. If justice is "simply speaking the truth and paying whatever debt one has incurred," as Cephalus believes, then he must believe that it is just to return a weapon to a madman, despite the fact that he believes it unjust to do so.[330] Socrates refutes this definition of justice by showing how it entails a belief that contradicts one more deeply held. Choosing to preserve the more deeply-held belief, and reject the definition, the audience—which includes us—implicitly applies the principle of consistency. For it is this principle which forbids both at once; it is this principle which demands we choose one or the other (or neither). However complex our souls, then, our self must be the part which respects this demand. In other words, *we* must be the part of the soul that heeds the principle of consistency. Reason alone eschews whatever "turned out both to be and not to be at the same time,"[331] the mutable and contradictory things accessible to the senses and mere belief. We are this reason.

A second argument, more subtle than the first, may be reconstructed from a combination of dialogues. *Phaedo* taught that we cannot judge anything imperfectly equal unless we are already acquainted, however dimly, with perfect equality.[332] To judge anything imperfectly equal, "we must then have acquired the knowledge of the Equal."[333] Yet this is only one example of such knowledge;[334] another should be self-knowledge. After all, *Phaedrus* teaches that self-knowledge is the most fundamental sort.[335] According to Socrates, there and elsewhere, we philosophers must begin with the recognition that we do not know ourselves, that our self-knowledge is imperfect. We cannot judge our self-knowledge imperfect, however, unless we are already acquainted, however dimly, with perfect self-knowledge. But what is this? What is perfect self-knowledge? Although Plato never answers this question directly, the passage of *Republic* just quoted—according to which "neither knowledge nor ignorance would deal with" anything which turned out "both to be and not to be at the same time"—taught that knowledge is an exercise of the principle of consistency over objects that satisfy this principle.[336] The knowing self, the subject of perfect self-knowledge, must therefore exercise this principle. The self known, the object of perfect self-knowledge, must correlatively satisfy it.

Symposium, among other dialogues, taught that only something eternal can satisfy the principle of consistency.[337] For, everything in time must suffer contradiction at each moment, rendering it unknowable by subjects exercising this principle. At first glance, this dialogue seems to make our very selves victims of time's flux. "A person," Plato writes, "never consists of the same things, though he is called the same, but he is always being renewed and in other respects passing away, in his hair and flesh and bones and blood and his entire body."[338] That his body suffers such flux comes as no surprise. What is surprising is that we find this Heraclitean condition "not just in his body, but in his soul, too."[339] Remembering the tripartite soul of the other dialogues we have examined, we might have expected to find this flux in the soul's inferior capacities—"his manners, customs, opinions, desires, pleasures, pains, or fears," none of which remains, "but some are coming to be in him while others are passing away."[340] Little, however, prepares us for the next claim. "And what is still far stranger than that," Plato acknowledges, "is that not only does one branch of knowledge come to be in us while another passes away and that we are never the same even in respect of our knowledge, but that each single piece of knowledge has the same fate."[341]

More precisely, these claims are made by Diotima, who apparently considers us mortal, not immortal as Socrates so often argues elsewhere. According to her, humans preserve their knowledge by perpetually renewing it with study, "and in that way everything mortal is preserved, not, like the divine, by always being the same in every way, but because what is departing and aging leaves behind something new, something such as it had been."[342] We could see here a departure from Plato's cherished doctrine of immortality, but Diotima never says that our selves are mortal, only that human knowledge is among our many mortal capacities. Were we to confuse our selves with this capacity, or any of the others like it, we would indeed believe that our immortality "is possible in one way only: by reproduction, because it always leaves behind a new young one in place of the old."[343] But we should not confuse our selves with this sort of knowledge—the sort we study, recalling its words and concepts—let alone any of the other mortal capacities she mentions, for they all depend on representations. We should recognize the imperfection of such representations, and thus the imperfection of the knowledge Diotima describes. Her epistemology and eschatology would contradict Plato's only if she were describing his perfect and immortal archetype: pure reason's union with eternal Form.

Tarrying below, where embodiment in time fetters reason's ascent, let us return one last time to the point in *Phaedo* from which we began this final argument.[344] Recall that we cannot judge representational knowledge imperfect unless we already possess, however dimly, its perfect archetype. If we already possess this archetype, if we are already pure reason united to eternal Form, the mortal nature Diotima describes in this passage cannot ultimately be us. She describes instead our imperfect image—in a word, our humanity—and not by any error, for she is goading us to ascend to the Form of Beauty, aware that we must begin this ascent from the confusions to which embodied reason is heir. To purify this reason, then, we must begin by recognizing it as impure and imperfect. But to recognize it as such, paradoxically, we must already somehow know ourselves perfectly. In perfect self-knowledge, we as subjects must exercise the principle of consistency upon ourselves as objects. In order to satisfy this principle, though, our selfsame self must be consistent and therefore outside of time. Our perfect self is therefore an eternal exercise of the principle of consistency upon our eternally consistent self. What is the "self itself"?[345] Who are we really?

Not human, but divine; not dying, but living forever; not ever changing in any way, but in every way staying always the same. We are pure reason: thinking thinking thinking.

Chapter 5

Conclusion

Many of the philosophers we have considered in this volume have enjoined us to become divine; others, to become immortal. In the midst of archaic and classical Greece, where gods alone lived forever, these twin injunctions were in fact one.[1] Also one was the road they followed to immortal divinity: reason.[2] Describing this road, however, they diverged from each other. Reason makes us divine, but what is reason? For Heraclitus, it is chiastic; for Parmenides, consistent.[3] Condensing the structure of reason into a principle, the one formulated a principle of chiasmus, the other a principle of consistency. We are more familiar with Parmenides' principle, but this is primarily because Plato promoted it.[4] Enriching the austere monism of Parmenides with the Pythagorean program of purification and divinization, he showed how consistency could form a whole way of life.[5] With his ascetic rejection of sensation, emotion, and everything embodied in time, Plato showed us how to pursue eternal consistency in order to become divine.[6] But could he make sense of becoming itself?

Becoming, for Parmenides, is supposed to be an illusion, an appearance apart from reality. Such a gap would require non-being, however, and non-being cannot be. His goddess urges her initiate to travel the road of immortal truth, to forswear the road of mortal opinion, yet her principle will not tolerate the being of any road but the true one. Nor will it tolerate any movement along that road. To move, to change, to become: these are impossible; only being can be. The problem with becoming—and thus all injunction, which summons us to become what we are not—is that it requires non-being.[7] This problem is most stark in Parmenides, whose purification of contradiction is so stringent that only one, static, homogenous being survives.[8] This being is pure reason, the principle of consistency itself, but purification is a temporal process and thus inconsistent.[9] Pure reason cannot accommodate its own purification; the eternal cannot encompass the temporal.

The problem persists into Plato's synthesis of Parmenides with the Pythagoreans. To appreciate its tenacity, let us review the main points of the Platonic synthesis, juxtaposing them with the main points of the Heraclitean logos. Stepping back from the textual thickets, we may find a road leading through them to its solution.

Aside from the principle of consistency, Plato assumes two additional principles: one of perfection, another of unity. According to the first, imperfection presupposes perfection.[10] If there is imperfect equality here in time, there must be perfect Equality in eternity. Because there is imperfect beauty here, Beauty must be perfect there. And so on. This principle works together with the principle of consistency to motivate the doctrine of Forms: everything in time is imperfect because it is inconsistent, and so there must be perfect and consistent paradigms in eternity.[11] Surrounded as we are by imperfection and inconsistency, we cannot know anything unless we be already acquainted with that realm of perfect consistency, the immortal and divine Forms. Plato's third fundamental principle is that of unity: multiplicity presupposes it.[12] Superior to all the many Forms in rank and power, then, is the one Good. Reaching it by contemplation, the philosopher sees no longer through a glass darkly, but face to face.[13]

Were you to arrive there, however, you would find that you had never really left. To know yourself imperfectly—as you do right now, presumably, traveling the road to self-knowledge—you must already be acquainted with your perfect self.[14] To become a self-knower, in other words, you must already be one. This perfect self-knower is the eternal activity of the principle of consistency turned upon itself: thinking thinking thinking. This perfect self is unchanging and immortal, a divinity. To become it, then, you must already be it. How is this possible? How can you become who you are? How can eternal being become anything at all? Plato's images, so helpful when we wish to envision his doctrines, tantalize us with this possibility.[15] You are like Glaucus, whose eternal glory has been dimmed by barnacles and seaweed; to perfect your divinity, you need only scrape off the encrustations acquired during your immersion here in the sea of time.[16] Purify yourself of appetite and ambition. Reason purely. Restore your immortality. But divinity cannot be perfected, nor immortality restored. Possessed once, they must forever be and forever have been yours. Nothing eternal can participate in the temporal activity of purification. Nothing that does only one thing—thinking of itself—can change. Being, in short, cannot become. Not, at any rate, without contradiction.

Heraclitus's philosophy makes better sense of becoming by expanding the three Platonic principles, showing Plato's versions to be limited components of a more capacious logos. If multiplicity presupposes unity, then so too must unity presuppose multiplicity.[17] If pure inconsistency must be prohibited, then so too must pure consistency.[18] Finally, if imperfection entails perfection, then so too must perfection entail imperfection.[19] Preferring concrete examples to such abstract principles, Heraclitus provided three that proved especially helpful to illustrate these expansions. The river's being depends on its becoming: if it has any claim to perfect being, this presupposes the imperfect flow of water.[20] The lyre's being depends on an internal inconsistency: if it has any claim to consistent being, it requires the contrary pulls of bow and strings.[21] The fire condenses these two examples and thereby epitomizes the Heraclitean logos. Like the lyre, its being depends on an internal inconsistency: at each moment of its burning it must be need and satiety.[22] Like the river, its being depends on its becoming, the perpetual burning of fuel. The being of fire, in sum, depends on the inconsistency present at each moment of its becoming.

This logos is most manifest in fire, but it is also everywhere else here in time.[23] The cosmos, or ordering, is fire everliving, kindled in measures and in measures quenched. Every moment in the becoming of fiery time is inconsistent. To say, as Heraclitus does, that conflict is justice or that war is the father of all is only to say that time is the supreme divinity. From its unity come all things, and from their succession comes its unity. Each of its moments is a contradiction of being and non-being, but its becoming forms a chiasmus: wholes and not-wholes, consonant dissonant, convergent divergent, from all things one and from one all things.[24] This chiasmus is god: day night, winter summer, war peace, satiety hunger.[25] It is also the self we grasp in our search for ourselves.[26] At each moment it is present and absent, as contradictory then as the need and satiety of a frozen fire. But the self is no more fully itself at any one moment than fire truly burns in an instant. It is not-whole in every now, whole through the flow of time alone. Neither one nor the other, it is a unity in opposition: opposed at once, unified nonetheless, then opposing unity and opposition it is unified once again. And so on.[27] You will not discover its limits, traveling every road, so deep is its logos.[28] Along its infinite way, you become who you are, just as time, just as god.[29]

Whereas Plato privileges perfection, consistency, and unity, Heraclitus juxtaposes each with imperfection, opposition, and multiplicity. No more static than the world his logos reports, however, his divine chiasmus refuses to settle into a set of perfectly balanced antitheses. The moment it achieves so perfectly unified a structure, it must oppose multiplicity to this unity, imperfection to this perfection. Opposing itself, it becomes a chiasmus of chiasmus, then a chiasmus of chiasmus of chiasmus, to infinity.[30] Opposing itself, however, it remains forever a chiasmus. Heraclitus hints at such opposition when he urges us to recognize the wise one, set apart from all, both willing and unwilling to be called by the name of Zeus.[31] This is the becoming god, the one structure of divine chiasmus, and it is willing to be recognized as such a transcendent unity.[32] But in the very moment it reveals itself as one it must conceal itself behind many. Perfection contradicts its own chiastic profession of imperfection. In the very moment it achieves perfect unity, then, it must also fragment into imperfect multiplicity.

This is the elusive dialectic of time, neither privileging consistency nor abandoning it altogether. For in one perfect moment it must contradict itself with imperfection and multiplicity. Yet in this same moment it moves to reconstitute itself as a perfectly consistent one.

As obscure as this logos appears—at least to the rival tradition that makes pure consistency the hallmark of clarity—it alone makes sense of becoming. Were we pure reason, as Parmenides and Plato would have us, we could not go in search of ourselves, let alone become divine. By contrast, as impure reason, as chiasmus, we can. In this divine activity, in fact, we are becoming god. If Heraclitus enjoins us to do anything, it is to recognize ourselves as such. Recognizing this demands more than accepting a principle, even the principle of chiasmus. It requires chiasmus itself, not as a static principle but as a perpetual activity. Each moment's synthesis must be attended by a correlative analysis, while this analysis must summon forth another synthesis. It must be a thinking about itself, and thus a thinking about this thinking. It must be thinking thinking thinking, only now in time. It must be the recognition, ultimately, that the thinker is this very time. It must be contradictory, but can we affirm it nonetheless? Maybe now this once: Yes.

Notes

Chapter 1

[1] DK 31B112 (D.L., 8.62). See also DK 31B146 (Clement, *Miscellanies* 4.23.150.1). Empedocles was from Sicily and lived ca. 490–430.

[2] Dodds 1951:10. See also Burkert 1985:121–22, 162, 298; Guthrie 1955:115, 239; Kingsley 1995:222–23; and Kahn 1979:218–19, citing Herodotus 2.61. Greek texts making this point are plentiful, but here are typical examples we shall mention below: Pindar, *Pythian Ode* 3.61 and *Isthmian Ode* 5.14; Euripides, *Alcestis* 799; and Epicharmus, DK 23B20 (quoted by Aristotle at *Rhetoric* 1394b25).

[3] DK 45D2, Iamblichus, *Life of Pythagoras* 137; trans. Cornford 1922, 142.

[4] These distinctions appear throughout the Platonic dialogues, but each of the following passages is a good candidate for the *locus classicus* of one of them: *Phaedo* 80b1–5 (soul and body), *Philebus* 23c9–10 (limit and unlimited), and *Timaeus* 30a2–6 (a good cosmic principle and something that resists this good).

[5] *Theaetetus* 176a8–b2; all translations of Plato are from Cooper 1997, unless otherwise indicated. For a discussion of this passage, see Sedley 1999a. For another discussion of becoming godlike in Plato, see Annas 1999:52.

[6] *Phaedo* 82b10–11. See also *Phaedo* 85a2.

[7] Ibid. 6.500c9–d2.

[8] *Alcibiades* 133b7–10.

[9] *Alcibiades* 132e4–133b7; cf. *Republic* 420c–d.

[10] *Alcibiades* 133c1–2.

[11] *Alcibiades* 133c4–6.

[12] *Alcibiades* 133c13–16. These passages (133c8–17 and 134d1–e7) are now omitted from the standard translations (e.g., Cooper 1997:592, 594).

[13] *Ennead* 1.2.6.2–3. See also: 2.3.9, 2.9.9, 3.2.8, 3.7.5, 3.7.12, 4.3.32, 4.4.2, 6.4.14, 6.7.5, 6.7.34–36, 6.8.14–15, 6.9.8–11.

[14] On reason both purifying and pure, see *Ennead* 1.1.13, 3.6.5, 5.1.10, 6.7.36, 6.9.9. On self-inquiry and self-knowledge, see *Ennead* 1.1.13, 2.1.1, 3.7.5, 3.9.6–7, 4.4.2, 5.3.1, 5.3.4, 6.7.41, 6.9.11.

[15] *Nicomachean Ethics* 1177b26–28; trans. PLM.

[16] 1177b30–31; trans. PLM.

[17] 1177b31–34; trans. PLM; cf. *Metaphysics* 982b29–983a11. For the consummation of his theology, see *Metaphysics* 12.9. For that of his psychology, *On the Soul* 3.5.

[18] *Metaphysics* 1074b1–14.

[19] *Ennead* 1.1.12. For some other examples of Plotinus exhibiting this hermeneutic, see 4.3.1–17, 5.1.7 and 5.5.3.

[20] *Odyssey* 11.601–2.

21 *Ennead* 1.1.12.38–40; trans. Armstrong 2000:121.

22 Kingsley 1995:276.

23 For Heracles' Italian travels, see Kingsley 2004:29, with a citations on 238. For an association between Heracles and Tarentum, particularly its prominent Pythagorean leader, Archytas, see Huffman 2005:305. For Heracles' psychagogical travels, see Euripides' *Alcestis* 1072–158, as well as Diodorus Siculus 4.26.1 (cited by Kinglsey 2004:61–62). For Persephone's welcome, see Kingsley 2004:94, with a citation on 243.

24 *Olympian Odes* 2.65–66; trans. Race 1997a:71.

25 Burkert 1985:211. Dionysus played a similar role according to Burkert. In this connection, see Kingsley 1995:269.

26 Kingsley 1995:225–26, 253, 274.

27 *Pythian Ode* 3.61; trans. Race 1997a:251. "Do not seek to become Zeus," he wrote in *Isthmian Ode* 5.14; trans. Race 1997b:177. See also Euripides (*Alcestis* 799) and Epicharmus (DK 23B20, quoted by Aristotle at *Rhetoric* 1394b25).

28 *Isthmian Ode* 7.42–44; trans. Race 1997b201.

29 *Isthmian Ode* 7.44–47.

30 For a fuller account of the following interpretation of Sophocles' *Oedipus Tyrannus*, see Miller 2006.

31 *Oedipus Tyrannus* 398–99.

32 For the full argument, which draws equally upon mythology and philosophy, see Goux 1993.

33 Goux 1993:135.

34 For a fuller comparison of Oedipus and Athenian democracy, epitomized by Pericles, see Knox 1957 (especially page 77).

35 Thucydides 2.48.1–2.

36 DK 59B12 (Simplicius, *Commentary on Aristotle's* Physics 164.24–25; 156.13–157.4).

37 Aristotle, *Metaphysics* 984b17.

38 Guthrie 1965(2):268 lists and discusses some sources for this story. These include Plato (*Apology* 26d6), Plutarch (*Life of Pericles* 32), and Diodorus (12.39).

39 Race 2000:102–3 enumerates two of these similarities, along with three others: "(1) both receive an enigmatic oracle from Delphi; (2) both devise logical plans to avoid fulfilling it; (3) both ironically fulfill it in the very act of trying to avoid it; (4) both discover in the process the limitations of human knowledge; and (5) both become *paradeigmata* for their fellow human beings." Contra (2), Socrates does not try to avoid fulfilling the oracle—that he is the wisest of the Greeks—although he does investigate it critically in order to understand what it means. See Plato, *Apology* 21b, as well as Kahn 1979:123 and Reeve 1989:21–28.

40 Plato, *Republic* 9.588b–e; Goux 1993:150–58.

41 *Oedipus Coloneus* 10.

42 *Oedipus Coloneus* 576–79.

43 *Oedipus Tyrannus* 1076 ff.

44 *Oedipus Tyrranus* 1331–32.

45 *Oedipus Coloneus* 1627–30.

46 *Oedipus Coloneus* 1662–64.

47 Remarkably, Oedipus's confusion about the circumstances of Laius's murder stems in part from discrepancies between different reports of the number of

murderers: one or many? The problem of the one and the many was a central preoccupation of Greek philosophy—especially in its earliest period, perhaps most of all among Heraclitus (B10, B50) and Parmenides (B8), but also in its latest period, most notably in Plotinus (5.1.8)—and Oedipus seems to contribute to it with his argument that "one cannot become equal to many" (845; for a discussion, see Miller 2006:230–31).

48 *Metaphysics* 1005b19–21.

49 *Metaphysics* 1005b23–24. See also *Topics* 159b30–33, *Physics* 185b19–25, *Metaphysics* 1012a24–26, and 1012a33 ff.

50 *Metaphysics* 1006a15–16, 1008b10–12.

51 *Republic* 4.436b7–9. See also *Republic* 5.477a2–b1 and *Theaetetus* 183a.

52 *Republic* 5.477a, 5.479e8; *Phaedo* 78d3–4, 80b1–2; *Symposium* 211e1–3; *Phaedrus* 247c6–7.

53 DK 28B2 (Proclus, *Commentary on Plato's* Timaeus 1.345.18).

54 DK 28B8.5 (Simplicius, *Commentary on Aristotle's* Physics 145.1–146.25).

55 DK 28B6.7–9 (Simplicius, *Commentary on Aristotle's* Physics 86.27–28; 117.4–13).

56 DK 22B51 (Hippolytus, *Refutation* 9.9.2). Unless otherwise noted, all translations of Heraclitus are from Kahn 1979.

57 *Othello* 3.3.170.

58 *Paradise Lost* 3.141–42. This interpretation of this verse is indebted to Eriksen 2000:42, 141. For an explicit account of Milton's Christology, see *The Christian Doctrine* 1.5. Despite its evident differences from Heraclitean theology, Milton's too must wrestle with the question of the one and the many.

59 DK 22B90 (Plutarch, *De E apud Delphous* 388D–E).

60 *Puros antamoibē ta panta kai pur hapantōn hokōsper chrusou chrēmata kai chrēmata kai chrēmatōn chrusos.*

61 DK 22B10 (Aristotle, *On the World* 5.396b20).

62 *On the Parts of Animals* 1.5.645a20–21. (Irwin and Fine 1995:217).

63 The precise dates of Heraclitus, like the dates of most Greek philosophers who wrote before Plato, are unknown, but the best approximation for his birth is 540.

64 DK 22B67 (Hippolytus, *Refutation of All Heresies*, 9.10.8); translation revised from Kahn 1979:276.

65 Dodds 1951:10. See also Kahn 1979:218–19, citing Herodotus 2.61.

66 DK 22B62 (Hippolytus, *Refutation of All Heresies* 9.10.6); Kahn 1979:216.

67 *Metaphysics* 1074b34–35.

68 See Long 1996:35–57.

69 *Meditations* 5.23.

70 *Meditations* 4.43.

71 *Meditations* 10.17; see also 10.18.

72 Plato, *Timaeus* 27d–28b, 37c–e.

73 *Meditations* 7.9.

74 E.g., *Meditations* 4.14.

75 Kant, *Foundations of the Metaphysics of Morals* 389; trans. Beck 1990:5.

76 Kant, *Foundations of the Metaphysics of Morals* 424; trans. Beck 1990:40.

77 Kant, *Lectures on Ethics*; trans. Heath, eds. Heath and Schneewind 1997:155. Cited in Reeve 2005:6–7.

[78] Ibid.

[79] Nietzsche, "Of Immaculate Perception," *Thus Spoke Zarathustra* (Pearson and Large 2006:272).

[80] Nietzsche 1962:79, *Philosophy in the Tragic Age of the Greeks*, Chapter 10.

[81] Ibid. 80.

[82] Ibid. 80.

[83] Ibid. 80.

[84] *Genealogy of Morality* 3.12 (Pearson and Large 2006:427).

[85] Nietzsche, "Of Immaculate Perception," *Thus Spoke Zarathustra* (Pearson and Large 2006:272–73).

[86] Nietzsche 1962:68, *Philosophy in the Tragic Age of the Greeks*, Chapter 8

Chapter 2

[1] Diogenes Laertius, *Lives of Eminent Philosophers* 2.22. All translations of Diogenes Laertius are from Hicks (2000), unless otherwise noted.

[2] DK 22B1 (Sextus Empiricus, *Against the Professors* 8.132). All translations of Heraclitus are from Kahn 1979, unless otherwise noted. In this one, the original *logos* has been preserved instead of Kahn's "account."

[3] To exacerbate the paradox, *aiei* ("forever") plays an ambiguous grammatical role in the original Greek: does it belong with what precedes it or what follows it (*tou de logou toud' eontos* aiei *axunetoi ginontai anthrōpoi*)? Aristotle complained of this ambiguity (*Rhetoric* 3.5.1407b11 ff. = DK 22A4, cited by Kahn 1979:93). If it belongs with what precedes it, on one hand, an appropriate translation would be: "Although this *logos* holds forever, men fail to comprehend it." If *aiei* belongs with what follows it, on the other hand, an appropriate translation would be: "Although this *logos* is true, men ever fail to comprehend it." Kahn's delicate translation preserves both senses by repeating the idea in both clauses ("forever" in the first, "ever" in the second). What this translation loses—as Kahn is well aware—is an ambiguity that turns out to be characteristic of the logos itself.

[4] The authority Heraclitus grants the logos, according to Edward Hussey, is "none other than the impersonal kind of authority that is intrinsic to *reason* or *rationality*" (Hussey 1999:93). A discussion of the meanings of *logos*, both in Heraclitus and later Greek authors, is available in Peters 1967:110–12. An exhaustive list of meanings can be found in Liddell et al. (1940:1057–59).

[5] DK 22B12 (Arius Didymus fr. 39.2).

[6] Both points are made by Charles Kahn (1979:167). He interprets the sounds of the aphorism differently—the interpretation advanced here is closer to Daniel Graham's (2008:173), although not identical to his. However differently we interpret the significance of these sounds, we cannot deny that Heraclitus intends to signal something with them.

[7] Graham 2008:180.

[8] Kahn 1979:320, n.196. Graham (2008:179–81) develops the point, focusing especially on syntactic ambiguity.

[9] Graham (2008:180) provides several convincing reasons for seeing the syntactic ambiguity in this aphorism as deliberate.

[10] DK 22B49a (Heraclitus Homericus, *Homeric Questions* 24, Oelmann [Schleier-macher fr. 72]). Although many commentators, including Diels, accept this fragment as authentic, Kahn rejects it as a syncretism of several other aphorisms (Kahn 1979:288–89; see also n. 431). It is consistent with our conclusions, in any case, about the Heraclitean logos and self.

[11] DK 22B30 (Clement, *Miscellanies* 5.103.6); translation revised from Kahn.

[12] See Long 1996:35–57. Thales lived in the late seventh and early sixth centuries. The dates of Anaximenes are c. 585–525.

[13] DK 22B65 (Hippolytus, *Refutation of All Heresies* 9.10.7).

[14] *Metaphysics* 1005b19–21.

[15] *Metaphysics* 1005b23–24. See also *Topics* 159b30–33, *Physics* 185b19–25, *Metaphysics* 1012a24–26, and 1012a33ff. See also Plato's *Theaetetus* 183a.

[16] For Plato's formulation, see *Republic* 5.476e4–480a13 (cf. 4.436b8–c1). For Parmenides', DK 28B2.3 (Proclus, *Commentary on Plato's Timaeus* 1.345.18).

[17] (i) is DK 22B60 (Hippolytus, *Refutation* 9.10.4); (ii) is DK 22B61 (ibid. 9.10.5); (iii) is DK 22B126 (Tzetzes, *Scholia to the Exegesis of the Iliad* p. 126). The transla-tions are all Richard McKirahan's (1994:123). McKirahan (1994: 121–24) also arranges the Heraclitean aphorisms on opposition into one large group (Group V, Fragments on Opposition). Moreover, he subdivides this group, roughly as we have, according to the type of opposition in question.

[18] A recent example is Daniel Graham 2006:118–22. As for the charge of obscurity, Diogenes Laertius (9.6) records a verse of Timon (c.325–c.235) calling Heraclitus "riddling" (*ochloloidoros*). Others echoed the charge: Cicero (*On Goals* 2.15); Lucretius (1.638–44); Strabo (14.25); Hippolytus (*Refutation*, 6.9.4, 9.8.5–6, 9.10).

[19] Fuller discussions of the Stoic (mis)appropriation of the Heraclitean fire aphorisms are available in Kirk 1962:303–328, Kahn 1979:147–53, and Long 1996:40–42.

[20] Nemesius reports the Stoic doctrine that "There will be another Socrates, a Plato, and every man with the same friends and the same fellow citizens . . . and this renewal will not happen once, but several times; rather, all things will be repeated eternally" (*On the Nature of Man* ch. 38; *Stoicorum Veterum Fragmenta* 2.625; quoted in Hadot 1998:76). Marcus Aurelius writes more tentatively of "the periodic rebirth of the Whole" (*Meditations* 11.1.3; see also 2.14, 5.13, 5.32, 9.35; all transla-tions of Marcus are from Grube 1983, unless otherwise indicated), but Hadot interprets this as a spiritual exercise rather than as a cosmological doctrine (1998:41, 48–51, 75–76, 144–45, 177–78, 267). As for Nietzsche, the most explicit references are from his unpublished notes, which should be ignored, as Robert Solomon has argued. From the published works, the key passages are: *The Gay Science* 4.341; *Thus Spoke Zarathustra* 3, "On the Vision and the Riddle" (2), and "The Convalescent"; also *Ecce Homo* ("The Birth of Tragedy," 3; "Thus Spoke Zarathustra," 1).

[21] For a fuller account of this interpretation of Nietzsche, see Miller 2010a.

[22] Kahn 1979:23.

[23] *Physics* 218a9–30.

[24] A parallel question could be asked—although Aristotle does not ask it—about when a moment that comes into being does so. In which moment? Not in itself, for then it would have to precede its own existence, when it would both exist and

not exist; nor in any other moment, for then it would be simultaneous with a different moment.

25 Plato's *Parmenides* (127a–128d) depicts Zeno (b. c. 490) as not only the student but also the boyfriend of Parmenides.

26 DK 29A27 (Aristotle, *Physics* 6.9.239b5–7, 30–33). For a fuller discussion see McKirahan 1999:151–55.

27 *Physics* 239b5 –7.

28 *Physics* 239b31–32; DK 29A27.

29 *Physics* 239b7–8.

30 *Physics* 220a25–31.

31 DK 22B50 (Hippolytus, *Refutation* 9.9.1). There is an important ambiguity in the Greek of this aphorism that we shall not raise until section 2.8 of this chapter.

32 DK 22B53 (Hippolytus, *Refutation* 9.9.4). See also DK 22A22.

33 *Iliad* 1.544. Perhaps aware of Heraclitus's writing, Pindar calls time the father of all things (*Olympian Odes* 2.18). For a short discussion, see Kahn 1979:206.

34 DK 22B80 (Origen, *Against Celsus* 6.28).

35 For Homer, see *Iliad* 28.107; for Hesiod, see *Works and Days* 11–26. For Heraclitus's critique of "the poets of the people," generally, see DK 22B104; for his particular critiques of Homer and Hesiod, see DK 22B40, B42, B56, B57, and B106.

36 DK 22B51 (Hippolytus, *Refutation* 9.9.4). Kahn translates *harmoniē* as "attunement."

37 Kahn 1979:196–97, complete with citations of source texts.

38 Kahn 1979:197–99. When Plato and Aristotle testify to B51, they both interpret it as a comment about musical harmony, neglecting the other semantic overtones and thereby flattening it. (For Plato, *Symposium* 187a–b; for Aristotle, *Nicomachean Ethics* 8.1.1155b4.)

39 DK 22B54 (Hippolytus, *Refutation* 9.9.5); trans. PLM. For a more extensive commentary, see Kahn 1979:202–4.

40 Kahn 1979:203 discusses the latter two meanings, noticing especially the appropriation of Pythagorean doctrine with the musical one. Although Heraclitus criticized Pythagoras harshly (DK 22B129, but also DK 22B40), Kahn notes how he nonetheless adapted Pythagorean psychology. The murky chronology of Pythagoreanism makes it difficult to decide who influenced whom. It is possible, as Kahn himself observes (1979:204) that later Pythagoreans, such as Philolaus, appropriated Heraclitean doctrines.

41 DK 22B124 (Theophrastus, *Metaphysics* 15 [p. 16, Ross and Fobes]).

42 Kahn 1979:203.

43 Kahn 1979:203.

44 Kahn 1979:203–04, citing DK 22B114.

45 DK 22B1; see also B2, B17, and B34.

46 DK 22B51. By using *palintropos*, a deliberate substitution for the customary *palintonos*, this aphorism also resonates with all the other aphorisms about cyclical reversions (DK 22B31a, B94, B120), characteristically exhibiting the very *logos* it describes (Kahn 1979:199).

47 "The immortal gods think only of the lyre and song" (*Homeric Hymn to (Pythian) Apollo* 3.188). See also *Homeric Hymn to Hermes* (4.480–82).

[48] "Il faut donc considérer non pas l'instrument inerte mais le couple," writes Marcel Conche, "le tout formé par l'instrument et celui qui s'en sert" (Conche 1998:429). Similarly, Kahn (1979:198) cites Lewis Campbell, who "took his inspiration from Plato's remark at *Republic* 439b." 439b uses the example of an archer to help explain a version of the principle of non-contradiction.

[49] Accented on the iota, it means life; on the omicron, bow.

[50] DK 22B48 (*Etymologicum Magnum*, s.v. *bios*). Here is a transliteration of the aphorism: *to toxō onoma bios, ergon de thanatos.*

[51] See DK 22B67, where the opposition of war and peace makes a list that characterize "the god." We discuss this aphorism in the next section.

[52] *Homeric Hymn to Apollo* 3.131–32.

[53] DK 22B93 (Plutarch, *On the Pythian Oracles* 404D).

[54] For the aphorism that invokes the oracular style of Apollo, DK 22B93, Kahn distinguishes "the obvious sense (applying to Heraclitus' own style) and the *hyponoia* that emerges only upon reflection (applying the nature of things understood as *logos*)" (1979:124). In this way, he adds, "the semantic complexity that is *described*" by this aphorism "in reference to Apollo is also illustrated by these words in their reference to our double *logos*: the discourse of Heraclitus and the structure of reality" (1979:124).

[55] DK 22B123 (Themistius, *Orations* 5.69b).

[56] See, e.g., *Oedipus at Colonus* 486–87.

[57] DK 22B32 (Clement, *Miscellanies* 5.115.1): *hen to sophon mounon legesthai ouk ethelei kai ethelei Zēnos onoma.*

[58] DK 22B41 (Diogenes Laertius, 9.1): *hen to sophon; epistasthai gnōmē hokēkubernēsai panta dia pantōn.*

[59] Kahn (1979:171) justifies both "plan" and "insight" as translations of *gnōmē*, also reminding us of the relevant aphorisms on the logos (DK 22B2 and B50).

[60] DK 22B50.

[61] Graham 2008:178–81. The simplest example is also arguably the deepest: *ēthos anthrōpōi daimōn* ("character human destiny"). DK 22B119 (Stobaeus 4.40.23 = Plutarch, *Quaestiones Platonicae* 999E, etc.); trans. PLM. The middle word is a dative of reference, but the roles of subject or predicate in an accurate translation could be played either of the other two words. After discussing the meaning of *daimōn*, which can mean "divinity," even in Heraclitus himself (DK 22B79), Kahn renders this aphorism as follows: "Man's character is his fate" (Kahn 1979:260–61). Uniting our character and our destiny—or, alternately, our character and our divinity—humanity grasps an aphorism, like the world it describes, balancing opposites and thereby exemplifying divine harmonia. The full depth of this aphorism will not become clear until we have considered several others on mortality and immortality, grasping and selfhood. Yet we can already see how its paradigmatic technique of syntactic ambiguity works: rather than forcing us to choose between syntactic roles, it encourages us to hold both in mind at once, so that we might recognize their unity in opposition.

[62] DK 21B11, B14–16, B23–26.

[63] DK 21B23 (Clement, *Miscellanies* 5.109).

[64] DK 22B40.

[65] Kahn 1979:136, 145–46, 203–04, 239, 269. Anaximander reportedly said that his Boundless "contains all things and steers them all" (DK 12A15; Aristotle, *Physics*

203b11). If this is an accurate report, as Kahn observes (1979:272), Heraclitus likely has it in mind when we writes that his Wise One "steers all things through all" (DK 22B41).

66 Kahn (1979:269) describes how to construct such a composite paraphrase, but does not provide it himself.

67 Justice (*Dikē*) is named among the daughters of Zeus and Themis by Hesiod (*Theogony* 902).

68 DK 22B30; translation revised from Kahn. Kahn has "ordering" for *kosmos*, a translation he justifies while nonetheless recognizing "cosmos" (in the sense of a world-order) as a deeper meaning of the aphorism (1979:132–34).

69 DK 22B41.

70 Kahn 1979:137.

71 See Chapter 3, sections 3.1–2.

72 DK 22B64 (Hippolytus, *Refutation* 9.10.7).

73 For a discussion of thunderbolt (*keraunos*), especially as purest fire, see Conche 1986:302–5 (citing DK 22B31 and B90).

74 DK 22B66 (Hippolytus, *Refutation* 9.10.7). See also DK 22B28b, as well as B16, which Kahn (1979:274) reads as a reference to omnipresent divine fire.

75 DK 22B67; translation revised from Kahn 1979:276. Kahn inserts "and" between each of the opposing pairs in the first sentence of this aphorism, but there is no equivalent in the Greek, and the severe asyndeton of the original heightens the confusion of opposites that is the aphorism's point. Kahn translates *hēdonē* as "pleasure," the common meaning of the word in the fifth century, while noting "the old technical use of *hēdonē* for a flavor or perfume" (1979:280). Although odd, this translation does keep before our minds the subjective contribution of the namer when naming the one god according to a false dichotomy. In later sections of this chapter we shall examine the deliberate confusion of subject and object in the Heraclitean account of thinking and speaking about the world.

76 Conche (1986:381) discusses in detail the image of an altar fire mixed with perfumes, citing Pindar and Hippolytus.

77 See DK 22B5, B14, B15, B96. To these criticisms of popular piety, we must add the criticisms of Homer and Hesiod (DK 22B40, B42, B57, B106), whose texts underwrote so much of Greek religion (Burkert 1985:120).

78 The more famous god of war is Ares (see *Iliad* 5.889–98); lesser known is Peace (*Eirēnē*), whom Hesiod makes the daughter of Zeus and Themis (*Theogony* 902).

79 DK 22B53. See also DK22A22.

80 *Theogony* 748–57.

81 DK 22B57 (Hippolytus, *Refutation* 9.10.2).

82 Conche 1998:380–81.

83 DK 22B17 (Clement, *Miscellanies* 2.8.1).

84 Kahn (1979:278) describes in more detail the complex arrangement presented in the next paragraph. Conche (1998:382) discusses the same arrangement, citing Deichgräber and Serra.

85 DK 22B2 (Sextus Empiricus, *Against the Professors* 8.133).

86 *The Gay Science* 354; see also *Twilight of the Idols* ("Reason in Philosophy," 5).

87 *Genealogy of Morality* 1.13.

88 *Genealogy of Morality* 1.13.25–26.

89 Kahn 1979:276–77.

⁹⁰ See, e.g., Heidegger 1999:4.

⁹¹ Kahn 1979:277.

⁹² DK 22B84a (Plotinus, *Enneads* 4.8.1).

⁹³ DK 22B101 (Plutarch, *Against Colotes* 1118C).

⁹⁴ Kahn 1979:116.

⁹⁵ *Against the Professors* 7.310–12. Sextus flourished in the second century of the common era. For earlier versions in Plato and Aristotle, see *Charmides* 167a–169c and *On the Soul* 3.2, 425b12–28.

⁹⁶ DK 22B34 (Clement, *Miscellanies* 5.115.3).

⁹⁷ Hussey 1999:105.

⁹⁸ DK 22B115 and B45; slightly rev. from Kahn's translations. In both translations, "self" renders *psychēs*, which Kahn translates more literally as "soul."

⁹⁹ DK 22B10 ([Aristotle], *On the World* 5.396b20).

¹⁰⁰ DK 22B67.

¹⁰¹ Kahn 1979:281.

¹⁰² Kahn 1979:283.

¹⁰³ DK 22B110–11, B88. Of the last, we should notice how it shares formal features with both the logos of god and the logos of graspings. It lists concrete oppositions of the human life-cycle, like the logos of god, then follows this list with a chiasmus, like the logos of graspings: "The same . . . : living and dead, and the waking and the sleeping, and young and old. For these transposed are those, and those transposed again are these." We shall discuss the figure of chiasmus more fully below, in time making it our translation of *syllapsies*.

¹⁰⁴ Many of the better manuscripts have *synapsies*, as Kirk observes (1962:170), but he thinks *syllapsies* preferable. Marcovich writes that "the difference in meaning between the two words is minimal" (1967:105). Both are cited by Conche (1986:433–34), who favors *synapsies*. Kahn opts for *syllapsies*. He does not discuss any textual grounds for doing so, saying only that the alternative "is rejected in most recent editions of the text" (1979:338, n.423). He thinks the best translation of *syllapsies* is "graspings" because it makes the aphorism about both the subject and object of thinking.

¹⁰⁵ See DK 22B40, B104, and B114. In two of these aphorisms, Heraclitus denies *nous* to those whom others celebrate for their wisdom: specifically Hesiod, Pythagoras, Xenophanes, and Hecataeus (B40); but more generally, popular poets and the mob who celebrate them (B104). In the other aphorism (B114), he describes those who speak with *nous* as those who "hold fast to what is shared (*xunōi*) by all." This is presumably the logos that is said in B2 to be "shared" (*xunou*).

¹⁰⁶ Graham 2008:181. (For Wittgenstein, see *Philosophical Investigations* 2.11. The drawing first appeared in a German humor magazine in 1892, then again in *Harper's* the same year. A Gestalt psychologist, J. Jastrow, introduced it to academic psychology in 1899.) Graham compares *nous* to the vision of the duck-rabbit drawing, and his own interpretation of *nous* has been helpful in the development of the interpretation advanced here, but our interpretation departs somewhat from his. According to Graham, *nous* grants "*insight* into the world and its complexity" (2008:181). With the help of Heraclitean aphorisms, more specifically, "we perceive suddenly the complexity of the representation, and also its unity"

(2008:182). Graham thus describes these aphorisms as "exercises in intuition, in right-brain logic, in synthetic intelligence" (2008:183). In our interpretation, however, that is only half the story. Just as he thinks that an observer can view the duck-rabbit drawing as a duck or a rabbit, "though not as both at the same time," Graham also claims that Heraclitus's deliberate ambiguities "can be construed one way or the other, but not both ways at the same time" (2008:179). Our interpretation goes farther and argues—both of the drawing and of the ambiguities of the aphorisms, not to mention of the world whose logos they report—that perception of both ways at the same time is possible. Our example of a Bach fugue, below in the main text, is an example of this possibility. Analogously, we add, sound thinking's combination of analysis and synthesis is also possible.

[107] Kahn 1979:282. "There is a kind of isomorphism between the knower and the known," agrees Graham, "inasmuch as they share a structure" (2008:184).

[108] The Greek original, *syllapsies*, is plural, our adapted form singular, in order to facilitate speaking of one activity. However, the so-called "river" fragment (B12) also uses plurals, as Kahn observes (1979:166–67), and presumably this is deliberate. The plural in this case seems to indicate that there are two sorts of graspings, those in thinking's subject ("comprehensions"), and those in the world that is thinking's object ("collections"). But in the end the deeper point is that these two sorts of graspings are really identical, two sides of the same mind–world coin. Although we favor the singular with our provisional adaptation of "syllapsis," we shall always be sensitive to both of these points, the one initially revealed and the other more deeply concealed. Indeed, we shall soon consider the difficult relation between one and many in Heraclitus, when we investigate the final phrase of the logos of graspings: "from all things one and from one thing all." Our interpretation of this relation will confirm, however, that the singular adaptation of *syllapsies* is as accurate as the plural, if not more so because it helps to reveal the concealed meaning.

[109] Marcus Aurelius, *Meditations* 10.31; cf. 4.1.

[110] DK 22B101.

[111] In Chapter 4 (section 4.9), on Plato, we shall consider his influential treatment of inner conflict, which he highlights in tandem with the principle of non-contradiction in order to divide the self into parts. (Earlier in *Republic* [408d–409b], he neglects the importance of frustration and inner conflict for self-knowledge, arguing that although the best physician would have experienced many illnesses, the best judge should be pure of vice.) Other famous instances of this philosophical strategy—not treated in this book on ancient Greek philosophy, but nonetheless downstream from its conclusions—are found in Augustine's *Confessions* and Freud's *The Ego and the Id*.

[112] DK 22B10.

[113] See Chapter 3, section 3.1. The chronological order of Heraclitus's and Parmenides' writings has been hotly contested since Hegel first claimed that Parmenides wrote first. The majority of scholars now subscribe to the opposite order. Graham surveys the state of this scholarship and argues that Heraclitus wrote first (2002:27–44). For another view, see Nehamas in the same volume (2002:4–64).

[114] *Thus Spoke Zarathustra*, Second Part, "On Redemption."

[115] *Thus Spoke Zarathustra*, Second Part, "On Redemption." For a fuller picture of the diagnosis, see First Part, "On the Hinterworldly," and Second Part, "On the Blessed Isles."

[116] For a discussion of the misunderstandings and an alternate interpretation, see Miller 2010a.

[117] *Meditations* 10.18.

[118] This is especially true of Books 2 and 3; see Hadot 1998:264–65.

[119] Kahn 1979:216.

[120] DK 22B62; Kahn 1979:216.

[121] Kahn's analysis of this chiasmus is quite similar. Commenting also on the numerical pattern of the Greek words, he concludes: "The two-to-two, four-to-four structuring of these twelve words points to some tight pattern of unity between life and death whose exact content is not easy to make out" (Kahn 1979:217).

[122] "*Athanatos* (immortal) . . . means god and nothing else" (Guthrie 1955:115; see also 239). O'Cleirigh and Barrell 2000:50–53 discuss the equation of immortality and divinity, as well as other unique features of the traditional Greek notion of *theos*. See also Burkert 1985:121–22, 162, and 298; Kingsley 1995:222–23; Dodds 1951:10; and Kahn 1979:218–19.

[123] Kahn (1979:217–18) calls these the "weak" and "strong" readings, respectively, considering the first the "revealed" and the second the "concealed" meanings. According to the first, we mortals die and the immortals live on somehow thanks to our deaths. According to the second, death is any change at all—night lives the death of day, cold the death of warm, and so on—so that anything in time, which is to say everything, is mortal inasmuch as it changes, but immortal inasmuch as its logos remains the same.

[124] Kahn 1979:226–27.

[125] For Marcus, see especially *Meditations* 4.48; for Nietzsche, *Thus Spoke Zarathustra*, Fourth and Final Part, "The Sleepwalker Song" (10).

[126] *Meditations* 10.17.

[127] *Meditations* 10.21.

[128] *Thus Spoke Zarathustra*, Fourth and Final Part, "The Sleepwalker Song" (10).

[129] *Thus Spoke Zarathustra*, Fourth and Final Part, "The Sleepwalker Song" (10).

[130] The most relevant passages of Marcus are 2.14, 5.13, 5.32, 9.35, and 11.1; Hadot has detailed discussions of the question (1998:41, 48–51, 75–76, 144–45, 177–78, 267). For the relevant passages from Nietzsche, as well as a discussion, see Miller 2010a.

[131] To Marcus's several quotations of Heraclitus in *Meditations* 4.46, we owe this fragment, DK 22B72, as well as B73. This section also quotes or paraphrases DK 22B36, B74, and B76. Kahn thinks all of these fragments are quoted from unreliable memory (1979:104), and thereby suspect.

[132] See Long 1996:35–57.

[133] *Meditations* 5.23.

[134] *Meditations* 4.43.

[135] *Thus Spoke Zarathustra*, Third Part, "On Old and New Tablets" (8). "Everything is in flux" is a translation of the most famous paraphrase of Heraclitean philosophy: *panta rhei*. Plato and Aristotle use this wording in several passages (e.g., *Cratylus* 440c and *On the Heavens* 3.1.298b30), as do other ancient authors (e.g., Theophrastus and Simplicius). But it is never attributed to Heraclitus as a

quotation, and so it is not usually included among his authentic aphorisms. Conche nevertheless includes it, providing a full list of its ancient citations (1986:467–70).

[136] *Thus Spoke Zarathustra*, Third Part, "On Old and New Tablets" (8).

[137] *Philosophy in the Tragic Age of the Greeks*, Chapter 8 (Nietzsche 1962:68). See also *Genealogy of Morality* 2.16.

[138] On opposition alone, e.g.: DK 22B18, B26, B31, B34, B36, B48, B53, B59, B60, B61, B65, B80, B91, B110–11, B123, B126 On unity alone, e.g.: DKB1, B33, B41, B54, B57, B108, B113–14.

[139] There are several such "key" aphorisms, testifying to unity in opposition (DK 22B10, B30, B32, B50, B51, B54, B62, B67, B88, B101). These are consequently the aphorisms to which we have dedicated most of our attention.

[140] DK 22B10; translation revised from Kahn 1979:85, 281.

[141] See Chapter 2, sections 2.6–7.

[142] In terms of unity and plurality, here is an analysis of these stages: additional contradiction (one-many and yet one); further reconciliation (the one that is somehow one-many-and-yet-one); another conflict (one-many-one and yet one); a higher unity (the one that is somehow one-many-one and one); and so on.

[143] Hussey 1999:105.

[144] DK 22B1 and B2.

[145] DK 22B32.

[146] DK 22B50. We have already witnessed Kahn speaking of Heraclitus's "monism with vengeance" (1979:137). Addressing himself to the "programmatic declaration" of this specific aphorism (B50), Hussey thinks it "already suggests that Heraclitus harbors monistic ambitions" (1999:96).

[147] Another common translation, by Richard McKirahan, is almost exactly the same: "Listening not to me but to the *logos* it is wise to agree that all things are one" (Curd 1996:34).

[148] The observation belongs to Ronald Polansky.

[149] DK 22B1.

[150] Neither Kahn (1979:131–32) nor Conche (1986:25–27) raises the possibility of this meaning.

[151] Herodotus (1.53). Although the historian wrote in the century after Heraclitus, neither he nor his century invented this sort of story—consulting an oracle, only to hear its obvious meaning to the exclusion of its concealed meaning, and thereby ruining oneself. Consider the story of Oedipus.

[152] DK 22B93.

[153] Herodotus 1.53.3; trans. Waterfield 1998:23.

[154] The English conveys the same ambiguity without the same grammatical trick, for in the end Croesus does destroy a great empire: his own.

[155] DK 22B108.

[156] DK 22B41; see also B32.

[157] Kahn 1979:116, with citations of Plato (*Charmides* 164e7) and two modern scholars (North and Wilamowitz). Other common translations would be: be temperate, be moderate, be humble, and so on.

[158] DK 22B116 (Stobaeus, 3.5.6).

[159] DK 22B93.

[160] DK 22B34.

[161] Respectively: DK 22B1 and B2.

[162] Kahn 1979:116.

[163] DK 22B103 (Porphyry, *Homeric Questions*, on Iliad 14.200); cf. B2 (*xunou*), but also B1 (*axunetoi*) and B34 (*axunetoi*).

[164] DK 22B79 (Origen, *Against Celsus* 6.12) and DK 22B78 (Origen, ibid.); translation of the second revised from Kahn (1979:172), following the interpretation he himself provides (1979:173).

[165] DK 22B53 (see Kahn 1979:209).

[166] See Aristotle, *On the World* (396b20), and Cicero, *On Goals* 2.5.15.

Chapter 3

[1] DK 28B1 (Sextus Empiricus, *Against the Professors* 7.111–14). Unless otherwise noted, all translations of Parmenides in this chapter are from Curd 1996.

[2] DK 28B1.28–30 (Simplicius, *Commentary on Aristotle's* On the Heavens 557.25–558.2).

[3] DK 28B2 (Proclus, *Commentary on Plato's* Timaeus 1.345.18).

[4] Among its many difficulties, the verb "to be"—in Greek, *einai*—can function in several different ways. For example, we can say that god is, existentially, in the sense that god exists; we can also say that god is just, predicatively, in the sense that justice is one of god's qualities. There are at least two other senses, that of identity and veracity: "god is love," forges an identity between two subjects, whereas "it is god who loves," claims a truth. Parmenides uses *einai* in an unspecified way, as do the other philosophical authors of his period, and David Sedley writes that it is "probably harmless for us to gloss Parmenidean being as existence" (1999b:115). In this chapter we shall try to remain faithful to the unspecified use.

[5] A third answer—that there is no subject, in the manner of "it is raining"—was suggested by Raven and Fränkel, but Owen "pertinently objected that something more definite must be intended 'because Parmenides goes on to prove various characteristics of the subject of his *esti*' " (Guthrie 1965:15). For simplicity's sake, we shall not consider this answer.

[6] See DK 28A6.1, 7.1, 8.7, 8.12, [8.19], 8.24, 8.25, 8.32, 8.33, 8.35, 8.46, 8.47.

[7] See DK 28A6.1 See also DK 28A8.8–9, 8.16, 8.34.

[8] As mentioned earlier in this volume, the canonical form of this principle arrives with Aristotle (*Metaphysics* 1005b19–21). But a form intermediate between Parmenides and Aristotle can be found in Plato (*Republic* 5.476e4–480a13; cf. 4.436b8–c1). See Chapter 4, section 4.3.

[9] Guthrie 1965:15.

[10] DK 28B6.4 (Simplicius, *Commentary on Aristotle's* Physics. 86.27–28, 117.4–13).

[11] DK 28B6.7–9.

[12] DK 22B34 (Clement, *Miscellanies* 5.115.3).

[13] DK 22B107 (Sextus Empiricus, *Against the Professors* 8.126). See also DK 22B34.

[14] DK 22B51 (Hippolytus, *Refutation* 9.9.2).

[15] Graham 2002:27–44.

[16] DK 22B10 (Aristotle, *On the World* 5.396b20). See, especially, 2.8–9.

[17] For other, fuller discussions of these arguments, see Gallop 1984:12–19, Sedley 1999b:113–23, Crystal 2002:28–38, and McKirahan 2008:189–229.

[18] This assumption ignores the distinction between qualities and substances, we should note, since the changes of a man from tan to pale or from pale to tan, say, differs from the changes in which he is born or annihilated. Formal recognition of this distinction, however, would await Plato's *Sophist* (261e–263d) and, later, Aristotle's *Physics* (1.8). In the meantime, the longstanding confusion of qualities and substances permitted Anaxagoras, on one hand, to speak of mixtures of hot and earth, as though there were no difference of kind between the two (DK 59B4b); on the other hand, sophists exploited the confusion to fashion beguiling pseudo-paradoxes (*Sophist* 251a–c).

[19] DK 28B8.7–9 (Simplicius, *Commentary on Aristotle's* Physics 145.1–146.25).

[20] DK 28B8.13–14.

[21] One reading of the manuscript for B8.36–38, accepted by Sedley (1999:120) and Coxon (1986:71,73), yields this explicit prohibition of time: "And time is not nor will be another thing alongside Being, since this was bound fast by fate to be entire and changeless" (trans. Coxon 1986:70,72).

[22] See, especially, Chapter 2, section 2.2.

[23] DK 28B8.3–4; trans. McKirahan, in Curd 1996:47, slightly rev. by Miller ("perfect" for "complete").

[24] DK 28B8.5–6.

[25] DK 28B6.1.

[26] DK 28B2.8 (Proclus, *Commentary on Plato's* Timaeus 1.345.18); trans. Gallop 1984:55.

[27] Russell 1905.

[28] DK 28B8.8–9; italics removed from trans. Gallop 1984:65.

[29] DK 28B5 (Proclus, *Commentary on Plato's* Parmenides 1.708 [16 Cousin]). Long thinks this epistemological circularity explains, and is explained by, the ontological sphericity of Parmenides' being (1996:144). Though fanciful, as Long admits, the thought is consistent with the interpretation that Parmenides equated thinking and being.

[30] Clement, *Miscellanies* 6.23; Plotinus, *Ennead* 5.1.8 = DK 28B3. Translations of this fragment differ markedly, as we shall discuss. Here is a transliteration of Parmenides' Greek: *to gar auto noein estin te kai einai.*

[31] Coxon 2003:210. Accordingly, Coxon calls their reading "the traditional understanding of the phrase."

[32] Long 1996:132. The correlative German translation is: *Dasselbe ist Denken und Sein.* Gatti (1999:23) quotes Hegel calling Neoplatonism "a recovery of the spirit of man, indeed of the spirit of the world," but without citation.

[33] Coxon 2003:210.

[34] Zeller 1923. For champions of the traditional reading, we shall consider Long 1996 and Sedley 1999.

[35] Sedley 1999:120.

[36] E.g., Cornford 1939:34, n. 1; cited in Guthrie 1965:42. That the mind/being identity reading does not attribute to Parmenides *idealism* (in the sense customary in discussions of modern philosophy), see Long 1996:146.

[37] Zeller 1923:678(1); cited in Coxon 2003:210. The correlative German translation is: *Dasselbe kann gedacht werden und sein.*

[38] It is impossible to be sure of the case of the Greek infinitives, since they lack the article of an articular infinitive that would reveal their case. Coxon (2003:210–11) thus argues that the traditional reading "is at least questionable, since it postulates a substantival use of the infinitive with no article, which would be unparalleled in the first half of the fifth century, and even later." The argument is challenged, however, by numerous passages listed in Smyth 1980:441–50. The whole section is entitled "The Infinitive without the Article," and includes a chapter, "As Subject, Predicate, and Appositive" (ss. 1984–88), which cites Thucydides, among others.

[39] Long 1996:137, especially n. 24.

[40] Coxon 2003:211 mentions Aeschylus (*Persians* 419) and Plato (*Sophist* 259a), and then cites fragments of Eupolis (139, 2K) and Ephippus (15, 5K), which appear in Coxon 1986:174. See also Coxon 1986:180. He might also have cited Xenophanes, B32 (*nephos . . . idesthai*), or even Homer, *Iliad* 5.725, 10.439, 18.83, 18.377 (*thauma idesthai*).

[41] Coxon (2003:211) reminds us of Zeller's parallels from DK 28B2.2 (*eisi noēsai*, translated as "can be thought"), as well as DKB2.3, 6.1, 8.34, and 8.36.

[42] For example, Coxon renders fr. 2.3 (*ouk esti mē einai*) as "it is not for not being," but it may be translated more naturally as "not-being is not." Similarly, Coxon renders 6.1 (*esti gar einai*) "it is for being," whereas "being exists" is again more natural.

[43] Gallop 1984:71. Here is a transliteration of the Greek: *tauton d' esti noein te kai houneken esti noēma.* Also rendering the infinitive as a dative, Coxon translates this passage as follows: "the same thing is for thinking as is the cause of thought," which is difficult to understand. Sedley's version renders the infinitive as a nominative and is far more natural: "thinking is identical to that with which thought is concerned" (1999:120). Speaking of this version in particular, though, Coxon says that "no rendering is acceptable which . . . makes *noein* the subject of the sentence" (2003:211). But Coxon seems to have neglected Smyth (1980:441–50).

[44] Long 1996:136.

[45] Parmenides' thinking being anticipates the god of Aristotle insofar as it is thinking thinking of thinking (*noēsis . . . noēseōs noēsis*; *Metaphysics* 1074b34–35).

[46] Vlastos 1953:168; quoted in Long 1996:139.

[47] DK 28B8.22.

[48] Guthrie 1965:42.

[49] Long 1996:135.

[50] As Long writes, "there can be no gap between being *qua* thinking subject and being *qua* object" (1996:135).

[51] Long 1996:131.

[52] DK 31B28 (Simplicius, *Commentary on Aristotle's* Physics 1184.12–13); trans. McKirahan 1994:241.

[53] Hippolytus, *Refutation* 7.29.14–23.

[54] DK 59B12 (Simplicius, *Commentary on Aristotle's* Physics 164.24–25; 156.13–157.4).

[55] Long 1996:131. The text of Long's article has "Parmenides" in this sentence instead of "Empedocles," but this must be a typographical error.

[56] See, e.g., Graham 2006:148–85. Graham does not question the allegiance of these so-called Pluralists to Parmenides, indeed he argues for it, but he emphasizes

different facets of the allegiance in order to defend a very different reading of Parmenides from the one advanced here. According to Graham's reading, Parmenides was not a monist; instead, his Truth established necessary conditions of being—by a proto-transcendental argument, so to speak—which the views of his Doxa then sought to respect. For a critical appraisal of this reading of Parmenides, see my review of Graham 2006 in *Ancient Philosophy* (forthcoming). Among other problems, Graham must downplay the testimonies of Parmenides' successors, Zeno and Melissus.

[57] "Although a Samian," writes McKirahan, "Melissus is philosophically an Eleatic" (1994:295).

[58] DK 30B7 (Simplicius, *Commentary on Aristotle's* Physics 111.18–112.15). "Absence of physical and mental pain," writes Long (1996:141), "are defining characteristics of the divine in Greek thought." For another view, however, see Morford and Lenardon 1999:85, or, for that matter *Iliad* 5.336–54 (Diomedes wounds Aphrodite) and *Iliad* 16.432–61 (Zeus grieves over Sarpedon's death).

[59] McKirahan 1994:299.

[60] DK 29A30; quoted in Long 1996:141.

[61] Had Parmenides proposed a lifeless or mindless cosmos, argues Long, he would have anticipated by a generation the Atomists, whom scholars acknowledge as the first to do so (Long 1996:140). This argument begs the question against the mind/being non-identity reading, however, since this reading inherently challenges this scholarly consensus. The value of the argument is nonetheless the attention it draws to the animation and divinity so freely bestowed upon the cosmos by most early Greek philosophers.

[62] DK 11A22 (Aristotle, *On the Soul* 411a7–8).

[63] DK 13A10 (Cicero, *On the Nature of the Gods* 1.10.26).

[64] Ibid. Long (1996:143) quotes Coxon on Parmenides' appropriation of Xenophanes. "Xenophanes' account of God as a mind transcending human minds in its power (frr. 23–25)," writes Coxon, "since it is the immediate pattern for part of P.'s account of Being (fr. 8, 27–28), may also be regarded as suggesting that P. envisaged Being as Intelligence."

[65] See, especially, Chapter 2, sections 2.5–9.

[66] DK 28A32 (Aëtius 1.25.3 [*Doxographi Graeci* 321]); trans. Gallop 1984:114.

[67] DK 28B8.43.

[68] Long 1996:143.

[69] Burkert 1969:5; cited in Kingsley 2004:62.

[70] DK 28B1.3. The first translation is McKirahan's (Curd 1996:44); the second Coxon's (1986:44).

[71] Kingsley 2004:61–76. The next few pages rely heavily on Kingsley's account of Parmenides' proem.

[72] Sophocles, *Oedipus Coloneus* 683, 1548; cited by Kingsley 2004:243. Kingsley also cites there a score of other witnesses, both ancient and modern. His unusual book combines the accessibility of a detective story with the research of a scholarly monograph by, among other stylistic choices, trading footnotes for a compressed section of references at the end. When the list of such references is as long as this particular one, we cannot recapitulate them all here. To make it easier for anyone who wishes to pursue these points further, though, we shall adopt the following method. When we refer to Kingsley 2004 we shall cite first the

place in it where he mentions or discusses the point in question (in this case, 2004:95), and then cite the precise page(s) of its appendices where he lists his sources. Whenever the list is not too long, we shall also repeat his citations.

73   Kingsley 2004:63, with citations on 241 following "Right hand in the underworld": O. Weinreich, *Antike Heilungswunder* (Giessen 1909) 41–5; A. M. Kropp *Ausgewählte Koptische Zaubertexte* 2 (Brussels 1931) 17–18; G. Zuntz, *Persephone* (Oxford 1971) 367; West, *Zeitschrift für Papyrologie und Epigraphik* 18 (1975) 229–30; C. Brăiloiu, *Problems of Ethnomusicology* (Cambridge 1984) 295; W. M. Brashear, *Magica Varia* (Brussels 1991) 43.

74   Ibid. 212–13, with citations on 254 following "Justice, laws and the cave of night": O. Kern, *Orphicorum Fragmenta* (Berlin 1922) 168–69, s. 105; West, *The Orphic Poems* (Oxford 1983) 72–73, 109–10, 124, 213–14.

75   Ibid. 29, with a citations on 238 following "Posidonia and Heracles": J. Jehasse, *Revue des Études Anciennes* 64 (1962) 252; J. G. Pedley, *Paestum* (London 1990) 66–67. For an association between Heracles and Tarentum, particularly its prominent Pythagorean leader, Archytas, see Huffman 2005:305.

76   Diodorus Siculus 4.26.1; cited by Kinglsey 2004:61–62.

77   Kingsley 2004:94, with a citation on 243 following "Her right hand": *Lexicon Iconographicum Mythologiae Classicae* 8 / 1 (1997) 972 ss. 272, 274. Outside of eschatological contexts, the right hand was at least a pledge of trust. Before Parmenides, it appears in Homer (*Iliad*, 14.137); afterwards, in Euripides (*Medea* 21–22).

78   Kingsley 2004:74, with citations on 242 following "Divine *kouros* and *kourai*, Apollo": A. Brelich, *Paides e Parthenoi* 1 (Rome 1969) 435–36; West, *Hesiod, Theogony* (Oxford 1966) 263–64 and *Hesiod, Works and Days* (1978) 372.

79   Kingsley 2004:68, with citations on 241 following "Sun and underworld": A. Laumonier, *Les Cultes Indigènes en Carie* (Paris 1958) 580; W. Burkert, "Das Proömium des Parmenides und die Katabasis des Pythagoras," *Phronesis* 14 (1969) 9, 21; B. Otto in *Akten des XIII. Internationalen Kongresses für Klassische Archäologie* (Mainz am Rhein 1990) 400; G. Cerri, *La Parola del Passato* (Naples) 444–45; Kingsley 1995:49–68.

80   Kingsley 2004:69, with citations on 241. For a fuller discussion, see Kingsley 1995:50–213, and especially 252 n. 6.

81   Kingsley 2004:72, citing W. Burkert, "Das Proömium des Parmenides und die Katabasis des Pythagoras," *Phronesis* 14 (1969) 14 n.

82   Kingsley 2004:71–73, with many citations on 241.

83   Kingsley 2004:72.

84   Kingsley 2004:126–34, with citations on 246–47.

85   Kingsley 2004:206, with citations on 253 following "The four vocations": DK 31B146; A. D. Nock and A.-J. Festugière, *Corpus Hermeticum* 4 (Paris 1954) 13 s. 42; G. Zuntz, *Persephone* (Oxford 1971) 232–34; Kingsley 1995:343–46.

86   Kingsley 2004:147, 205. Several citations on 248 following "Parmenides as *hērōs ktistēs*," and many others on 252–53 following "Parmenides and Zeno as lawgivers."

87   Kingsley 2004:105, with citations on 244 following "Parmenides, incubation and experts at incubation": H. Diels, *Parmenides, Lehrgedicht* (Berlin 1897) 13–22; H. Demoulin, *Épiménide de Crète* (Brussels 1901) 99; J. S. Morrison, *Journal of Hellenic Studies* 75 (1955) 59–60; *Gnomon* 35 (1963) 239–40; W. Burkert, *Lore and Science in Ancient Pythagoreanism* (Cambridge, MA 1972) 283–84; Culianu, *Studi Storico Religiosi* 4 (1980) 295, 300; A. Francotte in *Mélanges Ph. Marçais* (Paris 1985) 30–37.

88 Kingsley 2004:107, citing (on 244 following "The inscription"): *La Parola del Passato* 25 (Naples 1970), 247, 262.

89 Kingsley 2004:107–10, with many citations on 244 following "Ouliadēs" and "Iatromantis."

90 Kingsley 2004:140, with citations on 248 following "The Parmenides inscription": P. Ebner, *Rassegna Storica Salernitana* 23 (1962) 6, *Apollo* 2 (1962) 128–29; M. Napoli, *Filosofia e Scienze in Magna Graecia. Atti del Quinto Convegno di Studi Sulla Magna Graecia* (Naples 1966) 140–41.

91 See Longrigg 1998:5–83, and Jouanna 1999:181–285. The most famous of the early philosopher-physicians were Philolaus and Alcmaeon—both of Croton, in southern Italy—as well as Empedocles (from Sicily). All were associated with the Pythagoreanism, but Kingsley argues that Parmenides was too (2004:180, 186, 206). Moreover, the fusion of medicine and philosophy was not unique to Pythagoreans. Democritus was said to have written medical works, and some Hippocratic treatises dealt in places with philosophical topics (e.g., *The Sacred Disease*, *The Nature of Man*, and *Ancient Medicine*). Much later, in the Roman era, Sextus Empiricus and Galen were both physicians and philosophers. The latter even wrote a treatise entitled *The Best Doctor is Also a Philosopher*.

92 Kingsley 2004:119–20, with many citations on 246.

93 For Empedocles' claim to these roles, see DK 31B146.

94 See Chapter 2, section 2.10.

95 DK 28B8.13. The same language of prohibition is used of Necessity (B8.30–31) and Fate (B8.37–38)

96 DK 28B1.26–28.

97 DK 28B6.4–8.

98 DK 28B8.49–52.

99 For a detailed survey of the major commentators and their views, see Tarán 1965:202–230.

100 For a short discussion of the relative lengths of the two sections of Parmenides' poem, see Curd 1998:98, n. 1, with citations.

101 Parmenides seems to have discovered that the moon borrowed its light from the sun. The other discovery, according to the citation of Stobaeus, was that the Morning Star and the Evening Star are identical (Stobaeus, *Selections* I xxiv 2e; trans. Barnes 2001:89). Both Popper (1992:14) and Sedley (1999:123) attribute the discovery about the moon to Parmenides. There was dispute even in antiquity, however, about the identity of the discoverer. Diogenes Laertius (9.23) says that Favorinus favored Parmenides, but that others preferred Pythagoras. Diogenes himself agrees with the latter (8.14).

102 DK 28B8.53–54 (Simplicius, *Commentary on Aristotle's* Physics 145.1–146.25).

103 DK 28B9.1 (Simplicius, *Commentary on Aristotle's* Physics 180.9).

104 In this respect, if not others, Parmenides agreed with Heraclitus, who likewise admonished those, like Hesiod, who "could not recognize day and night, for they are one" (DK22B57 [Hippolytus, *Refutation* 9.10.2]).

105 DK 28B8.61.

106 DK 28B1.31–32 (Simplicius, *Commentary on Aristotle's* On the Heavens, 557.25–558.2).

107 See Chapter 4, sections 4.1–4.

[108] Kingsley 2004:162, citing D.L. 9.21 = Sotion, fr. 27 (Wehrli). See also Kingsley 2004:156–57, 180, 186, 206.

[109] DK45D2, Iamblichus, *Life of Pythagoras* 137; trans. Cornford 1922, 142.

[110] Riedweg describes the intellectual climate of Samos in Pythagoras's early life (2005:45–46), as well as the earliest evidence (Heraclitus, DK 22B81) for his establishment of a school (2005:52).

[111] By neglecting to discuss Pythagoras, and instead discussing Pythagoreanism, we follow Aristotle, who "rarely mentions Pythagoras, more frequently speaking of 'those who are called Pythagoreans' or 'the Italians,' as though unwilling to attribute the doctrines he reports to Pythagoras himself" (McKirahan 1994:80).

[112] Huffman 1993:10.

[113] Hadot 2002:3.

[114] Ibid.

[115] The most famous Neopythagorean was Numenius of Apamea (second century C.E.).

[116] Kahn 1996:1284. Because of this importance of Plato to later Pythagoreanism, the Neopythagoreans became indistinguishable from Platonists, and *vice versa.* Kingsley (1995:217, 331) has disputed Burkert's point, arguing that Plato, especially in his myths, offers both as faithful and as eclectic a record of early Pythagorean ideas as does any other source.

[117] This is the method adopted by both Burkert and Huffman. "All the basic conceptual terms which Aristotle assigns to the Pythagoreans," Huffman thus writes, "are also found in Fragments 1–7 of Philolaus" (1993:28). Also helpful—especially when we come to Pythagorean psychology—will be fragments of Xenophanes (DK 21B7), Heraclitus (DK 22B40 and B129), and Ion (DK 36B4), as well as a comment of Herodotus (4.95). These passages appear together in McKirahan 1994:81–82. With so little contemporaneous evidence, a judicious use of later sources will sometimes be necessary to round out the picture. As for our two principal sources, Huffman (2003, 1.2) believes that they are one, that Aristotle based his account of Pythagoreanism on Philolaus's book. Riedweg (2005:79), by contrast, argues that Aristotle based his account on more than Philolaus.

[118] McEvilley 2002:85, citing Neugebauer 1957:36. See also Kahn 2001:32–33 and Burkert 2004:65.

[119] McEvilley 2002:67–97.

[120] DK 44B6a (Stobaeus, *Selections* 1.21.7d). See also Aristotle, fr. 162, quoted at Riedweg 2005:83. The series continues, so that 4:5 yields the major third, and 5:6 the minor third.

[121] Sextus Empiricus, *Against the Logicians* 7.94–95, quoted and discussed at McKirahan 1994:93. Although Sextus is late, he appears to be borrowing from Posidonius (Kahn 2001:31, n. 16), and the doctrines he reports agree with the fragment of Philolaus already cited (Stobaeus, 1.21.7d = 44B6a). Another rationale for the perfection of 10 was that 1 represented a point; 2, a line; 3, a plane figure (the triangle); and 4, a solid (the pyramid). "All these are primary and the starting points for the other figures of each kind," wrote Speusippus (fr. 4 [Lang] = DK 44A13), quoted and discussed at McKirahan 1994:100.

[122] See, e.g., DK 58B4 (Aristotle, *Metaphysics* 985b28–33); and Alexander, *Commentary on the* Metaphysics 38.10–39.20. For discussions, see McKirahan 1994:108–13 and Kahn 2001:32–33.

[123] Other sources attributed the coinage to Anaximander or Anaximenes (Peters 1967:108–9), whereas Diogenes Laertius (8.48) and Aëtius (2.1.1) attribute it to Pythagoras. We have already discussed its earliest known appearance, in Heraclitus DK 22B30.

[124] Aristotle, *Metaphysics* 1090a20–25.

[125] McKirahan 1994:93. See Chapter 2, section 2.3.

[126] DK 58B4 (Aristotle, *Metaphysics* 986a2–12); trans. McKirahan 1994:105.

[127] For brief introductions to Pythagorean astronomy and its controversies, see Kahn 2001:25–27 and McKirahan 1994:104–07. These discussions credit Aristotle's account. For a very different treatment, which begins with a rejection of Aristotle's testimony, see Kingsley 1995:172–213.

[128] Stobaeus 1.22.1d; cited in Barnes 2001:179.

[129] Kingsley 1995:172–94.

[130] Huffman 1993:283.

[131] The analogy is Aristotle's (*On the Heavens* 290b12–19).

[132] DK44B6a (Stobaeus 1.21.7d); unless otherwise noted, all translations of Presocratic fragments from DK in the remainder of this chapter are from Curd 1996.

[133] *Metaphysics* 986a21.

[134] Ibid. 987a20 = DK58B8; trans. Ross, in Barnes 1995:1561. See also *Metaphysics* 986a16–17.

[135] Ibid. 1080b17–21; trans. Ross, in Barnes 1995:1708.

[136] See, e.g., Huffman 1993:57–64. For a concise summary, see Huffman 2003 (section 3).

[137] Huffman 1993:205; cited in Kahn 2001:27.

[138] Kahn 2001:27; see also Schibli 1996.

[139] Stobaeus 1.21.8 (1.189.17 Wachsmuth); trans. Huffman 1993:227. Italics added.

[140] *Metaphysics* 983a24–32 distinguishes the four causes, but they are more thoroughly distinguished at *Physics* 194b16–195a3, and then again at 198a14–21. For a more thorough explanation, see Shields 2007:36–97.

[141] *Physics* 195b22–25.

[142] See *Metaphysics* 1.3–6. This text begins "We must inquire of what kind are the causes," and then proceeds to tell a short history of Greek philosophy. On the anachronism of Aristotle's causal analysis of the Presocratics, see Guthrie 1962:63. For a more recent, and more favorable, discussion of Aristotle's use of his causal theory as a framework for his history of preceding philosophy, see Collobert 2002.

[143] DK 11A12 (Aristotle, *Metaphysics* 1.3.983b6–27).

[144] DK 13B2 (Aëtius, 1.3.4).

[145] DK 21B29 (Philoponus, *Commentary on Aristotle's* Physics 1.5.125). See also DK 21B33.

[146] DK 21B25 (Simplicius, *Commentary on Aristotle's* Physics 23.19).

[147] *Metaphysics* 1.3.984b15–20.

[148] DK 59B1 (Simplicius, *Commentary on Aristotle's* Physics 155.26).

[149] DK 59B9 (Simplicius, *Commentary on Aristotle's* Physics 35.14–16).

[150] Ibid.

[151] *Metaphysics* 988b6–15. See also *Phaedo* 96a–99d; *Republic* 508e–509a, 511b–c, 530a6; *Timaeus* 47e4; and *Sophist* 265c4. For a comprehensive account of the

relationship between Plato's *nous*, demiurge, and the Form of the Good, see Menn 1995 (especially 6–18, 45–46).

[152] *Metaphysics* 987b10–11.

[153] Kahn 2001:28.

[154] Kahn 2001:28.

[155] Plato, *Philebus* 23c9–10.

[156] See, e.g., *Metaphysics* 986a23. The only exception was the number one, which was of both types (986a20). As for the Greek terms, a comment is in order about their translation. The first evokes Anaximander, whose *archē* was the *apeiron*, which is most often translated as the "indefinite." In order to appreciate the continuity of Pythagorean thought with its precedents, then, it will be helpful to remember that the term persists, even though it is usually given a different translation in discussions of Pythagoreanism—namely, "unlimited." Translators seem to choose this English approximation because the second Greek term with which it is contrasted above, *peperasmenon*, derives from *peras*, which is best translated as "limit."

[157] Huffman 1993:39.

[158] DK 44B1 (D.L. 8.85); slightly rev. from trans. McKirahan, in Curd 1996:22. The Greek verb is *harmozō*, and it exhibits the same range of meanings as *harmonia*: "to join," "to compose," and also "to harmonize."

[159] Kahn 1974, 173; cited in Huffman 1993 (204).

[160] Aristotle, *Physics* 213b25–26; trans. R. P. Hardie and R. K. Gaye, in Barnes 1995:363.

[161] Cornford 1922:145. Cited in Guthrie 1962:248.

[162] *Nicomachean Ethics* 1106b29–30. For the equation of justice with number, see DK 58B4 (*Metaphysics* 985b28–33).

[163] This translation and arrangement of *Metaphysics* 986a22–26 appears in McKirahan 1994:107. For a discussion of *archē* (pl., *archai*), a central concept in early Greek philosophy, see Guthrie 1962:57 and Peters 1967:23–25. From this word, which we shall translate as "principle," we derive "archaic," "archaeology," "architecture," etc.

[164] At *Metaphysics* 986b4–6, Aristotle writes: "how these principles can be brought together under the causes we have named has not been clearly stated by them" (trans. W. D. Ross, in Barnes 1995:1560). But he also says that "the principles in the second column are indefinite because they are privative," a notion he then proceeds to explain (*Physics* 201b25–26; trans. Ross, in Barnes 1995:344). For a modern treatment, see McKirahan 1994:108.

[165] The articles of Cornford (1922, 1923) made the biggest strides. The chapters of Guthrie 1962 (212–306) and McKirahan 1994 (79–116, but especially 94–97) summarize the progress that has been made in the meantime.

[166] From this system we derive some of our own mathematical terminology. The square root of a number, for example, is the length of its sides when it is formed as a square.

[167] Explanations for some of the other oppositions can be found in McKirahan 1994:94–108, but especially 107–08.

[168] Cornford 1922:141.

[169] See Cornford 1903:441, Notopoulos 1944a:165–67, Notopoulos 1944b:229 n. 97, and especially Classen 1965.

[170] Boyce 1984:45.

[171] *Bundahišn* 1.1; trans. Boyce 1984:45. See also *Bundahishn* 1.39–42.

[172] Skjærvø 2010:57.

[173] West 1971:30.

[174] E.g., *Yasna* 30.

[175] Skjærvø 2010:55.

[176] Nigosian 2003:16.

[177] These accounts are: Cicero (whose dates are: 106–43), Strabo (63–21), Plutarch (50–120), Apuleius (120–170), Clement of Alexandria (150–216), Hippolytus (170–236), Porphyry (234–305), and Iamblichus (245–325). For full citations and discussion see Guthrie 1962:217–18, 253–54.

[178] Guthrie 1962:249–50.

[179] West 1971:32. Hippolytus (fr. 13 Wehrli, *Refutation* 1.2.12) attributes the story to Aristoxenus and Diodorus of Eretria. "Zaratas," adds West, "is of course Zoroaster" (1971:32, n. 2).

[180] Guthrie 1962:250.

[181] Skjærvø 2010:58; citing *Yasna* 28.2, 43.3 and 53.6. See also *Greater Bundahišn* 1.13–14.

[182] Nigosian 2003:84–89.

[183] Skjærvø 2010:65; see also Nigosian 2003:82.

[184] Supra note 139.

[185] The Zoroastrian 'models' also anticipate in some ways Plato's Forms—which were perfect models for everything in the sensible world, and which his philosophers were to contemplate and emulate, as we shall see in chapter 4.

[186] Choksy 1989:8. For a discussion of the many rituals see Choksy, chapters 2–4; for a brief summary, see Nigosian 2003:104–09.

[187] Nigosian 2003:91. Although written in Sasanian times, some of the *Vidēvdāt's* prohibitions appear in classical authors. Choksy (1989:85, 87) cites Xenophon and Ammianus Marcellinus.

[188] Nigosian 2003:91, 118.

[189] Nigosian 2003:111.

[190] Choksy 1989:9.

[191] For translations of the most important passages, see Nigosian 2003:54–57.

[192] Choksy 1989:18; see also Nigosian 2003:108.

[193] Choksy 1989:80, citing *Vidēvdāt* 17:1–10.

[194] DK 58C3 (Aristotle fr. 195 [Rose], quoted in D.L. 8.34 ff.).

[195] D.L. 8.17.

[196] Douglas 2004:42, 64.

[197] Douglas 2004:xvii.

[198] Douglas 2004:44, 50.

[199] Douglas 2004:5, 7.

[200] Douglas 2004:117.

[201] Ibid.

[202] D.L. 8.17. Kahn admits that the Pythagorean *akousmata*, or sayings, are mysterious, suggesting that they "seem to have served as observances and passwords to mark membership in the Pythagorean community" (2001:10).

[203] Nigosian 2003:113.

[204] *Vidēvdāt* 8.79–80; cited in West 1971:185.

[205] *Yasna* 36; trans. Boyce 1984:54. For the Platonic notion of a Form of Forms, as well as its analogy with the sun, see Chapter 4, section 4.6–7.

[206] Choksy 1989:13. See *Yasna* 25.7, 36.1; *Ataxsh Niyayishn* 1.1; and *Zadspram* 3.82–83. See also Nigosian 2003:113.

[207] Nigosian 2003:88.

[208] *Vidēvdāt (Vendidad)* 19.32; trans. Boyce 1984:80. See also *Arda Viraz Namag* 12.1–2.

[209] McEvilley 2002:5.

[210] DK 11A5 (Herodotus 1.74). For the "beginning" of Presocratic philosophy, see, e.g., Curd 1996:1.

[211] McEvilley 2002:6, n.22; McKirahan 1994:24–25.

[212] 1.1 –5; trans. Alexander Heidel 1963:18.

[213] Naddaf 2005:39. See also McEvilley 2002:29.

[214] Buchanan Gray 1964:9–10.

[215] "La préexistence des âmes n'est attestée en Iran que tardivement." Duchesne-Guillemin 1953:101; cited in Guthrie 1962:254–55.

[216] West 1971:89.

[217] DK 12A15 (Aristotle, *Physics* 203b10–15).

[218] DK 12B1 + A9 (Simplicius, *Commentary on Aristotle's* Physics 24.13–21).

[219] In addition to the Upaniṣadic passages we shall quote, West 1971:93–94 supplies several others. In other words, there is no shortage of evidence for a resemblance between Anaximander and early Indian philosophy.

[220] *Bṛhadāraṇyaka Upaniṣad* 4.4.20; trans. R. E. Hume, in S. Radhakrishnan and C. A. Moore 1989:88. Unless otherwise indicated, all translations of the Upaniṣads are from Radhakrishnan and Moore 1989.

[221] McEvilley 2002:60, with citations.

[222] *Kaṭha Upaniṣad* 2.18.

[223] *Śvetāśvatara Upaniṣad* 3.7.

[224] *Kaṭha Upaniṣad* 5.12.

[225] *Bṛhadāraṇyaka Upaniṣad* 4.5.15. See also 4.4.20.

[226] *Bṛhadāraṇyaka Upaniṣad* 4.4.19.

[227] See, e.g., *Muṇḍaka Upaniṣad* 1.1.7, 3.2.7–8; *Chāndogya Upaniṣad* 6.10.1, 8.7.4; *Bṛhadāraṇyaka Upaniṣad* 2.3.1; *Śvetāśvatara Upaniṣad* 4.9.

[228] McEvilley 2002:59 lists eight general parallels between early Greek and Indian philosophies. Chapter 2 (pages 23–66) discusses many specific parallels. These latter, in particular, are specific and numerous enough to dismiss the obvious objection—*post hoc ergo propter hoc*—to the hypothesis of Indian influence over early Greek philosophy.

[229] West 1971:201–02. For the abundant similarities between Heraclitus and Eastern ideas, see West 1971:165–202. For a summary of his similarities with the Upaniṣads, see McEvilley 2002:36–44.

[230] McEvilley 2002:5–18.

[231] Herodotus, 4.44. "Scylax's book, along with the later work of Ctesias of Cnidus, who was himself in Persian service in the late fifth century B.C., was one of 'the two standard descriptions of India before Alexander the Great'" (McEvilley 2002:8, citing Halbfass 1988:11).

[232] McEvilley 2002:60, n. 68.

[233] McEvilley 2002:16.

234 Herodotus 3.120–28, 139–49.

235 D.L. 8.3.

236 Herodotus 3.129–37.

237 Democedes seems to have acquired his original training in Croton. Within one year of emigrating, he was recognized in Aegina, his new residence, as the best of the island's physicians (Herodotus 3.131).

238 It is likely that Darius kept physicians of different nationalities in his court, for Democedes displaced the Egyptians who had tried to treat Darius before him (Herodotus 3.132).

239 McEvilley 2002:16; see also 208–12.

240 Herodotus 6.20 and 6.119. See McEvilley 2002:8–9.

241 These were called *kurtash*, writes McEvilley (2002:8), and "among the *kurtash* were individuals from conquered populations, including both Ionians and Bactrians."

242 3.38; trans. Robin Waterfield 1998:186–87; see McEvilley 2002:6–7.

243 Eusebius, *Preparation for the Gospel* 11.3.8; cited in McEvilley 2002:10. See also McEvilley 2002:16–18.

244 4.4.22.

245 Ibid.

246 McEvilley 2002:117. See also 2002:111, 118.

247 McEvilley 2002:117.

248 *Chāndogya Upaniṣad* 2.23.3.

249 *Kaṭha Upaniṣad* 3.8.

250 *Bṛhadāraṇyaka Upaniṣad* 4.4.19.

251 *Muṇḍaka Upaniṣad* 6.18. See also *Kaṭha Upaniṣad* 6.6–15.

252 6.34.

253 *Bṛhadāraṇyaka Upaniṣad* 1.4.10; quoted in McEvilley 2002:100.

254 Guthrie 1962:251 cites Zeller and Ueberweg-Praechter.

255 Burkert 1985:299.

256 Kahn 2001:19. See also Gomperz 1920:126–27.

257 McEvilley 2002:98.

258 DK 21B7 (D.L., 8.36).

259 Moulinier 1975:119; trans. PLM.

260 DK 44B14 (Clement, *Miscellanies* 3.3.17.1); trans. Barnes 2001:181.

261 Phi, 214; McEvilley 202:103 also mentions Cicero, *Tusculan Disputations* 1.38, as indirect evidence.

262 West 1971:3.

263 He was said to have written a book that went by the name *Theokrasia*, which may be translated "Divine Mingling" (with Kirk et al. 1983:51), or even "Fusion with God" (with Lafontaine 1986:49).

264 D.L. 8.2.

265 Riedweg 2005:9.

266 DK 36B4 (D.L., 1.120).

267 For a list of them, see Riedweg 2005:52–53.

268 In the late sixth century, the two major Pythagorean settlements were Croton and Metapontum. At the beginning of the fifth century, however, Pythagoreans there suffered a political catastrophe in which many of them were murdered. Nevertheless, their intellectual influence in the region lingered after they lost political power (Huffman 2005:8–18). Tarentum, for instance, was lead by

Archytas, one of the three most important Pythagoreans of antiquity (along with Philolaus, and of course Pythagoras himself). "It is quite plausible to regard Tarentum as one of the most powerful of all Greek city-states in this period" (Huffman 2006:11, citing Purcell 1994:388).

269 Kingsley 1995:257.

270 *Olympian Odes* 2.65–66; trans. Race 1997a:71.

271 *Orphic Fragments* 60–235. For complete citations and discussion, see Burkert 1985:297–98, n. 15). See also Bluck 1964:278–79. For a complete treatment of Pindar's eschatology, see Lloyd-Jones 1990:80–103.

272 Plato, *Meno* 81b8–c4. Pindar fr. 133, Snell; Race 1997b:369.

273 D.L. 8.54–56.

274 DK 31B129 (Porphyry, *Life of Pythagoras* 30); trans. Barnes 2001:161. There is some controversy about the object of this praise. Riedweg (2005:54–55) makes a good case for Pythagoras.

275 Ibid.

276 DK 31B117 (Hippolytus, *Refutation* 1.3.2; trans. Barnes 2001:157. McEvilley (2002:107) has noticed that each of the animal species may represent an Empedoclean element: earth (bush), water, (fish), air (bird). Having been a girl, moreover, he had lived as each gender.

277 DK 31B127 (Aelian, *On the Nature of Animals* 12.7); trans. Barnes 2001:157.

278 McEvilley 2002:141–42; cf. Herodotus, 2.123.

279 For the action of Love and Strife, see the fragments quoted by Barnes (2001:132–34), namely DK 31B16, B35, B71, B73, B75, B86–87, and B95. See also Aristotle, *Metaphysics* 985a21–b3.

280 *Metaphysics* 985a5–9; trans. Barnes 1995:1558.

281 DK 31B134 (Ammonius, *Commentary on Aristotle's* On Interpretation 249.1–10); trans. Barnes 2001:140. On the Empedoclean sphere, see the fragments collected in Barnes 2001:140–41. For Greek reverence of the sphere, see Guthrie 1962:351–54 and 1965:47.

282 DK 31B115.6 (Plutarch, *On Exile* 607CE); trans. Barnes 2001:113.

283 Ibid.

284 DK 31B35 (Simplicius, *Commentary of Aristotle's* On the Heavens 528.30–530.1); trans. Barnes 2001:133.

285 Hippolytus, *Refutation* 7.29.14–23; trans. Barnes 2001:115.

286 Plutarch, *Commentary on the Golden Verses* 24.2; trans. Barnes 2001, 145.

287 DK 31B17 (Simplicius, *Commentary on Aristotle's* Physics 157.25–159.10).

288 Ibid.; trans. Barnes 2001:121.

289 Hippolytus, *Refutation* 7.29.14–23; trans. Barnes 2001:115.

290 DK 31B137 (Sextus Empiricus, *Against the Logicians* 9.127–29); trans. Barnes 2001:158.

291 Hippolytus, *Refutation* 7.29.14–23; trans. Barnes 2001:115.

292 One of the most controversial questions of Empedoclean scholarship is whether Empedocles wrote two poems—*Peri Phuseōs* and *Katharmoi*—or one poem that went by these two names. Taking a position on this question is not our concern here, but discussions of it can be found in Inwood 2001 (8–21), favoring one poem, and Kingsley 1995 (363–70), favoring two.

293 DK 31B132 (Clement, *Miscellanies* 5.14.140.5); trans. Barnes 2001:117.

[294] DK 31B146 (Clement, *Miscellanies* 4.13.150.1). Empedocles was a political leader who prevented a tyranny in Agrigentum (D.L., 8.72). The isolation of certain stations as penultimate stages before immortalization recalls the Upaniṣad-doctrine that members of the highest caste, the Brahmins, were most likely to escape reincarnation (McEvilley 2002:113). Both doctrines anticipate Plato's belief, which we shall discuss in Chapter 4, that philosophers are the highest mortal stage before the divine.

[295] DK 31B147 (Clement, *Miscellanies* 5.14.122.3); trans. Barnes 2001:157.

[296] D.L. 8.69. For other references, see Kingsley 1995:233.

[297] For Greek purification by fire, see Kingsley 1995:252. For the volcano as a gateway to both the fiery underworld below and the fiery heavens above, see Kingsley 1995:50–53. Still more bizarre than the volcano was the shoe it was said to spew forth after Empedocles dove into its crater. "This one bronze sandal," writes Kingsley, "was the chief 'sign' or 'symbol' of Hecate who, as the 'controller of Tartarus' and mediator between this world and the next, grants the magician access to the underworld" (Kingsley 1995:238, which cites the work of A. Dietrich).

[298] DK 31B112 (D.L., 8.62).

[299] For Homer's portrait of the soul's life after death, see *Odyssey* 11, otherwise known as the *Nekyia*, or Book of the Dead. Helpful commentaries on Homeric psychology and eschatology include Snell 1960, Claus 1981, and Bremmer 1983.

[300] *Odyssey* 11.489–491; trans. Fagles 1996:265.

[301] As mentioned in n. 91, the most famous of the early philosopher-physicians were Pythagoreans, or at least associated with Pythagoreanism.

[302] DK 31B111 (D.L., 8.59); trans. Inwood 2001:219.

[303] Ibid.

[304] See *Iliad* 4.320–21, 9.445–446, *Odyssey* 13.59–60; cited and discussed by Kinglsey 1995:222.

[305] "*Athanatos* (immortal) . . . means god and nothing else" (Guthrie 1955:115; see also 239). O'Cleirigh and Barrell 2000:50–53 discuss the equation of immortality and divinity, as well as other unique features of the traditional Greek notion of *theos*. See also Burkert 1985:121–22, 162, and 298; Kingsley 1995:222–23; Dodds 1951:10; and Kahn 1979:218–19.

[306] Burkert 1985:203–15, especially 205. For an opposing view of Dionysus, see Kerényi 1996.

[307] Kingsley 1995:269.

[308] Burkert 1985:211.

[309] Kingsley 1995:274.

[310] Ibid., 225–26.

[311] Ibid., 253.

[312] *Pythian Ode* 3.61; trans. Race 1997a:251. "Do not seek to become Zeus," he wrote in *Isthmian Ode* 5.14; trans. Race 1997b:177. See also Euripides (*Alcestis* 799) and Epicharmus (DK 23B20, quoted by Aristotle at *Rhetoric* 1394b25).

[313] Euripides, *Alcestis* 1072–1158.

[314] Kingsley 1995:276.

[315] Ibid., 253.

[316] Ibid., 264. For other discussions, see Graf 1993 and Burkert 1985:293.

[317] Kingsley 1995:266, with citations.

[318] Supra note 271.

[319] Burkert 1985:162.

[320] Kingsley 1995:262, with citations. For skepticism about the connection between Archytas and Dionysus (as well as Orphism), see Huffman 2005:306–07.

[321] Burkert 1985:289 cites three sources: *Hymn to Demeter* 280–82, Pindar fr. 137a, and Sophocles fr. 837 (Pearson-Radt).

[322] Graf 1993:239–40.

[323] 73–107, especially 102.

[324] 948–54; trans. PLM.

[325] Aristophanes' *Frogs* (1032–33) mentions Orpheus in connection with mystic rites and abstinence from slaughter. Plato mentions "a noisy throng of books by Musaeus and Orpheus" (*Republic* 2.364e3).

[326] Burkert 1985:297. The touchstone for this point is the coincidence of the Gutenberg bible and the Protestant Reformation.

[327] D.L., 8.8; trans. Barnes 2001:29.

[328] Herodotus, 2.81; trans. Waterfield 1998:126.

[329] About the Egyptians, it must be said, Herodotus seems to be mistaken. Whether or not they were debarred from burial in wool, "current knowledge indicates that the Egyptians were not familiar with the doctrine of rebirth" (Riedweg 2005:56). For a more sympathetic reading, see Burkert 2004 (98).

[330] With an apt metaphor from geometry, Burkert describes them as three intersecting circles (1985:300). See also Cornford 1922:143 and Kahn 2001:20–22.

[331] Kingsley 1995:262–72 discusses the complicated relationship between them.

[332] Although Empedocles preached chastity, Pythagoras was said to be married (D.L. 8.42). If nothing else, the claim about Pythagoras's marriage indicates that later Pythagoreans were not celibate.

[333] Although Empedocles preached vegetarianism, Burkert has argued that early Pythagoreans tailored their dietary restrictions in order not to conflict with civic religion and its public sacrifices (Kahn 2001:9, with citations). There was debate in late antiquity about the origins and meanings of Pythagorean food taboos (e.g., D.L. 8.12–13).

[334] For other, still odder, prohibitions, see D.L., 8.17–20, and Iamblichus *Life of Pythagoras* 28.81–87. For a summary and discussion of Pythagorean dietary rules, see Riedweg 2005:67–71. See also Kingsley 1995:283–85.

[335] McEvilley 2002:101.

[336] That Anaximenes posited infinite (or "limitless": *apeiron*) air is testified by Hippolytus and Olympiodorus. See Barnes 2001:24, 26. The Pythagoreans adopted something like this view, believing that the world inhales the infinite fiery-air (*pneuma*) that surrounds it (Aristotle, *Physics* 213b22–26). Huffman (2003) also discusses Fr. 201, which describes the universe as drawing in time, breath, and void from the unlimited (2.1). Guthrie (1962:469–73) sees echoes of this view in Heraclitus, calling it "a common notion of the universe" shared by most of the Presocratics.

[337] DK 13A10 (Cicero, *Nature of the Gods* 1.10.26). Before Anaximenes, Thales had thought that "everything was full of gods" (*On the Soul*, 411a7–8; trans. Barnes 2001:12).

[338] DK 44B17 (Aristotle, fr. 201); trans. Huffman 1993:43.

³³⁹ Sextus Empiricus, *Against the Logicians* 7.92; trans. Barnes 2001:178. For Empedocles' similar 'like-to-like' theory of thinking, see 31B107 (Theophrastus, *On the Senses* 10); for his 'like-to-like' theory of nutrition, see 31B90. Kingsley (1995:298) argues that this theory had special significance for Empedocles; in any case, the theory of perception according to which "like is naturally apprehended by like" may date back to Pythagoras himself (Aëtius, 4.13.9–10 [*Doxographi Graeci* 404] = DK 28A48).

³⁴⁰ Many scholars believe that this fusion of religion and mathematics was not likely a feature of early Pythagoreanism. "It is universally recognized," writes Fritz Graf in the *Oxford Classical Dictionary*, "that scientific Pythagoreanism is a reform of its earlier, religious way ascribed to Hippasus of Metapontum around 450 BC." (1284). One prominent dissenter from this "universal" consensus is Kahn (2001:37–38).

³⁴¹ Not all Pythagoreans would maintain both aspects of this revolution. Sometime in the fifth century, according to later testimonies, a schism arose within their society (Iamblichus, *Life of Pythagoras* 81, 82; for a fuller account of the differences, see Guthrie 1962:191–93, McKirahan 1994:89–93, and Riedweg 2005:106–08. On one hand, those calling themselves *akousmatikoi* dogmatically preserved the moral and religious sayings, or *akousmata*, attributed to Pythagoras himself. (The Greek verb *akouein* means "to hear," so that an *akousma* means "something heard," and *akousmata* is its plural form. An *akousmatikos* is thus someone eager to hear something, and *akousmatikoi* its plural form.) Those calling themselves *mathēmatikoi*, on the other hand, continued in the spirit of innovation and learning, or *mathēma*, which they attributed to the founder. Although the *mathēmatikoi* accepted the legitimacy of their rivals, the *akousmatikoi* did not extend to theirs the same generosity. So long as the original synthesis of religion and philosophy persisted, however, the Pythagoreans urged more vigilant care of one's soul, and especially of one's thought, in ways that refashioned both fields.

³⁴² *Bṛhadāraṇyaka Upaniṣad* 4.4.20.

³⁴³ See, e.g., *Muṇḍaka Upaniṣad* 1.1.7, 3.2.7–8; *Chāndogya Upaniṣad* 6.10.1, 8.7.4; *Bṛhadāraṇyaka Upaniṣad* 2.3.1; *Śvetāśvatara Upaniṣad* 4.9.

Chapter 4

¹ *Phaedo* 82b10–11; trans. G. M. A. Grube, in Cooper 1997:72. (All translations of Plato are from Cooper 1997 unless otherwise indicated.) See also *Phaedo* 85a2.

² Ibid. 80c–84b.

³ Ibid. 96a7–8. The Greek translated here by "natural science" is *peri phuseōs historia*.

⁴ The dates of Presocratic lives are often estimates: Thales (ca. 625–545), Anaximander (ca. 610–540), Anaximenes (ca. 585–525), Xenophanes (ca. 570–478), Heraclitus (ca. 537–480), Parmenides (late sixth to mid-fifth century). Socrates, we know for sure, died in 399 B.C.; his birth year has been estimated at 470.

⁵ DK 11A12 (Aristotle, *Metaphysics* 983b20).

⁶ DK 12B1 + A9 (Simplicius, *Commentary on Aristotle's* Physics 24.12–21). For a recent account of Anaximander, see Naddaf 2005:63–112.

7 DK 13B2 (Aëtius, 1.3.4). For the association of *psychē* and breath, see Claus
   1981:61, citing *Iliad* 22.467. Diogenes Laertius, however, writes that Xenophanes
   "was the first to declare that . . . the soul is breath" (9.19). For a recent account
   of Anaximenes, see Graham 2006:45–84.

8 DK 13A5 (Theophrastus, quoted by Simplicius, *Commentary on Aristotle's* Physics
   24.26–25.1).

9 *Phaedo* 97c8. Italics added.

10 See, e.g., DK 68B9 (=B125) (Sextus Empiricus, *Against the Logicians* 7.135); and
   also DK 67A18 (Aristotle, *Metaphysics* 1071b33–35). The dates of Leucippus are
   very uncertain; in fact, there was some doubt even in antiquity whether he existed
   at all (D.L. 10.13 = DK 67A2). Those who believe that he did estimate that we was
   born in, perhaps, 470, and died in 390. Democritus's dates are more certain:
   460–370, making him a younger contemporary of Socrates. Plato's total neglect
   of him in the dialogues is therefore quite remarkable. Although their productive
   lives overlapped, Plato makes no explicit mention of him anywhere. That said, he
   does seem to have him in mind when he describes the intellectual battle between
   materialists and formalists, a battle he likens to the Gigantomachy (*Sophist*
   246a3–c3).

11 *Nous* has been translated by 'intelligence,' 'mind,' 'thought,' 'reason,' and
   'understanding,' among other English words. This diversity arises not only from
   the usual difficulties of translation, but more so from the long and distinguished
   career of the word and its cognates in Greek philosophy. Most notably, Plato
   appropriated it to name his highest epistemic state, as well as his highest god;
   Aristotle did the same, while also using it as the name of the highest part of the
   human soul; finally, Plotinus chose it as the name for his second hypostasis.
   Stephen Menn (1995:14–18) describes the difficulty of translating *nous* and
   exposes the inadequacy of the standard translations. To use one of them always,
   in the interests of an artificial consistency, would sometimes become awkward.
   We shall thus vary our translation when required by the context, but shall favor
   "thought" when appropriate. To begin with Anaxagoras, this is the translation
   favored by Barnes 2001:185–98.

12 *Phaedo* 97c2–6. *Nous* substituted for "Mind" in the Grube translation.

13 For the Aristotelian distinction among causes, see *Physics* 194b17–195a3 and
   Metaphysics 983b23–985b24. See also Chapter 3, note 140.

14 *Phaedo* 98b7–c2.

15 Ibid. 98c5–8.

16 See, e.g., DK 59B13 (Simplicius, *Commentary on Aristotle's* Physics 300.31–301.1).

17 *Phaedo* 99b2–4.

18 *Crito* 44e–46a.

19 Ibid. 50a–52d.

20 D.L. 8.46 = Aristoxenus fr. 19 Wehrli.

21 Simmias and Cebes are said to have spent time in the company of Philolaus
   (*Phaedo* 61d6–7). The dramatic locale is given at 57a. As for Echecrates, Diogenes
   Laertius (8.46) reports that "the last of the Pythagoreans, whom Aristoxenus
   in his time saw, were Xenophilus from Thracian Chalcidice, Phanton of Phlius,
   and Echecrates, Diocles, and Polymnastus, also of Phlius, who were pupils of
   Philolaus and Eurytus of Tarentum."

22 For the origins of the Pythagorean program of purification and divinization, see Chapter 3, especially section 3.6. For Parmenides' principle of non-contradiction, see especially section 3.1.

23 E.g. *Clouds* 228–34.

24 DK 11A9 (Plato, *Theaetetus* 174a4–5). All translations of Presocratic fragments in this chapter are from Curd 1996, unless otherwise indicated.

25 *Clouds* 173; trans. P. Meineck, in Reeve 2002:98. All translations of *Clouds* are from this edition, unless otherwise indicated.

26 *Clouds* 160–64. The butt of this joke is more immediately Diogenes of Apollonia, who adopted both Anaximenes' *archē* and his mechanism. See, e.g., DK 64A1 (D.L. 9.57).

27 *Clouds* 380.

28 DK 64B5 (Simplicius, *Commentary on Aristotle's* Physics 152.22–153.17). See Guthrie 1962:129–30. Diogenes' dates are 460–362.

29 *Clouds* 316–317. "Thought," said Diogenes, "is due to air that is pure and dry" (DK 64A19 [Theophrastus, *On the Senses* 39–45]). Here Diogenes echoes the views attributed earlier to Heraclitus (DK 22B118 [Stobaeus, *Selections* 3.5.8]). Both believed that inebriation moistened the soul (DK 22B117 and DK 64A19).

30 *Clouds* 229–230; trans. A. H. Sommerstein 1991:33.

31 For a mockery of Prodicus in particular, see 666. For Sophistic rhetoric more generally, see the clash of the two *logoi*: 889–1103.

32 *Clouds* 642–643.

33 Ibid. 258. Kenneth Dover discusses the specific rites to which these lines may be referring (1989:130–131). Cornford believed these references to be Orphic (1903:437, n. 2) and cites in this connection *Birds* 1555.

34 *Clouds* 140.

35 Guthrie 1962:149–50 cites Iamblichus's *Life of Pythagoras* 88 = DK 18,4.

36 *Apology* 33b6–9; trans. Reeve 2002:49. (All translations of *Apology* are from Reeve 2002, unless otherwise indicated.) The following interpretation of this dialogue owes much to Reeve 1989.

37 *Apology* 19b4–c1.

38 *Apology* 19c5.

39 Ibid. 19d7–20b6, 21d1–7. Socrates' confessions of ignorance are not unique to *Apology*; they can also be found in the following dialogues: *Euthyphro* 5a3–c7, 15c11–16a4; *Charmides* 165b4–c2, 166c7–d6; *Laches* 186b8–c5, d8–e3, 200e2–5; *Lysis* 212a4–7, 223b4–8; *Meno* 71a1–7, 80d1–4; *Greater Hippias* 286c8–e2, 304d4–e5; *Gorgias* 506a3–4, 509a5; and *Symposium* 216d1–4. The list is comprehensive according to Irwin 1977:39.

40 *Apology* 33a5. See also *Theaetetus* 150b–151b.

41 *Protagoras* 333a1–2, and 6–7.

42 *Gorgias* 483b7–c3.

43 *Apology* 20d7–8, 23a4–6, 23b1–3.

44 Ibid. 30a5, 33c4–6.

45 Cornford 1903:437.

46 *Sophist* 230d6–8; slightly rev. from trans. N. P. White, in Cooper 1997:251.

47 *Apology* 28e4–6.

48 Ibid. 29e1–2, 30b1–2.

[49] The classic paper on the novelty of Socratic psychology is Burnet 1916. Qualifications and challenges to Burnet's view have been advanced by Claus 1981 and Solmsen 1983. Speaking of DK 22B107, Kahn notices that Heraclitus identifies the psyche as "the cognitive or rational element in human beings," adding that "this intellectual conception of the psyche must be emphasized here, since it has been overlooked in several influential studies where the originality of Socrates in this respect has been grossly overstated" (Kahn 1979:127).

[50] See, e.g., *Republic* 2.377b–383c, *Laws* 4.717a–b.

[51] *Laws* 10.908a7–909d2.

[52] For his respect for oracles see, e.g., *Laws* 5.738b–c, 7.792d2–4. His eschatological myths come at the end of three dialogues: *Gorgias*, *Phaedo*, and *Republic*; *Phaedrus* 246a ff. narrates the ascent of the soul to the heavenly realm; *Timaeus* contributes a divine cosmogony.

[53] *Republic* 2.383c2–3. (All translations of this dialogue are from Reeve 2004, unless otherwise noted.) See also *Republic* 6.500c9–d1, 10.613a7–b1; *Phaedrus* 252e7–253a5; *Theaetetus* 176a8–b3, 176b8–c3; *Timaeus* 90b6–c6.

[54] *Apology* 23a6.

[55] *Gorgias* 509a5–7. Italics added.

[56] *Cratylus* 436c8–d2; see also *Republic* 7.533c2–5.

[57] *Gorgias* 483b4–c1.

[58] *Republic* 1.338c1–2. Although this claim about the stronger appears at odds with Callicles' about the weak, by "stronger" Thrasymachus means those who institute laws, the very people in a democracy such as Athens whom Callicles calls the weak.

[59] Marx and Nietzsche proposed two different diagnoses of the traditional beliefs about justice in their own society, diagnoses that resembled the critiques of Thrasymachus and Callicles respectively. According to Marx, on the one hand, traditional beliefs about justice preserve the *status quo* of property relations and thus serve the advantage of the stronger (*The German Ideology*, Part One). For Nietzsche, on the other, the naturally weak have fashioned traditional beliefs about justice and have promoted them through philosophy and religion in order to tame the naturally strong (*The Genealogy of Morality*, especially 1.14). In both cases, however, traditional beliefs about justice are a false ideology, whether preserved through "false consciousness" or "slave morality."

[60] C. D. C. Reeve first makes this point in Reeve 1988:10–16 and then again in Grube 1992:xiv–xvii.

[61] *Meno* 82b–86c. For a discussion, see Kahn 2001:54.

[62] *Meno* 80e3–5.

[63] *Topics* 183b7–8.

[64] *Metaphysics* 987b1–2, *Parts of Animals* 642a28–31.

[65] *Metaphysics* 987a32–b10, 1078b12–1079a4, 1086a37–b11. These citations of Aristotle concerning the difference between Socrates and Plato come from T. Irwin's fuller discussion of the subject in Irwin 1995:8–11.

[66] Cooper 1997:xv.

[67] For fuller discussions of the classification of Plato's dialogues, see Irwin 1995:11–13 and Cooper 1997:xii–xviii. There are three salient differences between these accounts. Generally, Irwin credits stylometry more than does Cooper. As a result,

Irwin divides the corpus more finely, into four groups rather than three, and adopts the chronological labels ("early," "second," "third," and "latest") that Cooper uses more gingerly (preferring the categories "Socratic," "second," and "latest," with no chronological sequence implied between the first two). For the sake of simplicity, this chapter adopts Cooper's scheme. For an altogether different approach to the order of the Platonic corpus, see Annas 1999.

68 By Cooper's reckoning, the dialogues of the second group include *Meno, Symposium, Phaedo, Republic, Phaedrus, Parmenides, Cratylus,* and *Theaetetus* (in no particular order). All of these will prove useful to us, as will passages from the latest group—*Timaeus, Sophist, Statesman, Philebus,* and *Laws.*

69 These include the Heraclitean understanding of time, Anaxagoras's doctrine of *nous,* Hippocratic medicine, and Sophistic rhetoric. We shall discuss Heraclitus and Anaxagoras all-too-briefly below. Now, however, let us say that the Hippocratic theory of health as a balance of humors (see, e.g., *Nature of Man*), which itself owes much to the Pythagoreans (especially Alcmaeon of Croton), corresponds neatly with the Platonic account of virtue as a harmony of soul-parts (*Republic* 4.444d3–e3). As for the Sophists, they appear often as characters in the dialogues; and despite Plato's numerous criticisms of them he occasionally adopts their ideas. For instance, the Sophistic diagnosis of god as the invention of a clever statesman (*Sisyphus,* DK 88B25) anticipates Plato's "noble lie" (*Republic* 3.414b–416d), both of which resemble the parade of shadows at the bottom of the Cave (*Republic* 514b1–515a1).

70 Socrates uses interrogative particles that suggest the correct answers—whether yes or no—to the slave. In the Greek, a positive answer is suggested by *oukoun* (83b3, e5; 85a1), but also in their contexts *ouchi* (83c3, 4; 85a5), *ēou* (83d1), and *ouch* (83d2), while *oud' ar'* suggests a negative answer. In English these particles are rendered by Grube (Cooper 1997) respectively as "is it not?" (suggested answer: it is) and "it cannot be, can it?" (suggested answer: it cannot).

71 Socrates never notices that a parallel paradox of recollection arises alongside Meno's paradox of learning. After all, if memory is like an aviary, as Plato imagines in *Theaetetus* (197b–199c), and recollection is akin to seeking and finding within it a particular bird, then recollection should require that we already know what we seek. We cannot find a particular bird unless we already know what it looks like. When the object of our search is knowledge, however, knowing what we seek is already to possess it. Recollection therefore appears as impossible as learning. Aristotle will later argue that neither are in fact impossible because both can proceed with only partial knowledge, whereas Meno's paradox assumes that they need total knowledge. Thus, for example, when I seek a particular bird in an aviary, I must know some things about it (e.g., what it looks like) but need not know others (e.g., where it is). "What is absurd," observed Aristotle, "is not that you should know in some sense what you are learning, but that you should know it in *this* sense, i.e., in the way and sense in which you are learning it" (*Posterior Analytics* 71b7–9). Aristotle's argument fails, however, if the objects of knowledge do not admit such different senses because they are simple unities, as Plato believes.

72 The most succinct statement of this argument can be found in *Phaedo* 72e2–73b2, a fuller version follows this, 73b3–77a5.

73 See Chapter 3, section 3.6.

74   *Meno* 81c5–d5.
75   Ibid.
76   *Phaedrus* 249c3–4.
77   Ibid. 249c1–3.
78   Ibid. 249d5–6. For a very similar account, see *Phaedo* 73b3–77a5. *Symposium* seems similar, inasmuch as the sight of bodily beauty ideally provokes one to contemplate higher beauties, arriving ultimately at Beauty itself. But the process of ascent in *Symposium* is not one of recollection, since the soul is said there to be mortal. *Republic* 7.523a–524e discusses an apparently different way in which sense perception may provoke the contemplation of eternal realities: by creating illusions that convince the perceiver to distrust his perception and instead summon his reason.
79   *Phaedrus* 249b5–c1.
80   Ibid. 250c4–5.
81   Ibid. 250b8–c1.
82   Ibid. 250c1–6.
83   Nehamas and Woodruff (1995:3, n. 8) provide a comprehensive list: "234d (Bacchic frenzy), 241e (possession by Nymphs), 244b and 248d–e (ecstasy of the oracles), 245a and 262d (possession by the Muses), and 250b–d (the ultimate vision after initiation into a cult)."
84   *Phaedo* 86c2–3.
85   Ibid. 92a6– c3.
86   For the defense of recollection, see *Phaedo* 72e2–77a5. For the discussion of equality in particular, see 74a9–75d5.
87   *Phaedo* 75c10–d2. The Greek being translated by "itself" is the idiosyncratic *auto ho esti*, which can be translated more literally by "itself what it is." Plato gives three Greek names to these things themselves: *eidos*, *idea*, and *genos*. In *Parmenides*, e.g., he uses all three: *eidos* (129a1), *idea* (132c4), *genos* (134b7). (Full descriptions of *eidos* and *genos* can be found in Peters 1967:46–51, 72.) He uses these names interchangeably, although he favors the first two, which are forms of the Greek verb *eidō*, "to see" or "to know." These etymological connections will prove important for our purposes, because the analogy between sight and knowledge has already been forged at the level of language. Accordingly, the most common English translations of these Greek terms are "Form" and "Idea," each preserving the notion of something seen or known.
88   See, e.g., Cicero's *Topics* 4.14.
89   *Symposium* 210a1.
90   Ibid. 211a1–2.
91   DK 28B8.5–6 (Simplicius, *Commentary on Aristotle's* Physics 145.1–146.25). See also DK 28B8.3–4, and 8.42–43.
92   See fragments 50–83 in Curd 1996:35–38, and especially DK 22B88, and 22B126. In this volume, see Chapter 2, especially sections 2.1–4.
93   *Symposium* 211a2–4.
94   *Republic* 4.436b7–9. As mentioned earlier in this volume, the canonical version of this principle arrives with Aristotle (*Metaphysics* 1005b19–21). Plato's is a version intermediate between Parmenides (DK 28B2) and Aristotle.
95   See Chapter 4, section 4.9.

[96] *Republic* 5.477c6–d5.

[97] Ibid. 5.477a2–b1.

[98] DK 28B2. See Chapter 3, section 3.1.

[99] DK 28B6.4–5 (Simplicius, *Commentary on Aristotle's* Physics. 86.27–28, 117.4–13).

[100] DK 28B6.6–9.

[101] See DK 22B51, and the discussion in 2.3.

[102] *Republic* 5.476b4.

[103] Ibid. 5.476c2–3.

[104] Ibid. 5.478e.1–2.

[105] For a fuller explanation of the relationship between time and contradiction, see Chapter 2, section 2.2.

[106] *Republic* 5.479d9.

[107] Ibid. 5.479c3–5.

[108] Ibid. 5.476a4–5; see also *Phaedo* 65d and 75c10–d2, quoted earlier.

[109] *Republic* 5.477a.

[110] Ibid. 5.479e8; see also *Phaedo* 78d.

[111] *Phaedo* 78d3–4.

[112] Ibid. 80b1–2.

[113] *Symposium* 211e1–3.

[114] *Phaedrus* 247c6–7.

[115] See *Parmenides* 130e5–131a2,132a1–4.

[116] *Sophist* 248a7–13.

[117] D.L. 8.6.

[118] *Cratylus* 440d7–e2.

[119] Aristotle himself confirms that Plato absorbed his Heracliteanism from Cratylus (*Metaphysics* 987a32–34).

[120] *Theaetetus* 179e2–181b7.

[121] See Chapter 3, section 3.3.

[122] *Timaeus* 37d.

[123] *Cratylus* 440a6–7.

[124] *Theaetetus* 183a2–b5.

[125] *Metaphysics* 1010a12.

[126] *Phaedo* 79d1–4.

[127] *Parmenides* 129d7–8.

[128] *Phaedo* 67b2. See also 69c–d, in which Plato says that philosophers are the true Bacchants.

[129] Ibid. 62b1–5, 81d9–e2, 82e1–2; see also 66b6, 66c6, 67a7, and 79c7–8.

[130] Ibid. 80b1–5.

[131] 58b5, 65e6, 66d8, 66e5, 67a5, 67a7, 67b2 (bis), 67c3, 67c5, 68b4, 69c1, 69c2, 69c6, 79d2, 80d6, 80e2, 81b1, 81d3, 82c1, 82d6, 83d9, 83e2, 108b4, 108c3, 109b7 (bis), 109d3, 110c2, 110e3, 111b6, 111d8, 114c1.

[132] *Phaedo* 61d–62c. Indeed, the alacrity with which he drinks the hemlock lends his arguments their full rhetorical force. Socrates' *daimōn* was his guardian angel, as it were—warning him not to take certain actions. See, e.g., *Apology* 31c8–d4 and Xenophon's *Memorabilia* 1.1.4, where its operation is wider. For a brief discussion, see Peters 1967:33; for a longer one, see Reeve 1989:68–70.

[133] *Phaedo* 64a4–6, 80e7–81a2.

[134] Ibid. 83a7–b2. Plato's Greek is no less awkward than this translation, signaling an important technical point.

[135] *Symposium* 210a–211d.

[136] *Republic* 6.490a8–b1.

[137] *Symposium* 211e4–212a2.

[138] *Republic* 6.490b2–4; trans. slightly rev. from Reeve 2004:183. Italics added. The Greek word faithfully translated by "grasps" is *haptomai.*

[139] *Republic* 6.490b5–8. In the passive voice, the Greek verb (*mignumi*), here translated by "has intercourse," can mean something either social or sexual, like the English verb itself. The next few lines make it clear, however, that Plato intends the sexual connotation.

[140] For the most famous comparison of philosophy to birth, see *Theaetetus* 150b–151b, in which Socrates compares himself to a midwife.

[141] *Symposium* 212a2–5; *Republic* 6.490b5–6. See also *Republic* 10.611e1–3.

[142] *Sophist* 226d1–228e5. The best remedy for the first, he supposes, is admonition; for the second, it is the purifying effect of cross-examination—in other words, the *elenchos* (229e4–230e3).

[143] *Republic* 9.585b–e. This argument is one of several for the superiority of intellectual over other pleasures found between 9.583b and 9.586b.

[144] For an explanation of this point, see Chapter 2, section 2.2.

[145] According to Plato's precise terminology, the pleasure gained is "true" and should be included among those pleasures for which there is no painful anticipation, the "pure" pleasures. See *Republic* 9.583b, 584c.

[146] Ibid. 9.586a4–6.

[147] *Phaedrus* 247d3–4.

[148] Ibid. 247c1–2.

[149] Ibid. 247c7–8; see also 248b7–c1.

[150] *Phaedo* 83a6–7.

[151] Ibid. 83a4. See also 65b1–4,65c5–7, and 79c2–8.

[152] *Timaeus* 47a1–2.

[153] See Chapter 3, sections 3.4 and 3.6.

[154] For Upaniṣadic asceticism, see *Bṛhadāraṇyaka Upaniṣad* 4.4.22. For the absence of asceticism in Zoroastrian, see Nigosian 2003:91, 118. For a discussion of both, see Chapter 3, section 3.5. For the Pythagorean variety, see Chapter 3, section 3.6.

[155] For Zoroastrian esteem of light, see Boyce 1984:45 and West 1971:32. For the parallel Pythagorean esteem, see Cornford 1903:441, Cornford 1922:141, Notopoulos 1944a:165–167, Notopoulos 1944b:229 n. 97, and especially Classen 1965. In this volume, see Chapter 3, section 3.1.

[156] See Aristotle, *Metaphysics* 986b22–26. In this volume, see Chapter 3, section 3.4.

[157] *Timaeus* 47a1–7.

[158] Ibid. 47a7–b2.

[159] *Republic* 5.477a7, 478d6–7, 479d5.

[160] Ibid. 6.507b–509d.

[161] *Republic* 6.509b8–10; slightly rev. from trans. Reeve 2004:205.

[162] Ibid. 6.508a4–8; see also *Laws* 10.899a7–b9.

[163] *Republic* 6.506e3–4; slightly rev. from trans. Reeve 2004:201; see also 507a3 and 508b12–13.

[164] Herodotus 1.131 and 2.59; Notopoulos 1944a:165 cites the first.

[165] These and many other such citations can be found in Notopoulos 1944a:165–67. These ones in particular are from: *Iliad* 3.277, *Works and Days* 267, *Agamemnon* 508, and *Oedipus Tyrannus* 1425.

[166] *Oedipus Tyrannus* 660; trans. PLM.

[167] Notopoulos 1944a:165.

[168] *Pythian* 8:95–97; trans. Race 1997a:337.

[169] "It is natural," writes Kahn (2001:55), to connect the Pythagoreanism of Plato's second group of dialogues with his "two later trips to Syracuse in 367 and 361, which afforded him the opportunity for more intimate contacts with Archytas and the Pythagoreans of Tarentum." For an exhaustive account of Archytas, see Huffman 2005.

[170] DK 31B84 (Aristotle, *On the Soul* 404b13–14); trans. PLM. For Empedocles' similar "like-to-like" theory of cognition, see 31B107 (Theophrastus, *On the Senses* 10); for his "like-to-like" theory of nutrition, see 31B90. Kingsley 1995:298 argues that this theory had special significance for Empedocles, which it may have, but the theory of perception according to which "like is naturally apprehended by like" was used also by Philolaus (Sextus Empiricus, *Against the Logicians* 7.92; see Barnes 2001:178), and perhaps even Pythagoras (DK 28A48 [Aëtius, 4.13.9–10 {*Doxographi Graeci*} 404]). On the lineage of the theory generally, see McEvilley 2002:101. As for this particular formulation by Empedocles, something should be said about Empedocles' Greek. We are accustomed to think of the four elements introduced by him as earth, water, air, and fire; but of the two Greek words roughly translated by "air," he uses not *aēr*—or mist, which Anaximenes chose for his first principle—but *aithēr*, which refers to the purer air of the heavens. The English derivative, "ether," is the best translation, especially as it conveys the connotation of purity. Anaxagoras called the *aithēr* "fine," *araios*, saying that it moved away from our location in the cosmos, where instead darkness and earth, wet and cold came to predominate (DK 59B15). Plato distinguishes *aēr* and *aithēr* at *Timaeus* 58d1–3: "The same goes for air. There is the brightest kind, that we call 'aether', and also the murkiest, 'mist' and 'darkness'." For a sustained discussion of Empedocles' *aithēr* and *aēr*, see Kingsley 1995:15–23, 24–35.

[171] DK 31B84 (Aristotle, *On the Senses* 437b32–438a2); trans. Barnes 1987:154.

[172] Ibid.

[173] *Hamlet* 2.1.100–2. Elaborating a creationist cosmogony, at least according to a more literal interpretation, *Timaeus* helped Christian theologians develop a philosophical account of *Genesis*. Thanks to the late antique translation of Calcidius, furthermore, it was the only Platonic dialogue available in Latin—and then only in part—until the twelfth century (Lesky 1996:536, Zeyl 2000:xiv). For the subsequent history of Plato's theory of light and vision, see Park 1997 (especially 2.4 and 4.1).

[174] *Timaeus* 45b1–3.

[175] Ibid. 45c7.

[176] Ibid. 45b6.

[177] Ibid. 45b7–c2.

[178] Ibid. 40a2–4.

[179] *Republic* 3.415a–417b.

[180] *Timaeus* 69e1–3. See also 69e–71e, and 72e–73a.

[181] Ibid. 92a4.

[182] Ibid. 92a7.
[183] *Timaeus* 90b1, *Republic* 7.519a8–b5, 9.586a1–8; cf. *Republic* 7.527b9–11,533d1–4, *Phaedrus* 247b3–6. Notopoulos 1944b analyzes Plato's metaphors of *up and down*, correlating them with the use of his two other most important metaphors: *light and dark*, and *image and reality*.
[184] *Timaeus* 90a2–6. For a similar association of posture, light, and ethics, see a passage that is often deleted from *First Alcibiades* as the addition of a later Neoplatonist scholar (134d1–e7).
[185] And consequently, the sphere above all other solids. See, e.g., *Timaeus* 33b2–7, or DK 31B134. Aristotle explains some of his reasons for privileging the circle over the line at *On the Heavens* 269a17–23.
[186] *Timaeus* 47c2–4.
[187] *Laws* 10.898a8–b2.
[188] Ibid.
[189] Ibid.
[190] *Timaeus* 43a4–5.
[191] Ibid. 44b3–6.
[192] Ibid.
[193] Speaking of astronomy and harmonics, Plato writes that "these two sciences are somehow akin, as the Pythagoreans say" (*Republic* 7.530d6–10). According to the Pythagoreans, the motions of the heavenly bodies produced a supreme harmony, the so-called harmony of the spheres. For similar praise of harmonics, see *Timaeus* 47c4–e2. For the similarity of seeing and hearing, on account of the fineness of their media (air and fire, respectively), see *Timaeus* 45b3–c7.
[194] See also *Republic* 6.508a, and *Laws* 11.930e–931a. In *Laws* 5.741b5–6, Plato also calls gods the lots by which property is distributed—a potent reminder of the mythological universe in which he still operates.
[195] *Republic* 7.530b3.
[196] At *Republic* 7.528e–529c, he says this satisfaction would allow that someone pursues "higher studies" simply by "leaning his head back and studying ornaments on a ceiling." At *Timaeus* 91d6–e1, similarly, he says that the souls of "men who studied the heavenly bodies but in their naiveté believed that the most reliable proofs concerning them could be based upon visual observation" are, in their next life, reincarnated as birds.
[197] *Republic* 7.533b2–3. For a brief summary of the philosopher's intellectual ascent, see also *Theaetetus* 173e1–174a2.
[198] *Republic* 7.529c–530c.
[199] Ibid. 7.533c8–d1.
[200] *Republic* 7.515b7, 517b2, 519d5.
[201] DK 44B14 (Clement, *Miscellanies* 3.3.17.1).
[202] *Republic* 7.514b8–515a1.
[203] Cornford 1903:436, 439.
[204] *Phaedrus* 250b1–c6. See also Notopoulos 1944a:238, especially n. 130.
[205] *Republic* 7.518c7–8.
[206] Ibid. 7.517b–c; 7.531c–534e.
[207] Ibid. 7.516a6–8.
[208] Ibid. 6.509d6–511e5.

[209] Ibid. 6.509d6–8.
[210] See Gerson 2003:180, n. 51.
[211] *Republic* 6.509d8–510a6, and 511d6–e4.
[212] Ibid. 6.510b3–511d5. The four faculties are catalogued twice at 511c3–e5.
[213] Ibid. 6.510b3–5. See also 6.510e1–511a1, and 511a5–7.
[214] Ibid. 6.510d7–8.
[215] Ibid. 7.532a5–b2 and 533c7–e1.
[216] Gerson 2003:82.
[217] For Epicurean representationalism, see *Letter to Herodotus* 46–51; for a summary of the Stoic variety, see Diogenes Laertius 7.49–53. The modern versions of representationalism were responding to the renewed belief that qualities such as color, so-called secondary qualities, are qualities that objects produce in subjects, but which objects themselves do not have. If this is correct, our perception or knowledge of color cannot be a reception of the object's own form, one of its so-called primary qualities. In the wake of both ancient and modern representationalism, skepticism inevitably arises. The two figures who founded the modern version, according to Richard Rorty's (1981) discussion and criticism of it, are Descartes, who introduces the metaphor of the mind as a mirror, and Locke, who portrays knowledge as accurate representations (or *ideas*) in the mirror. Rejecting ancient and medieval non-representationalist epistemologies, as well as the modern representationalist ones that are the target of his book, Rorty champions instead the post-modern, or "pragmatist," epistemologies he finds in the likes of Wittgenstein, Heidegger, and Dewey. See also Gerson 2003:81–82.
[218] Gerson 2003, chapter 2, adduces independent arguments for the plausibility of a non-representationalist epistemology. "One excellent reason for holding that knowledge is non-representational," he writes, "is that knowledge is an infallible state" (2003:82). "If knowledge were representational," he adds, "infallibility could in principle not be preserved because there would be no way of inferring from a representational state any objective state of affairs" (ibid.). He elaborates this line of argument in Gerson 2009.
[219] For Plotinus, see *Enneads* 1.4.9, 2.9.1, 3.8.8, 3.9.1.
[220] *On the Soul* 429a15–19; trans. PLM.
[221] Ibid. 430a4–5. Gerson 2005:151 cites this passage along with five others that make the same point, 430a19–20, 430b25–26, 431a1, 431b17, 431b22–23. See also *Metaphysics* 1072b20–23. To be precise, this identity must remain qualified so long as *nous* is embodied (Gerson 2005:157). "Unqualified identity," writes Gerson, "is available only for that which is cognitively identical with that which is not other than it," and this is true of disembodied *nous* alone (Gerson 2005:157).
[222] *Phaedo* 78b4–84b4. Detailed analyses of this argument are available in Gerson 1986:352–55, Shields 2001:141–44, Bostock 2001:259, and Gerson 2003:79–88.
[223] Gerson 2003:97.
[224] *Republic* 7.533a1–3.
[225] *Symposium* 211b1.
[226] *Republic* 6.511b6–7.
[227] Ibid. 6.509b6–8; slightly rev. from trans. Reeve 2004:205.
[228] Gerson 2003:175.

[229] *Parmenides* 129d7–8.

[230] *Republic* 7.516b4–6.

[231] *Republic* 6.506d7–8.

[232] Cooper 1977:155.

[233] *Gorgias* 506e1–2.

[234] See Douglas 2004:xvii, 5, 7, 42, 44, 50, 64, 117. See Chapter 3, section 3.5 of this volume.

[235] *Timaeus* 30a2–6. Reeve 2003:49 additionally cites *Gorgias* 507e6–508a8, and *Philebus* 66a6–7.

[236] Gerson 2003:176.

[237] *Laws* 896d10–e7.

[238] See Chapter 3, section 3.5.

[239] Gerson 2003:176.

[240] Ibid. 177.

[241] *Symposium* 211b1.

[242] Gerson 2003:175. Italics added.

[243] Ibid. 177.

[244] Ibid. 175.

[245] Ibid.

[246] *Republic* 509b6–8; slightly rev. from trans. Reeve 2004:205.

[247] Ibid. 6.509d6–511e5.

[248] *Phaedo* 98b7–c2.

[249] *Republic* 1.341d7–8, 342c1–2.

[250] Ibid. 10.601d4–5; slightly rev. from trans. Reeve 2004:305.

[251] *Republic* 10.601d5–6. For instance, a pruning knife is something whose use is to prune; if it prunes well, it is an excellent one (*Republic* 1.353d9–354a2). Or, a horse-breeding action is something whose purpose is to produce good horses; if it succeeds, it is a correct one (1.342c4). Finally, Plato argues, a human soul's purpose is to live; if it lives well—however that may be specified—it is a virtuous one (1.353d3–e12). The trick of the argument, needless to say, is the move from the uncontroversial ascription of use and purpose to artifacts, through their more questionable ascription to actions, to their ultimately dubious ascription to organisms. Other passages relevant to the Platonic conception of virtue include *Charmides* 161a8–9, *Euthyphro* 6d9–e1, *Gorgias* 506d2–4, *Protagoras* 332b4–6, and *Republic* 1.353d9–354a2. For short discussions of the Greek notion of *aretē*, see Cooper 1997:980, n. 8, and Reeve 2004:329. MacIntyre 1984 (especially pp. 57–59 and chapter 12) provides a fuller explanation of the notion, not to mention a spirited defense of a renovated version of it.

[252] *Republic* 7.517b6–8.

[253] He adduces the "recollection" argument of *Phaedo* (72e2–77a5). *Timaeus* sketches a related epistemological argument (51d3–5). In *Republic*, the point is made most forcefully at 5.475e–480a. Despite the confidence of these passages, Plato does have the Socrates of *Meno* (81d6–e2) reject the skeptical argument not because it is incoherent but because "it would make us idle . . . whereas my argument makes them energetic and keen on the search." Such reasoning appears to be moral rather than strictly epistemological. For other statements of Plato's

position on Forms, see *Republic* 10.596a, *Phaedo* 103b–e, *Cratylus* 389a–390a, and finally *Parmenides* 129a–e, 130e–131a, and 132a, d.

[254] *Nicomachean Ethics* 1.1094a2–3 and *Metaphysics* 982b5–8.

[255] See *Euthydemus* 290b10–c6, as well as *Republic* 6.511b3–e5, 7.531c9–535a2.

[256] *Euthydemus* 290d1–3; see Reeve 2003:45.

[257] 5.473c11–e2; see also *Euthydemus* 282c5–d3 and *Cratylus* 388d9–390d5.

[258] *Republic* 7.532a5–533d1; see Reeve 2003:49. See also *Statesman* 287c10–d4.

[259] *Republic* 7.537c1–7; see Reeve 2003:51.

[260] *Phaedo* 66a1–3.

[261] *Republic* 6.500c4–5.

[262] Ibid. 6.500c9–d2.

[263] *Timaeus* 90c2–3. See also *Theaetetus* 176b1–3.

[264] *Republic* 6.501b5–7. See also *Sophist* 216b8–c1.

[265] *Republic* 7.540b6–c2.

[266] Ibid.

[267] Ibid.

[268] *Phaedo* 83e1–3.

[269] Ibid. 81a9. See also 108c3–5.

[270] See O'Cleirigh and Barrell 2000:50–53 for the equation of immortality and divinity, as well as other unique features of the traditional Greek notion of *theos*. See also Burkert 1985:121–22, 162, and 298; Kingsley 1995:222–23; Dodds 1951:10; and Kahn 1979:218–19, citing Herodotus 2.61. Greek texts making this point are plentiful, but here are typical examples we discussed in Chapter 3: Pindar, *Pythian Ode* 3.61 and *Isthmian Ode* 5.14; Euripides, *Alcestis* 799; and Epicharmus, DK 23B20 (quoted by Aristotle at *Rhetoric* 1394b25).

[271] *Phaedo* 107c–114c.

[272] Ibid. 111b1–c3.

[273] *Sophist* 254a9–10.

[274] As Dionysus's mother, Semele, learned to her destruction (Euripides, *Bacchae* 1–12).

[275] *Phaedrus* 248c3.

[276] Ibid. 248c5.

[277] See Pindar, *Olympian Odes* 2.65–66; Plato, *Meno* 81b8–c4; Pindar fr. 133, Snell; DK 31B127 (Aelian, *On The Nature of Animals* 12.7); DK 31B147 (Clement, *Miscellanies* 5.14.122.3).

[278] See, e.g., *Theaetetus* 176e3–177a8, *Republic* 6.498d1–4, and of course the Myth of Er, *Republic* 10.614b–621b. Like Pindar's eschatology (e.g., *Olympian Odes* 2.56–60), Plato's includes punishments for those who fail to live a good life. If a man wastes his life in impurity, the penalty is reincarnation as a woman; for a recidivist (who, despite his feminine incarnation, somehow retains a male soul), the penalty is still further incarnation as "some wild animal that resembled the wicked character he had acquired" (*Timaeus* 42b5–c4).

[279] *Timaeus* 42b3–4.

[280] *Phaedo* 78c6–8. See also 78c10–d7.

[281] Ibid. 79d1–7.

[282] Ibid. 79a3–4.

[283] Ibid. 82c3.

[284] *Phaedrus* 245c8–9. See also *Laws* 895e10–896a4. Aristotle also claimed that his predecessors assumed, "naturally enough, that what is in its own nature originative of movement must be among what is primordial" (*On the Soul* 405a2–4). He seems, thus, to have in mind Plato and the Academics.

[285] For Aristotle, see *Physics* Book 8, especially 8.5–6. For Plato, and the first stage in this argument, see *Phaedrus* 245c5–246a2; for its full expression, see *Laws* 887c7–899d2.

[286] *Philebus* 35c6–7.

[287] Ibid. 35d2–3.

[288] *Phaedrus* 253d7–8.

[289] *Phaedrus* 254a4–5; slightly rev. from trans. Nehamas and Woodruff, in Cooper 1997:530–31.

[290] See *Republic* 9.588d3, 588c7.

[291] *Timaeus* 69c5–72d3.

[292] *Republic* presents at least two arguments for the tripartition of the soul. The first depends heavily on his tripartite division of city (*Republic* 4.434e3–436a3). To be precise, it does not begin with a version of the principle of non-contradiction, but is weak, and apparently not Plato's main argument. The second (4.436a8–441c7) does begin with a version of the principle of non-contradiction, is independent of politics, and has earned the careful examination of many recent scholars: Gerson 1986, Reeve 1988:118–40, F. Miller 1999, several papers collected in Wagner 2001 (Cooper, Shields, Smith, and Bobonich), Carone 2001, Bobonich 2002:219–57, Gerson 2003:100–24, Lorenz 2006a, Anagnostopoulos 2006, Lorenz 2006b, Ferrari 2007b, Moss 2008. Moss (2008 and 2007) has shown how Plato elaborates this second argument with the help of two passages later in *Republic*: 602c–603a, and 603e–605c. The additional arguments of these passages extend the second, rather than being new arguments, properly speaking, because they apply its strategy to inner conflicts elicited by perception and tragedy.

[293] *Republic* 4.436b8–9. The more famous, Aristotelian version of the principle of non-contradiction (PNC) can be found at *Metaphysics* 4.1005b11–33. Fred Miller (1999:92–93) distinguishes it from Plato's version (the principle of non-opposition, or PNO) by observing, essentially, that PNO precludes the simultaneous presence of contraries, whereas PNC precludes that of contradictories. Reeve offers a different view, writing that PNO "is simply the principle of noncontradiction, formulated in terms of properties rather than propositions, and restricted to properties that are relational forms" (1988:119). For the purposes of this volume—which sees Plato and Aristotle as exponents of the Parmenidean reaction (see Chapter 3, section 3.1) against Heraclitus—we shall treat these versions as effectively the same. Each requires consistency of thought and being, which must be pure of contraries as well as contradictories. Accordingly, we shall henceforth call this principle the principle of consistency.

[294] *Republic* 4.436b9–c1.

[295] The interpretation of these two challenges presented here is indebted to Christopher Bobonich (2002:227–32). Among its several virtues, Bobonich's interpretation can explain important details of the passage's Greek: Plato does not use the *kata*-idiom (which indicates respects) in the case of the first

challenge, that of the man, but does use it in the case of the second, that of the top; moreover, Plato speaks of spinning tops moving and standing still *holoi* ("as a whole") at 436d5 (for both points, see 2002:229). As discussed below, the second challenge will be handled by claiming that there are relevantly different respects, whereas the first challenge will be handled by claiming that the relevant subject is not the whole man, so these linguistic details are crucial.

[296] *Republic* 4.436c9; trans. Bobonich 2002:228.

[297] Although it may seem unnecessary at first, the qualification about the same respect (rectilinear motion) is necessary because a man could be standing still and moving in respect of different sorts of motion, as the next example (of the spinning top) shows.

[298] *Republic* 4.436c9–d1; trans. Bobonich 2002:228.

[299] Ibid. 4.436d4–6; trans. Bobonich 2002:228.

[300] The "here" in this case must be a point in space coincident with the spinning top's vertical axis. The "here" in the case of the man, by contrast, can be anywhere.

[301] *Republic* 4.436e1–4; trans. Bobonich 2002:228.

[302] As Bobonich observes, "the circumference" cannot mean points on the circumference in particular, for two reasons. First of all, Socrates said that spinning tops experience this opposite "as a whole" (*holoi*). Second, moving in a circle is shared by all the coaxial as well as the circumferential points (2002:230). The best interpretation of "in respect of the circumference" is thus "in the respect of circular motion," marking a neat contrast with "in the respect of the straight line" (understood as rectilinear motion, for the same two reasons, *mutatis mutandis*). Bobonich supplements this interpretation with evidence about the distinction between these two kinds of motion in *Timaeus* (2002:231).

[303] See *Protagoras* 352a8–358d4, and *Meno* 77b6–78b2. *Akrasia* combines an alpha-privative (equivalent to our "non-" or "un-") with a nominal form of *kratos* ("power," from which demo-cracy or auto-cracy, e.g., are derived.) Literally, then, it means "lacking power"; more specifically, it means lacking the power to act upon one's assessment of what is best. "Weakness of will" is the most common translation, but it is anachronistic. The philosophical notion of "will"—which after Paul (e.g., *Romans* 7) becomes so important to Christian thinkers such as Augustine (e.g., *On Free Choice of the Will*)—emerged from the Hellenistic debate between Stoics and Epicureans about the freedom or determinism of human action (see Cicero's *On Fate*, e.g., which summarizes this debate, though not always fairly). There are antecedents of the debate in Aristotle (*On Interpretation* 9), and as far back as a speech of Gorgias (*Encomium of Helen*), but nothing quite like the will, in its modern sense, appears in their discussions. A better, but no less anachronistic translation of *akrasia*, is Freud's concept "neurosis," which owes as much to Plato as it does to nineteenth century mechanics. To avoid anachronism, then, *akrasia* will remain transliterated and untranslated. For the inadequacy of other candidate translations, see Rorty 1981:283, n. 1.

[304] He makes this belief most explicit at *Meno* 87c11–88d3.

[305] *Republic* 9.588d9–11.

306 For Hippocratic medicine, see, e.g., *Regimen in Acute Diseases* 15. For the Platonic example, *Republic* 4.439c5–7.

307 *Republic* 4.439b3–6.

308 DK 22B51, but also B48. In this volume, see Chapter 2, section 2.3.

309 For a fuller account of Plato's psychological distinction between accepting appearances uncritically and calculating upon them, that is, between the irrational and rational parts of the soul, see Moss 2008.

310 *Republic* 4.439d4–8.

311 Ibid. 9.588c7–10.

312 See, e.g., *Republic* 8.559d9–10, which speaks of this part's multicolored (*pantodapas*) pleasures, and 8.561a3–5, which describes individual appetites rising to prominence in it as if according to lot.

313 This happens with the avarice of the oligarch (*Republic* 8.554a5–8) and the lust of the tyrant (*Republic* 9.572e4–573a2).

314 *Republic* 9.586b3–4. See Chapter 4, section 4.4.

315 Ibid. 10.602c4–603b2.

316 Ibid. 4.437d2–439a2.

317 Ibid. 4.439d4–8. The Greek is *to logistikon*, which is related to *logos*. For an exhaustive list of meanings and citations, see Guthrie 1962:420–24. For another *logos* of *logos*, see Peters 1967:110–12.

318 *Symposium* 212a3–5.

319 *Timaeus* 71a1–2.

320 On the purity of intellectual pleasure, see *Republic* 9.583b–586b. On the superiority of the Good, see *Republic* 6.509b8–10.

321 Ibid. 9.590d3–4.

322 *Timaeus* 69c5–8.

323 *Republic* 10.611d4–5.

324 Gerson 2003:145.

325 Ibid. 175.

326 *Republic* 10.611c2–3.

327 Gerson 2003:57.

328 *Republic* 9.588b9–e1.

329 *Phaedrus* 253d1–255a1.

330 *Republic* 1.331c1.

331 Ibid. 5.478d5–6.

332 *Phaedo* 74a9–75d5. See Chapter 4, section 4.2.

333 *Phaedo* 75c1.

334 Ibid. 75c10–d2.

335 *Phaedrus* 229e6. See also: *First Alcibiades* 124a7, 129a2, 130e7; *Charmides* 164d–170a; and *Apology* 38a.

336 *Republic* 5.478d5–9.

337 *Symposium* 211e1–3. See also: *Phaedrus* 247c6–7; *Republic* 5.479e8; and *Phaedo* 78d3–4, 80b1–2.

338 *Symposium* 207d6–e1.

339 Ibid. 207e1–2.

340 Ibid. 207e2–5.

341 Ibid. 207e5–208a3.

[342] Ibid. 208a7–b2.
[343] Ibid. 207d2–3.
[344] *Phaedo* 74a9–75d5.
[345] *First Alcibiades* 129b1.

Chapter 5

[1] See Chapter 1; Chapter 2, section 2.4; Chapter 3, section 3.6; and Chapter 4, section 4.8.

[2] See, especially, Chapter 2, sections 2.7, 2.9–10; Chapter 3, sections 3.1–3, 3.4, 3.6; and Chapter 4, sections 4.1–3, 4.6, 4.10.

[3] Compare Chapter 2, section 2.7 and 2.9 with Chapter 3, section 3.1.

[4] See Chapter 3, sections 3.1 and 4.3.

[5] See Chapter 4, sections 4.1–6.

[6] See Chapter 4, sections 4.7–10.

[7] For this criticism, see Chapter 3, section 3.3.

[8] See Chapter 3, section 3.1.

[9] See Chapter 3, sections 3.2–3.

[10] See Chapter 4, section 4.2.

[11] See Chapter 4, section 4.3.

[12] See Chapter 4, section 4.7.

[13] See Chapter 4, section 4.8.

[14] See Chapter 4, section 4.10.

[15] See Chapter 4, section 4.9.

[16] Ibid.

[17] See Chapter 2, sections 2.3–4, 2.7, 2.9–10.

[18] See Chapter 2, sections 2.2, 2.7, 2.9–10.

[19] See Chapter 2, sections 2.1–2, 2.7, 2.9–10.

[20] See Chapter 2, section 2.1.

[21] See Chapter 2, section 2.3.

[22] See Chapter 2, section, 2.2.

[23] See Chapter 2, section 2.5.

[24] See Chapter 2, section 2.7.

[25] See Chapter 2, section 2.9.

[26] See Chapter 2, section 2.6.

[27] See Chapter 2, sections 2.7 and 2.9.

[28] See Chapter 2, section 2.6.

[29] See Chapter 2, section 2.10.

[30] Here is an initial opposition of two contraries: $A : B$ (say, synthesis and analysis). The opposition is unified in chiasmus: $A : B :: B : A$. This chiasmus becomes a chiasmus of chiasmus as follows: $A : B :: B : A ::: A : B :: B : A$. Then: $A : B :: B : A ::: A : B :: B : A :::: A : B :: B : A ::: A : B :: B : A$. The pattern can be iterated infinitely, always remaining chiastic.

[31] See Chapter 2, section 2.4.

[32] See Chapter 2, section 2.9.

Works Cited

Anagnostopoulos, M. 2006. "The divided soul and the desire for good in Plato's *Republic.*" In Santas: 166–88.

Annas, J. 1999. *Platonic Ethics Old and New.* New York, NY: Cornell University Press.

Armstrong, A. H. 1966–88. *Plotinus* 7 vols. (Loeb Classical Library). Cambridge, MA: Harvard University Press.

Barnes, J., ed. 1995. *The Complete Works of Aristotle: The Revised Oxford Translation.* 2 vols. Bollingen Series. Princeton, NJ: Princeton University Press.

—. 2001. *Early Greek Philosophy.* 2nd edn. London: Penguin.

Bluck, R. S. 1964. *Plato's* Meno. Cambridge: Cambridge University Press.

Bobonich, C. 2002. *Plato's Utopia Recast.* Oxford: Clarendon Press.

Bostock, D. 2001. "The soul and immortality in Plato's *Phaedo.*" In Wagner 2001:241–62.

Boyce, M. 1984. *Textual Sources for the Study of Zoroastrianism.* Manchester: Manchester University Press.

Bremmer, J. 1983. *The Early Greek Concept of the Soul.* Princeton, NJ: Princeton University Press.

Buchanan Gray, G. 1964. "The foundation and extension of the Persian empire." In *The Cambridge Ancient History*, eds. J. B. Bury, S. A. Cook, and F. E. Adcock, vol. 4, 1–25. Cambridge: Cambridge University Press.

Burkert, W. 1969. "Das Proömium des Parmenides und die Katabasis des Pythagoras." *Phronesis* 14:1–30.

—. 1985 (1977). *Greek Religion.* Trans. J. Raffan. Cambridge, MA: Harvard University Press.

—. 2004. *Babylon, Memphis, Persepolis: Eastern Contexts of Greek Culture.* Cambridge, MA: Harvard University Press.

Burnet, J. 1916. "The Socratic doctrine of the soul." *Proceedings of the British Academy* 7:235–59.

Carone, G. R. 2001. "Akrasia in the *Republic*: does Plato change his mind?" *Oxford Studies in Ancient Philosophy* 20:107–48.

Caston, V. and D. W. Graham, eds. 2002. *Presocratic Philosophy.* Burlington, VT: Ashgate Publishing Company.

Choksy, J. K. 1989. *Purity and Pollution in Zoroastrianism: Triumph over Evil.* Austin, TX: University of Texas Press.

Classen, C. J. 1965. "Licht und Dunkel in der frühgriechischen Philosophie." *Studium Generale* 18:97–116.

Claus, D. B. 1981. *Toward the Soul.* New Haven, CT: Yale University Press.

Collobert, C. 2002. "Aristotle's review of the Presocratics: is Aristotle finally a historian of philosophy?" *Journal of the History of Philosophy* 40:281–95.

Conche, M. 1998. *Héraclite*, 4th edn. Paris: Presses Universitaire de France.

Cooper, J. M. 1977. "The psychology of justice in Plato." *American Philosophical Quarterly* 14:151–57.

— . ed. 1997. *Plato: Complete Works.* Indianapolis, IN: Hackett Publishing Company.

Copleston, F. 1985. *A History of Philosophy.* 9 vols. New York, NY: Doubleday.

Cornford, F. M. 1903. "Plato and Orpheus." *The Classical Review* 17:433–45.

—. 1922. "Mysticism and science in the Pythagorean tradition." *The Classical Quarterly* 16:137–50.

—. 1923. "Mysticism and science in the Pythagorean tradition." *The Classical Quarterly* 17:1–12.

Coxon, A. H. 1986. *The Fragments of Parmenides.* Wolfeboro, NH: Van Gorcum.

—. 2003. "Parmenides on thinking being." *Mnemosyne* 56:210–12.

Crystal, I. M. 2002. *Self-Intellection and its Epistemological Origins in Ancient Greek Thought.* Burlington, VT: Ashgate.

Curd, P., ed. 1996. *A Presocratics Reader.* Indianapolis, IN: Hackett Publishing Company.

—. 1998. *The Legacy of Parmenides.* Princeton, NJ: Princeton University Press.

— and D. W. Graham, eds. 2008. *The Oxford Handbook of Presocratic Philosophy.* New York, NY: Oxford University Press.

Dodds, E. R. 1951. *The Greeks and the Irrational.* Berkeley, CA: The University of California Press.

Douglas, M. 2004. *Purity and Danger.* New York: Routledge.

Dover, K. 1989. *Greek Homosexuality.* Cambridge, MA: Harvard University Press.

Duchesne-Guillemin, J. 1953. *Ormazd et Ahriman: l'aventure dualiste dans l'antiquité.* Paris: F. Vieweg.

Eriksen, R. 2000. *The Building in the Text: from Alberti to Shakespeare and Milton.* University Park, PA: Pennsylvania State University Press.

Fagles, R., trans. 1996. *Homer: The Odyssey.* New York, NY: Viking.

Ferrari, G. R. F., ed. 2007a. *The Cambridge Companion to Plato's* Republic. New York, NY: Cambridge University Press.

—. 2007b. "The three part soul." In Ferrari 2007a:165–201.

Fontaine, P. F. M. 1986–2003. *The Light and the Dark: A Cultural History of Dualism.* 18 vols. Amsterdam: J. C. Gieben.

Gallop, D. 1984. *Parmenides of Elea: Fragments.* Toronto: University of Toronto Press.

Gatti, M. L. 1999. "Plotinus: the Platonic tradition and the foundation of Neoplatonism." In Gerson 1999: 10–37.

Gerson, L. P. 1986. "Platonic dualism." *Monist* 69:352–69.

— . ed. 1999. *The Cambridge Companion to Plotinus.* New York, NY: Cambridge University Press.

—. 2003. *Knowing Persons.* New York, NY: Oxford University Press.

—. 2005. *Aristotle and Other Platonists.* Ithaca, NY: Cornell University Press.

—. 2009. *Ancient Epistemology.* Cambridge: Cambridge University Press.

Gomperz, T. 1920. *The Greek Thinkers: A History of Ancient Philosophy.* 4 vols. London: John Murray.

Goux, J. J. 1993 (1992). *Oedipus, Philosopher.* Trans. C. Porter. Stanford, CA: Stanford University Press.

Graf, F. 1993. "Dionysian and Orphic eschatology: new texts and old questions." In *Masks of Dionysus,* eds. T. H. Carpenter and C. A. Faraone, 239–58. Ithaca, NY: Cornell University Press.

—. 1996. "Pythagoreanism (religious aspects)." In Hornblower and Spawforth, 1996:1284–85.

Graham, D. W. 2002. "Heraclitus and Parmenides." In Caston and Graham 2002:27–44.

—. 2006. *Explaining the Cosmos: The Ionian Tradition of Scientific Philosophy*. Princeton, NJ: Princeton University Press.

—. 2008. "Heraclitus: flux, order, and knowledge." In Curd and Graham 2008:169–88.

Grube, G. M. A., trans. 1983. *Marcus Aurelius: The Meditations*. Indianapolis, IN: Hackett Publishing Company.

—. trans. 1992. *Plato: Republic*. Revised by C. D. C. Reeve. Indianapolis, IN: Hackett Publishing Company.

Guthrie, W. K. C. 1955. *The Greeks and their Gods*. Boston, MA: Beacon Press.

—. 1962–1981. *A History of Greek Philosophy*. 6 vols. Cambridge: Cambridge University Press.

Hadot, P. 1998 (1992). *The Inner Citadel: The Meditations of Marcus Aurelius*. Trans. M. Chase. Cambridge, MA: Harvard University Press.

—. 2002. *What is Ancient Philosophy?* Trans. M. Chase. Cambridge, MA: Belknap Press.

Heidegger, M. 1999 (1936–38). *Contributions to Philosophy (From Enowning)*. Trans. P. Emad and K. Maly. Bloomington, IN: Indiana University Press.

Heidel, A. 1963. *The Babylonian Genesis*. Chicago, IL: University of Chicago Press.

Hicks, R. D., trans. 2000 (1925). *Diogenes Laertius: The Lives of the Eminent Philosophers*. 2 vols. Loeb Classical Library. Cambridge, MA: Harvard University Press.

Hornblower, S. and A. Spawforth, eds. 1996. *The Oxford Classical Dictionary*, 3rd edn. New York, NY: Oxford University Press.

Huffman, C. 1993. *Philolaus of Croton: Pythagorean and Presocratic*. Cambridge: Cambridge University Press.

—. 2003. "Philolaus." The Stanford Encyclopedia of Philosophy, ed. E. N. Zalta. Available at: http://plato.stanford.edu/archives/fall2003/entries/philolaus/.

—. 2005. *Archytas of Tarentum: Pythagorean, Philosopher, and Mathematician King*. New York, NY: Cambridge University Press.

Hussey, E. 1999. "Heraclitus." In Long 1999:88–112.

Inwood, B. 2001. *The Poem of Empedocles*. Revised ed. Toronto: University of Toronto Press.

Irwin, T. 1977. *Plato's Moral Theory*. Oxford: Oxford University Press.

—. 1995. *Plato's Ethics*. Oxford: Oxford University Press.

Irwin, T. and G. Fine, trans. 1995. *Aristotle: Selections*. Indianapolis, IN: Hackett Publishing Company.

Jouanna, J. 1998. *Hippocrates*. Trans. M. B. DeBevoise. Baltimore, MA: Johns Hopkins University Press.

Kahn, C. 1974. "Pythagorean philosophy before Plato." In *The Pre-Socratics: A Collection of Critical Essays*, ed. A. P. D. Mourelatos, 161–85. Garden City, NY: Anchor Press.

—. 1979. *The Art and Thought of Heraclitus*. New York, NY: Cambridge University Press.

—. 1996. "Pythagoras." In Hornblower and Spawforth 1996:1283–84.

—. 2001. *Pythagoras and the Pythagoreans: A Brief History*. Indianapolis, IN: Hackett Publishing Company.

Kant, I. 1990 (1785). *Foundations of the Metaphysics of Morals*. 2nd edn. Trans. L. W. Beck. New York, NY: Macmillan Publishing Company.

—. 1997. *Lectures on Ethics*. Trans. P. Heath. Eds. P. Heath and J. Schneewind. New York, NY: Cambridge University Press.

Kerényi, K. 1996. *Dionysos: Archetypal Image of Indestructible Life*. Trans. R. Manheim. Princeton, NJ: Princeton University Press.

Kingsley, P. 1995. *Ancient Philosophy, Mystery, and Magic: Empedocles and Pythagorean Tradition*. New York, NY: Oxford University Press.

—. 2004. *In the Dark Places of Wisdom*. Inverness, CA: The Golden Sufi Center.

Kirk, G. S. 1962. *Heraclitus: The Cosmic Fragments*. Reprint with corrections of the 1954 ed. Cambridge, UK: Cambridge University Press.

Kirk, G. S., J. E. Raven, and M. Schofield. 1983. *The Presocratic Philosophers*. 2nd edn. Cambridge: Cambridge University Press.

Knox, B. 1957. *Oedipus at Thebes*. New Haven, CT: Yale University Press.

Lange, A., E. Meyers, and R. Styers, eds. 2010. *Light against Darkness: Dualism in Ancient Mediterranean Religion and the Contemporary World*. Göttingen: Vandenhoeck & Ruprecht.

Lesher, J. H. 1992. *Xenophanes: Fragments*. Toronto: University of Toronto Press.

Lesky, A. 1996. *A History of Greek Literature*. Trans. C. de Heer and J. Willis. Indianapolis, IN: Hackett Publishing Company.

Lewis, D. M., et al., eds. 1994. *The Cambridge Ancient History*. Vol. 6, *The Fourth Century BC*. New York, NY: Cambridge University Press.

Liddell, H. G., et al. 1940. *A Greek-English Lexicon*. 9th edn. Oxford, UK: Clarendon Press.

Lloyd-Jones, H. 1990. "Pindar and the Afterlife." In *Greek Epic, Lyric, and Tragedy*, 80–103. Oxford: Clarendon Press.

Long, A. A. 1996. *Stoic Studies*. Berkeley, CA: University of California Press.

—. ed. 1999. *The Cambridge Companion to Early Greek Philosophy*. New York, NY: Cambridge University Press.

Longrigg, J. 1998. *Greek Medicine From the Heroic to the Hellenistic Age: A Sourcebook*. New York, NY: Routledge.

Lorenz, H. 2006a. "The analysis of the soul in Plato's *Republic*." In Santas 2006:146–65.

—. 2006b. *The Brute Within: Appetitive Desire in Plato and Aristotle*. New York, NY: Oxford University Press.

MacIntyre, A. 1984. *After Virtue*. 2nd edn. Notre Dame, IN: University of Notre Dame Press.

—. 1990. *Three Rival Versions of Moral Enquiry: Encyclopaedia, Genealogy, and Tradition*. Notre Dame, IN: University of Notre Dame Press.

Marcovich, M. 1967. *Heraclitus: Greek Text with a Short Commentary*. Merida, Venezuela: Los Andes University Press.

McEvilley, T. 2002. *The Shape of Ancient Thought: Comparative Studies in Greek and Indian Philosophies*. New York, NY: Allworth Press.

McKirahan, R. D. 1994. *Philosophy Before Socrates*. Indianapolis, IN: Hackett Publishing Company.

—. 1999. "Zeno." In Long 1999:134–58.

—. 2008. "Signs and arguments in Parmenides B8." In Curd and Graham 2008:189–229.

Menn, S. 1995. *Plato on God as Nous*. Carbondale, IL: Southern Illinois University Press.

Miller, F. 1999. "Plato on parts of the soul." In *Plato and Platonism*, ed. J. M. Van Ophujisen, 84–101. Washington, DC: Catholic University Press.

Miller, P. L. 2006. "*Oedipus rex* revisited." *Modern Psychoanalysis* 31:229–50.

—. 2010a. "Immanent spirituality." *Philosophy Today* 54 (Supplement 2010):74–83.

—. 2010b. "Greek philosophical dualism." In Lange et al. 2010:123–66.

Morford, M. P. O. and R. J. Lenardon, 1999. *Classical Mythology*, 6th edn. New York, NY: Oxford University Press.

Moss, J. 2007. "What is imitative poetry and why is it bad?" In Ferrari 2007a: 415–44.

—. 2008. "Appearances and calculations: Plato's division of the soul." *Oxford Studies in Ancient Philosophy* 34:35–68.

Moulinier, L. 1975. *Le pur et l'impur dans la pensée des Grecs*. New York, NY: Arno Press.

Naddaf, G. 2005. *The Greek Concept of Nature*. Albany, NY: State University of New York Press.

Nehamas, A. 2002. "Parmenidean being/Heraclitean fire." In Caston and Graham 2002:45–64.

Nehamas, A. and P. Woodruff, trans. 1995. *Plato: Phaedrus*. Indianapolis, IN: Hackett Publishing Company.

Neugebauer, O. 1957. *The Exact Sciences in Antiquity*. Providence, RI: Brown University Press.

Nietzsche, F. 1962 (1873). *Philosophy in the Tragic Age of the Greeks*. Trans. M. Cowan. Washington, D.C.: Regnery Publishing Inc.

—. 1974 (1882–87). *The Gay Science*. Trans. W. Kaufmann. New York, NY: Vintage Books.

—. 1997 (1888). *Twilight of the Idols*. Trans. R. Polt. Indianapolis, IN: Hackett Publishing Company.

—. 1998 (1887). *Genealogy of Morality*. Trans. M. Clark and A. J. Swensen. Indianapolis, IN: Hackett Publishing Company.

—. 2006 (1883–85). *Thus Spoke Zarathustra*. Ed. A. Del Caro and R. Pippin. Trans. A. Del Caro. New York, NY: Cambridge University Press.

Nigosian, S. A. 2003. *The Zoroastrian Faith: Tradition & Modern Research*. Montréal: McGill-Queen's University Press.

Notopoulos, J. A. 1944a. "The symbolism of the sun and light in the Republic of Plato. I." *Classical Philology* 39:163–72.

—. 1944b. "The symbolism of the sun and light in the Republic of Plato. II." *Classical Philology* 39:223–40.

O'Cleirigh, P. and R. Barrell. 2000. *An Introduction to Greek Mythology*. Lewiston, NY: The Edwin Mellen Press.

Park, D. 1997. *The Fire within the Eye: A Historical Essay on the Nature and Meaning of Light*. Princeton, NJ: Princeton University Press.

Pearson, K. A. and D. Large. 2006. *The Nietzsche Reader.* Malden, MA: Blackwell Publishing Ltd.

Peters, F. E. 1967. *Greek Philosophical Terms: A Historical Lexicon.* New York, NY: New York University Press.

Popper, K. R. 1992. "How the moon might throw some of her light upon the two ways of Parmenides." *The Classical Quarterly* 42:12–19.

Purcell, N. 1994. "South Italy in the Fourth Century BC." In *The Cambridge Ancient History*, ed. D. M. Lewis et al. 1994:381–403.

Race, W. H. 1997a. *Pindar: Nemean Odes, Isthmian Odes, Fragments.* Loeb Classical Library. Cambridge, MA: Harvard University Press.

—. 1997b. *Pindar: Olympian Odes, Pythian Odes.* Loeb Classical Library. Cambridge, MA: Harvard University Press.

—. 2000. "The limitations of rationalism: Sophocles' Oedipus and Plato's Socrates." *Syllecta Classica* 11:89–104.

Radhakrishnan, S. and C. A. Moore, eds. 1989. *A Source Book in Indian Philosophy.* Princeton, NJ: Princeton University Press.

Reeve, C. D. C. 1988. *Philosopher-Kings.* Princeton, NJ: Princeton University Press.

—. 1989. *Socrates in the Apology.* Indianapolis, IN: Hackett Publishing Company.

—. ed. 2002. *The Trials of Socrates.* Indianapolis, IN: Hackett Publishing Company.

—. 2003. "Plato's metaphysics of morals." *Oxford Studies in Ancient Philosophy* 25:39–58.

—. trans. 2004. *Plato: Republic.* Indianapolis, IN: Hackett Publishing Company.

—. 2005. *Love's Confusions.* Cambridge, MA: Harvard University Press.

Riedweg, C. 2005 (2002). *Pythagoras: His Life, Teaching, and Influence.* Trans. S. Rendall. Ithaca, New York: Cornell University Press.

Rorty, R. 1981. *Philosophy and the Mirror of Nature.* Princeton, NJ: Princeton University Press.

Russell, B. 1905. "On denoting." *Mind* 14:479–93.

Santas, G., ed. 2006. *The Blackwell Guide to Plato's* Republic. Malden, MA: Blackwell Publishing Ltd.

Schibli, H. S. 1996. "On *the one* in Philolaus, fragment 7." *The Classical Quarterly* 46:114–30.

Sedley, D. 1999a. "The ideal of godlikeness." In *Plato 2: Ethics, Politics, Religion, and the Soul*, ed. G. Fine, 309–28. Oxford: Oxford University Press.

—. 1999b. "Parmenides and Melissus." In Long 1999:113–33.

Shields, C. 2001. "Simple souls." In Wagner 2001:137–56.

—. 2007. *Aristotle.* New York, NY: Routledge.

Skjærvø, P. O. 2010. In Lange et al. 2010:54–103.

Smyth, H. W. 1980. *Greek Grammar.* Cambridge, MA: Harvard University Press.

Snell, B. 1960. *The Discovery of the Mind.* New York, NY: Harper & Row.

Solmsen, F. 1983. "Plato and the concept of the soul (*psyche*): some historical perspectives." *Journal of the History of Ideas* 44:355–67.

Sommerstein, A. H., trans. 1991. *Aristophanes: Clouds.* Warminster, England: Aris & Phillips Ltd.

Tarán, L. 1965. *Parmenides.* Princeton, NJ: Princeton University Press.

Wagner, E., ed. 2001. *Essays on Plato's Psychology.* Lanham, MD: Lexington Books.

Waterfield, R., trans. 1998. *Herodotus: The Histories.* New York, NY: Oxford University Press.

West, M. L. 1971. *Early Greek Philosophy and the Orient.* Oxford: Oxford University Press.

Wittgenstein, L. 1953. *Philosophical Investigations.* Trans. G. E. M. Anscombe. Oxford: Blackwell Publishing Ltd.

Zeller, E. 1923. *Die Philosophie der Griechen.* Leipzig: Reisland.

Zeyl, D. J., trans. 2000. *Plato: Timaeus.* Indianapolis, IN: Hackett Publishing Company.

Index

Lightning Source UK Ltd.
Milton Keynes UK
UKOW04f1223140914

238570UK00001B/5/P